DISAPPEARING WORLD

Scyld Berry

DISAPPEARING
WORLD

The 18 First-Class Cricket Counties

First published by Pitch Publishing, 2023

Pitch Publishing
9 Donnington Park,
85 Birdham Road,
Chichester,
West Sussex,
PO20 7AJ
www.pitchpublishing.co.uk
info@pitchpublishing.co.uk

Introduction © Scyld Berry 2023
The Life and Times of County Cricket by Scyld Berry
© Telegraph Media Group 2020

The Publishers shall endeavour to include in any contract with any licensee concerning the Work an undertaking that the same notice shall be included in or on every edition published or further licensed by the licensee.

All rights reserved. No part of this book may be reproduced, sold or utilised in any form or transmitted in any form or by any means, electronic or mechanical, including photocopying, recording or by any information storage and retrieval system, without prior permission in writing from the Publisher.

A CIP catalogue record is available for this book from the British Library.

ISBN 978 1 80150 554 3

Typesetting and origination by Pitch Publishing
Printed and bound in Great Britain by TJ Books, Padstow

Contents

Introduction	9
Acknowledgements	19
Derbyshire	21
Durham	36
Essex	52
Glamorgan	67
Gloucestershire	81
Hampshire	94
Kent	109
Lancashire	122
Leicestershire	136
Middlesex	154
Northamptonshire	168
Nottinghamshire	184
Somerset	198
Surrey	213
Sussex	224
Warwickshire	243
Worcestershire	258
Yorkshire	272

Dedication

To press box colleagues whose company and humour have made almost 50 years of reporting fly by.

Introduction

A FRIEND was driving his seven-year-old child – a boy but it could have been a girl – past Lord's cricket ground. 'Look!' the boy said, as he stared at the floodlights and stands which must have assumed gigantic proportions in his eyes. 'That's the home of London Spirit!'

Not the home of Middlesex. Not the home of Marylebone Cricket Club. Not even the home of the England cricket team. What is more, this brief encounter occurred before The Hundred had even been launched and a ball bowled in the new format. Yet this young cricket enthusiast was already identifying with not a first-class county, nor even his country, but a franchise.

This story could be interpreted as a triumph of branding: of how successfully The Hundred's advertising campaign captured new and young imaginations. Deliberately, the marketing people did not appeal to traditional loyalties which, in English domestic cricket, had hitherto been based on county boundaries. They based the identity of The Hundred teams on three cities (London, Birmingham and Manchester), three regions (Northern, Trent and Southern), one ground (the Oval) and one country (Wales).

When I was a seven-year-old I identified with Yorkshire; my eyes were set on Bramall Lane in Sheffield. A Test match could be momentous: we were on holiday in a fishing village in the north of Scotland in 1961 when England crumbled on our fuzzy television on the final afternoon at Old Trafford against Richie Benaud. But every Yorkshire match was dramatic from the moment you walked down Bramall Lane, past factories and terraced houses black with soot. As if it were yesterday, I can remember pushing through the turnstiles – like the crash barriers they were painted bright red – and running up the steps of the stand at the Shoreham Street end, then down the terraces on the other side until I could see – below the roof of the football stand – white figures on the field and the scoreboard. I shouted out the score to my mother trailing behind, carrying her knitting and our tea. (Most of Yorkshire's matches at Bramall Lane took place in term-time, as the ground would have to be handed back to Sheffield United during August, so we usually arrived in mid-afternoon.) In my life I have not been happier, provided Yorkshire were winning the County Championship which they usually did in the 1960s: six times out of ten.

Once upon a time another first-class cricket county existed: London County. The Crystal Palace Company lured W.G. Grace from Gloucestershire as captain and manager for £600 a year – not bad for an amateur cricketer – from 1899, and London County played first-class matches until 1904. MCC, however, would not allow London County to join the Championship; and they had only one asset with which to compete with Lord's and the Oval, and WG was already 50 by the time the promoters started their venture.

If we could look through the eyes of a seven-year-old at the broader sweep of life in Britain now, the county or shire would not loom so large. Administrative boundaries which had applied for a millennium have been several times redrawn. If you inhabit the city of Bristol, you ceased to live in Gloucestershire or Somerset, but in Avon, then in the

INTRODUCTION

County of Bristol. If you inhabit Birmingham, you no longer live in Warwickshire but the West Midlands; Mancunians come from Greater Manchester, not Lancashire. It is a fact of life that many councils, police, fire and ambulance services are no longer based on, or named after, the traditional shire.

In Anglo-Saxon and Norman times the King's men had drawn lines on a map of England to decide the areas where he would be represented by a Lord Lieutenant and a Sheriff; and their quills did not always have natural boundaries or contours to follow. Cross the long bridge over the River Tamar and the distinction between Devon and Cornwall flows in front of your eyes: Cornwall is Cornwall. Elsewhere in England and Wales one can walk or drive from many a county into its neighbour without seeing any difference in the terrain, architecture or people.

It is against this inexorable drift, towards new identities, which county cricket struggles. Children grow up not knowing that they were born in a part of Britain which used to be called a county, and people arriving from abroad can settle in a part of Britain which used to be a county but they will be unaware that it ever existed. Hence the appeal of new identities to which they can relate, like Birmingham Bears or London Spirit.

We should not ignore, however, a benevolent aunt or uncle who is falling on hard times. To the majority of people in England and Wales, perhaps, county cricket no longer has significance; and yet, to a substantial minority, it continues to mean so much. Our lives have been interwoven with cricket seasons: we will always remember that we were born, or married, in the year Loamshire won their first Championship. We need county cricket, and the Championship in particular, to provide continuity and a sense of stability, as an integral part of an existence that technology makes ever more complicated. If only for a few minutes over breakfast, the scores of county cricket matches – the doings of men whom we may never see live – are conducive to our well-being.

It would be wrong to think that county cricket has always been about winning and should be judged accordingly. Maybe it has become so: every one-per-center is now analysed by every county in pursuit of success, not least because the coaches' jobs depend on it. But as the traditional shape of the county cricketer's day would suggest, it was not ever thus. Players would turn up at 10.30am to change into their flannels and have tea; bowlers would flex their arms when walking out to field and limber up gradually during their first spell; players would drink beer at lunchtime into the 1960s; and until a decade or two ago they would drink copiously after close of play, with team-mates and opponents.

By night, who can say for sure what used to happen when the evidence is anecdotal? But for many county cricketers, the away game was a chance to play shots. Practical jokes for a start. One pace bowler in the 1950s locked his fellow new-ball partner in a cupboard all night: there were no warm-ups, stretching exercises and practice overs in the nets to be missed next morning. Sexual encounters too: the more knowing professionals, from past experiences, would be familiar with where to go and whom to meet. All sorts of fun and games, on and off the field; money was never the sole motivation. The annual average pay in the UK in 1936, for example, was £153 and most professionals probably earned about the same; by the 1960s the average UK wage had risen above £700, and most professional cricketers earned less.

County cricket's traditional ethos was best summarised by Micky Stewart in conversation with Stephen Chalke in their book about *The Changing Face of Cricket*. 'At Surrey we always set out each summer to win the Championship, just

INTRODUCTION

as Yorkshire did. Maybe Glamorgan did when Wilf Wooller was captain, though for most of the time they didn't have the resources. But very few of the other counties did. I talked to John Murray about it. I said to him, "When you were playing for Middlesex, at the start of the summer, did you talk about winning the Championship?" He said, "No, never. Most counties, they just had this lovely existence where they went round the country, playing the games. In many ways it was an extension of club cricket.'" Pure entertainment.

This book celebrates county cricket while we can. A High Performance review, conducted on behalf of the England and Wales Cricket Board by Sir Andrew Strauss, recommended that the County Championship should be reduced by two-sevenths, to only ten four-day matches per year, in a season which has become extended to six months. The panel was composed of experts from other sports who genuinely wanted the England cricket team to become the best in the world in every format (apart from The Hundred). Championship cricket was to be dovetailed to this purpose and this purpose alone. 'Existential threat' was the catch-phrase of their opponents.

Since Edwardian times the benevolent aunt or uncle that is county cricket has usually been hard up, and its parlous state has often been the subject of the Editor's Notes in Wisden Cricketers' Almanack. Gloucestershire and Worcestershire were on the verge of dropping out of the Championship when the First World War intervened. The simple sums have not added up: crowds have never been large enough to support most of the counties most of the time. Always a local landowner has had to dip a hand into his pocket; or else the county has depended on the quadrennial handout after an England tour of Australia; in the 1950s football pools were a lifeline briefly or it was sponsorship. Now the centre subsidises the counties through the broadcasting deals generated by the England team. And yet, being 'poor but respectable', the opposite of Premier League football, may well be a reason for county cricket's role in our affections.

Unfortunately, too, there is a tide in the affairs of men which includes professional cricketers. Only a generation ago, from the month of May until September, cricket was not played at a high first-class level anywhere except in England and Wales. The weather was too cold in the southern hemisphere and too hot in south Asia while it was the hurricane season in the West Indies. A professional cricketer headed to Britain if he wanted to make a living at this time of year. All roads led to county grounds. The stars of world cricket represented counties in every format.

This tide has ebbed. Cricketers around the world who want to make a living have T20 franchise tournaments from which to choose. Their predecessors – Sir Garfield Sobers, Mike Procter, Sir Vivian Richards, Allan Border, Imran Khan and Malcolm Marshall to name the very finest – played dozens of innings for their counties and/or bowled hundreds of overs every summer, in addition to the winter workload for their countries. Their successors today can earn more in a year while bowling 100 balls, or by hitting 200 balls a long way, and their agents will be offering them so many tournaments between September and May that the ideal period for them to take a break may be the height of the English season.

When neither The Hundred nor the counties' 20-over competition (the Vitality Blast) is in progress during the English summer, solely the Championship, more and more county cricketers will fly away to play in franchise tournaments outside England. The most promising county players will, surely, continue to aim to represent their country at Test cricket, for that is still the pinnacle by almost every estimation, especially after the revolution led by England's captain and head coach, Ben Stokes and Brendon McCullum, when they mixed traditional red-ball skills with white-ball techniques in a compelling new blend. County cricketers will be more attracted to stay with the Championship when four-day matches replicate this revolution, and are no longer a war of attrition ending in a bore-draw. But once players realise they cannot reach Test level they will opt for 20-over franchises to make more money and to have a longer career – because of the lesser workload – than if they stayed on the county circuit.

The benefit, which the counties granted to senior players normally after ten years of service, is worth no more than a one-off contract to play in the Abu Dhabi T10 or in the 20-over tournaments staged in Australia, Bangladesh, India, Pakistan, South Africa, Sri Lanka, the United Arab Emirates and the West Indies. The United States of America will soon host cricket on turf pitches at the height of the English season, reviving the sport there after more than a century of decline.

Memberships have to be an objective measurement of the amount of interest in county cricket. Twenty years ago the total of county members was reliably estimated at 150,000 and is now at 70,000. We should factor in Covid-19 as a partial cause: it was reasonable for anyone cash-strapped to cancel his or her subscription when there was no chance of attending a game all season, as was the case in 2020. But some counties accelerated the expansion of their live-streaming service during covid as compensation for their members.

Before 1980 county cricket amounted to about half the amount of high-class cricket that was played worldwide. That proportion has shrunk because the sport has been growing at an unprecedented rate. Just browse the Cricinfo website and its series archive to appreciate how much professional cricket is being played, and the surge in the amateur game too. Just look at Tours and Minor Tours in 2022: from the India tour of England and the Uganda tour of Namibia to the Serbia Women tour of Romania and the Cook Islands tour of Vanuatu. About a hundred cricket tours are listed, and this is during the English summer alone, excluding what happened in the previous and subsequent winters. Cricket itself is booming as never before.

But if county cricket is diminishing, if only as a proportion of the whole, so too I guess is much of what we value most on Earth. Glaciers, rainforests, wetlands, marshes and coral reefs are also disappearing, and should be treasured and celebrated in order that we may preserve them.

I have watched the first-class counties play cricket at 50 grounds from Bramall Lane, where I grew up one mile away, to Bristol, where I now live two miles from the ground. From there I have come to know one of the most overlooked regions of England and Wales: the River Severn, so broad as to be almost Gangetic in its sweep.

Between the Severn's banks, Ivor Gurney let his imagination roam: not a famous name any more, but it was in his day, as a composer, poet and librettist. He had been born in a tradesman's house in Gloucester in 1890, became a chorister in the cathedral and won a scholarship to the Royal College of Music in 1911 before the First World War summoned him to the trenches, which were not the ideal place for someone with bipolar disorder.

Gurney often watched Gloucestershire in his youth, as the team then played at Cheltenham College and Gloucester's Spa ground. County cricket meant much to him before the Great War, and during it, and afterwards. As well as any of his contemporaries – Edward Blunden, Wilfred Owen, Siegfried Sassoon and Edward Thomas – Gurney captured those horrors which were, for most people, unutterable.

INTRODUCTION

And the consolations which Gurney sought were rooted in 'my county, Gloucester, that whether I live or die stays always with me'. His fame flared briefly after the war: not only his poems but 'Five Preludes' for piano, and the premiere of his 'String Quartet in D Minor', and music to go with the words of A.E. Housman, before he was declared insane in 1922 and spent the last 15 years of his life in psychiatric hospitals.

Yet he continued to compose verse and music, even more prolifically; and the Gloucestershire cricketers of his youth recur. In 'Iliad and Badminton', which is like a sonnet and a half, Gurney recalls: 'A sight of Jessop at his crouch'. This memory:

Stays with me still, though my arm with the rudder have racked.
Shot a hole through a German maybe, Vermands hill.

Vermand is the site of one of the Great War cemeteries. Then another memory recurs and fades:

… I saw the burly
Past Cricket figure of him, W.G. of Graces.
Out soon – a venerable figure …

Gurney did not over-romanticise, from the comfort of his asylum, which was in Dartford, all too far away from his favoured fields:

From dead Shrewsbury, as from the younger Grace
memory winces.

Winces, because Arthur Shrewsbury, the finest professional batsman of the late Victorian era, shot himself; and because Fred Grace died of pneumonia a fortnight after his Test debut in 1880.

Other county cricketers spring to Gurney's increasingly demented mind, some of whom went on to represent England:

'Hobbs and Strudwick'; Ranjitsinhji; and 'Paliaret' as he mis-spelled Somerset's Palairet. In this poem they are all mixed up with the warriors of Ancient Greece and Troy, with Agamemnon, Priam and Hector. Or maybe they are not mixed up at all; maybe they are, to Gurney, all equal heroes.

Hector was valiant all, but Townsend defied courage.

If this is Charles Townsend, he was a sensation when he represented Gloucestershire as a schoolboy. In 1895 Townsend, while still a pupil at Clifton College, took more than a hundred first-class wickets in the school holidays with his leg-breaks, which were a novelty in that age of finger-spin; and, even after he became a solicitor, Townsend produced feats that inspired local schoolboys.

I cannot begin to understand everything which Gurney wanted to tell us. Yet, I think, I can understand the unceasing significance for him of county cricket. Our final thoughts will of course encompass our family, but they may also consist of memories of cricketers of our past.

Acknowledgements

THE FIRST book profiling each of the first-class counties, from my reading, was *To The Wicket* by Dudley Carew in the 1930s, containing some exquisite writing. More prosaic, and substantial, was *Championship Cricket* by Trevor Bailey, published in 1961. The king of books about county cricket is, of course, *Summer's Crown* by Stephen Chalke, the definitive work and more: like an ocean, before pollution, you only have to dip into it to find something absorbing.

I am indebted to Stephen for his help and advice also. My thanks to everyone at Pitch Publishing – Jane Camillin, Dean Rockett, who made helpful suggestions at the editing stage, and Duncan Olner, for his evocative cover. Also to Bruce Talbot, who introduced me to Pitch and helped with the editing process.

I was introduced to the work of Ivor Gurney by Dr Richard Leach. As members of the Ivor Gurney Society are none too numerous, I am fortunate to have Richard as a friend and mentor.

Left-arm spinners are renowned for being unerringly reliable and steady. A prime example is David Luxton, of the world's number one cricket literary agency. My heartfelt thanks to him.

Derbyshire

'THERE IS no finer county in England than Derbyshire,' Jane Austen declared in *Pride and Prejudice*. More than two centuries later, her argument remains tenable.

Since Austen's time indeed the Peak District has become finer still, and for more people, because mass trespassing on Kinder Scout in the 1930s made it the beacon of freedom for fell-walkers. Chatsworth, the inspiration for Mr Darcy's estate, has been further extended, both House and gardens; and Dovedale is still as beautiful as it sounds. If in future more people prefer to holiday at home than abroad, Buxton and Matlock Spa may even become fashionable again, staging ballroom dances of which Jane herself would approve.

The view of Derbyshire from Lord's, however, is not perhaps so affectionate as that of our most famous novelist. Before the pandemic, the ECB said that in ten years' time not all 18 first-class counties would exist in their current form – and when their strategists in the St John's Wood offices are debating, we can imagine their eyes focussed on Derbyshire, and perhaps Leicestershire, as their index fingers hover over the 'delete' button. Of county grounds, only the Oval and Lord's are in closer proximity than Derby and Trent Bridge, a dozen miles away in Nottingham, while Derbyshire's membership, around 1,200, might be the lowest in the country.

Popular imagination too finds something unattractive about Derby and Derbyshire, as if they were synonyms for dourness. Collieries have closed; our stock image, rather than the Peak District, is of Belper or Bolsover; and the county has an image of industrial decline even though Rolls-Royce is based in Derby, which claims to have a higher proportion of graduates than any other English city. Those baggy caps which Derbyshire cricketers wore, like a poor man's version of the Australian baggy green, only added to the dour impression. From Sheffield we looked south, and down:

> *Derbyshire born, Derbyshire bred,*
> *Strong in the arm, thick in the head.*

The reality, however, in cricket too, is brighter than one might suspect. Derbyshire have won the County Championship, which Northamptonshire and Somerset have not: they did it in 1936, with home-grown players, when county cricket was a far more level playing field. They have never won the T20 title, but they won the 60-over NatWest Trophy in 1981; and the 40-over Sunday League in 1990 and the 55-over Benson and Hedges Cup in 1993. Their pace attack under Kim Barnett's captaincy was as robust as it was when they claimed their Championship title.

Depending on your definition of 'produce', it can be argued that Derbyshire through the ages have produced as many pace bowlers for England as any other county, and they keep on surfacing, like miners of yore after a shift underground: when a Lions team is announced it could well include a Sam Connors or George Scrimshaw. More surprisingly, it can be argued that more top wicketkeepers have played for Derbyshire than for any other county bar Kent: it has not only been into the gloves of Bob Taylor that the ball has melted. Derbyshire has resources, in addition to the natural finery of its scenery: can they be maximised?

DERBYSHIRE

***

A personal interest has to be admitted. When I was about 12, I would take the train from Sheffield to Chesterfield then walk through the town past the crooked spire – I had heard, if not fully comprehended, the joke that it had bent when a virgin was married in the church and would straighten when another one was – to Queen's Park.

A wooden bench beneath the trees of this sylvan setting was a world from my normal upbringing on the terraces of Bramall Lane.

Derbyshire cricket, in truth, still tended to the dour side, before overseas players could be registered with immediate effect and without two years of residence, starting in 1968. While Nottinghamshire, down the road, signed the greatest post-war cricketer, Garfield Sobers, Derbyshire and Yorkshire did not sign any 'bloody foreigners' – to descend to the language of the day – for that first 'open' season. In 1970, however, Derbyshire relented and made what was, by their standards, an exotic signing.

When England made their last Test tour of South Africa, I heard more about Chris Wilkins and how he used to run down the pitch in the face of fast bowlers like Mike Procter, Garth le Roux and Vintcent van der Bijl, and hit them for six back over their heads – all without a helmet. Wilkins was a dasher as batsman and person. Peter Kirsten, who was soon to follow Wilkins as Derbyshire's overseas player, could be rated the best batsman the county has had, but 'Wilkins, from South Africa, gave the batting a lustre it had never possessed in post-war years,' *Wisden* recorded. 'He was the most successful newcomer in the history of Derbyshire cricket.' Wilkins could also keep wicket, or bowl pace, and was a 'gun fielder' in the covers: he would have made a mint in franchise cricket. Having played many shots, Wilkins was reported to have shot himself.

I have to admit to a second soft spot, beyond Queen's Park. At my Sheffield school was a boy called Arthur Morton, whose grandfather – of the same name – had been one of Derbyshire's most stalwart all-rounders. In 1920 Derbyshire had the worst record of any first-class county ever: they played 18, lost 17, and one match was abandoned. Northamptonshire went through several seasons in the 1930s without a victory but no county has been defeated in such a high proportion of Championship matches; and it was because they had only two decent players, Sam Cadman and Morton.

Cadman and Morton not only opened the bowling in 1920, they did almost the whole of it. Morton took 89 wickets and Cadman 58, both at 20 runs each; nobody else took more than ten. Then they had to pad up and coax their team-mates to make half a total. Nobody apart from them reached 300 runs that season, except the captain Leonard Oliver, who scored 170 in one innings. Otherwise, even though they averaged only 15 apiece, Cadman and Morton were Derbyshire's two best batsmen as well.

After watching a game at Trent Bridge with my mother, on the way back to Nottingham station, I had found a copy of the 1921 *Wisden* in a second-hand bookshop in Arkwright Street and lent it to Arthur Morton, who took it home to read about his grandfather, who had pre-deceased. I could see the family trait which the grandson had inherited: stockiness and a big backside, the ideal physique if you had to earn your living by walking through galleries of a non-artistic kind, the physique advocated by someone else who escaped the mines by playing cricket, Fred Trueman. Against Somerset, for instance, Morton opened the bowling and bowled throughout their first innings (36.4 overs, 20 maidens, 37 runs and eight wickets), then did the same in their second, for another 29 consecutive overs, until the game was lost.

Derbyshire's last home game in 1920, against Leicestershire, was not so much the finale they wanted as the epitome of their season. Morton opened the batting with Cadman, and scored 105, carrying his bat. Then he opened the bowling, with Cadman, and bowled 49 overs of medium pace. When Derbyshire batted a second time, Cadman and Morton scored 35 runs – out of a total of 53. Derbyshire lost to Leicestershire by an innings. It might have been a sombre end-of-season dinner, and the awards ceremony brief.

***

Atop the all-time list of Derbyshire's bowlers, in every sense, is Les Jackson. He was not only *the* Derbyshire bowler; he was *the* English deck bowler. He was a miner from the age of 16, through the Second World War, and learned how to bowl in the Whitwell colliery team until he turned pro aged 27. He ran in close to the stumps, slightly round-arm, so the ball came down the line of your middle stump and there was not much room for manoeuvre thereafter, especially after it had jagged one way or the other off the seam. It is no coincidence the thigh pad became part of the English batsman's kit during Jackson's heyday in the 1950s.

Given the surfaces he needed by the Derby groundsman Walter Goodyear, Jackson took 1,670 first-class wickets for his county at only 17.11 each. His long fingers could also shape the new ball away. Many seasons he conceded less than two an over – and one of those runs might have come off an inside or outside edge. He played for England in 1949 and 1961, but there was a case for Jackson playing every home Test from 1949 to 1961, alongside Fred Trueman and Brian Statham. He should also have gone to Australia in 1950/51, but England's *eminence grise*, Gubby Allen, did not want another northern pro, especially a miner, so the selectors opted for John Warr (who averaged 281 in the Test series, with the ball unfortunately). If Jackson had been given a tour of Australia at a still-formative age, would he have altered his method, raised his release point, and found an extra yard? But then other 80mph bowlers, like James Anderson in 2010/11 or South Africa's Vernon Philander, did not have to speed up to succeed in Australia.

The one time I saw Jackson bowl was when he came out of retirement for a Sunday game against the International Cavaliers. It was at Queen's Park on a lovely afternoon and the ground was packed to see the local legend. Barry Richards opened for the Cavaliers, while Les bowled his allotment straight through with barely a run scored. Knowing Richards a little, I guess he did the decent thing and let Jackson bowl without going after him; yet it was still a master craftsman at work, going through his paces. You would not have wanted to be an 'abdominal protector' when he was bowling.

Josh Paxton, from Ilkeston, was the first pace bowler in Derbyshire's annals. He took 40 wickets in his six games in the mid-19th century against the All England XI, who banded together to play round the country as professionals, and were therefore far and away the best cricket team in England or the world. William Bestwick was so tough he opened the bowling for Derbyshire with his son in the 1920s; Bill Copson and Alf Pope were key to that Championship title in 1936, with younger brother George Pope to emerge the following year; Cliff Gladwin and Harold Rhodes partnered Jackson; Alan Ward was the fastest in the land around 1970; Mike Hendrick had something of Fred Trueman about his action and glower; Derbyshire gave Devon Malcolm his chance. Such great West Indian bowlers as Michael Holding and Ian Bishop chose Derby as their overseas home. Shacklock, back in Victorian times, is said to have inspired Conan Doyle with the name for his detective.

Top bowlers need top wicketkeepers and Derbyshire have produced them, although again the England selectors have not used them as often as they could have, perhaps because their batting was not the same standard. Both William Storer and Joe Humphries kept for England before World War One. Storer was so versatile that he not only played for Derby County, and kept wicket in six Tests for England, and scored almost 13,000 first-class runs at 28, he also took 232 wickets with leg spin! When Derbyshire's game against Nottinghamshire at Chesterfield was abandoned in 1920 without a ball being bowled, it was Humphries' benefit match and therefore a financial disaster.

Harry Elliott took over and missed one match – one single match – from 1920 to 1927; and contributed to their Championship title by not conceding a bye in the 25 innings completed by their opponents. George Dawkes admittedly came from Leicestershire originally, but still: of the 25 wicketkeepers who have made 1,000 first-class dismissals, three played for Derbyshire in Elliott, Dawkes and, prince of them all, Bob Taylor. 'Chat', the first England player to give me an interview on my first England tour (of Pakistan in late 1977) still stands – or squats – at the top of the all-time list with the mind-boggling total of 1,649 dismissals.

If you never saw Taylor in action, imagine Jamie Foster of Essex, or a shorter version of Ben Foakes. His feet were weightless, his pads light as air, his agility of footwork seemed to know no bounds; and every ball of an over would, at some stage, melt into his gloves, because he had the essential quality of the wicketkeeper who is born not made: he wanted the ball.

Taylor was a pioneer of the new English style. Traditionally keepers had not bothered to catch balls going down the leg side; that was the bowler's fault. Then Godfrey Evans threw himself to take the leg-side ball, at least if it was an England

Test or a big crowd were watching. Taylor, following the example of Keith Andrew at Northampton, developed his footwork to move down the leg side, unobtrusively, without diving, without showmanship: hence the saying that a keeper is never noticed when performing well. Nowadays, of course, the keeper has to combine quick footwork with the ability to throw himself at full stretch, thereby maximising his span.

***

Chris Wilkins was not, by any means, the first overseas player to represent Derbyshire. The first English team to tour the West Indies did so in 1895 – a good amateur side of Blues and MCC members – and they played in the Windward Island of St Vincent, in the capital Kingstown. I have on my desk (it is a bit cluttered) a photograph of the match staged there, taken by Morton Bros and Co, Kingstown. It was played at Victoria Park and shows a large crowd – with every spectator, every man and woman, wearing a hat or bonnet – as they stand and watch a stiff-legged batsman in a sola topee against a background of verdant hills.

St Vincent scored 139, the English team 63. The local fast bowler Charles Ollivierre proved too much of a handful for the tourists. He is often stated to have been born in St Vincent, but the Ollivierres came from the nearby island of Bequia, where they worked – at least seasonally – in whaling; and his birthplace has been revised to Bequia. When the first West Indian team toured England in 1900, Ollivierre was one of the black contingent who did the bowling and carried the bags. He must have been injured, because he ceased to bowl during the tour, when the team struggled in completely alien conditions. Yet by the end the most successful batsman to emerge was Charles Ollivierre, who took part in double-century opening partnerships against Leicestershire and Surrey. *Wisden* reported that he 'has strokes all round the wicket, and in some ways reminds one of Ranji'. Outstanding praise.

To that point, the only overseas players in county cricket had been a handful of Australians, all with familial ties to England, the wonder of the age that was Kumar Shri Ranjitsinhji, and a Parsi doctor who played one game for Middlesex, M.E. Pavri. But the cotton-mill magnate from Glossop who captained Derbyshire needed cricketers to lift his county off the bottom of the Championship table so, during that summer, Samuel Hill-Wood contracted Ollivierre to undertake two years of qualification by residence, then play for Derbyshire – *as an amateur.*

By using the amateur changing room, rather than the professionals', it seems that Ollivierre thereby avoided racial abuse. Rumour has it that Derbyshire's wicketkeeper William Storer was the outspoken professional on this subject, and he had 'previous'. It has recently emerged, from Australian newspaper sources, that he was reprimanded during the fifth Test of 1897/98 for saying to one of Australia's players: 'You are a cheat and you know it.'

A couple of sepia photographs of Ollivierre show a taller batsman than Ranji, with hands far apart, the right one well down the handle, and thus well-equipped to hit leg-side: this was the hitting zone which Ranji had been first to pioneer, in opposition to off-side orthodoxy, but he normally leg-glanced along the ground. Ollivierre looks lean, whippy, rubbery. His physique had enabled him to bowl quick and work in the whaling industry: you can see him throwing a long harpoon. Even in the 1980s when I visited Bequia, and the island was still allowed by the United Nations to catch three whales per year by traditional methods, the boat was one that Captain Ahab would have used, manned by oars, the harpooner standing in the prow braced to hurl. The cricketer growing up with such manual skills might well have been the first to introduce to England the strokes which we now call 'whippage'.

Having qualified for Derbyshire, Ollivierre played in what was described by the *Daily Telegraph* as 'the most astonishing victory in the history of cricket'; and only in the Ashes Test of 2019 at Headingley was it unarguably surpassed. It was staged in 1904 at Queen's Park, Chesterfield, which always seems to have had a quicker pitch than Derby. Essex totalled 595 and for Derbyshire, in reply, Ollivierre scored 229. In his definitive work on county cricket, *Summer's Crown*, Stephen Chalke quotes a newspaper account: 'He [Ollivierre] imparts into his late cut an extraordinary amount of energy. Few men affect a more commanding pose at the wicket.' We can see Ollivierre not merely strutting, he was flying. After Essex had collapsed in their second innings for 87, Ollivierre hit an unbeaten 92 against the clock to win the biggest of turnarounds by nine wickets.

It was not to be the start of great things; rather, it was the closest that Ollivierre came to a peak in the Peak District. Born in 1876, he was developing eye trouble by the time he was 30. Sir Samuel Hill-Wood, as he became, no doubt fixed him up with the best opticians. The first England Test cricketer to wear spectacles, Dick Young, was soon to do so, in 1907/08, but there might have been more to Ollivierre's affliction than short-sightedness. He soon retired, after a fruitless season in 1907, to live in Pontefract on the pension Hill-Wood provided. In the 1980s, after writing about Ollivierre, I received two letters from a Dutch cricketer of note who said that Ollivierre had spent his summers in the Netherlands, where he was a kind coach, before he died in 1949 – the first of a very distinguished line of players who went from the West Indies into county cricket and enlivened it.

Hill-Wood turned his attention from cricket to football. He signed up enough professional footballers to take Glossop into the second division, then the first, before settling on being the chairman of Arsenal after the First World War. Arsenal's crowds, at any rate in 1920, were probably larger than Derbyshire's.

***

'Few men have done so much for cricket.' This is some epitaph to be accorded by *Wisden Cricketers' Almanack*. This was said about another of Derbyshire's Taylors, William Taylor, who served as the club's secretary from 1908 to 1959, spanning two world wars, in the first of which he was badly wounded. No county has had a secretary who has served so long as his 51 years and it was his planning that led to that 1936 Championship title when, to lend continuity and stability, old Sam Cadman was coach.

As a lad William Taylor had been a medium-paced all-rounder, good enough to play a handful of games for the county, not good enough to become a regular. Instead, he carved his own niche. He acted as scorer for Derbyshire's away matches and, somehow, as 12th man as well. He was the son of a businessman who manufactured artificial fertiliser, and this knowledge was not wasted when it came to caring for the County Ground. Derby County FC, which had been founded by the county cricket club, had already transferred to the Baseball Ground before Taylor was appointed secretary, but there was still much to learn about the embryonic science of cricket groundsmanship. Under Taylor, Derbyshire enjoyed more continuity in the shape of Walter Goodyear, whose career as head groundsman at the Racecourse Ground in Derby spanned 44 years, but as he had already been head groundsman at Chesterfield for six years, let us round him up to half a century. It was Goodyear who designed the pitches for Derbyshire's seamers, both in the 1930s, when the Championship triumph was the climax, and for Les Jackson.

The strategy to win that title was not too crude or over the top in favouring seam. Derbyshire always played a spinner: Tommy Mitchell, their maverick wrist-spinner, took 121 wickets in 1936. He was a coalminer too, but he used his strength to rip the ball both ways. In this sense he was a forerunner of the Afghan wrist-spinners who have emerged on the T20 circuit: brought up in a highly physical culture, not a genteel or traditional cricket one, almost unable to bat, but able to rip through a side in a match-winning spell.

***

Although Derby County FC moved out, the horses stayed, as the old name of the Racecourse Ground implies. William Taylor no doubt warned the young pros, like Cadman and Morton, about the shadier side of horse racing but they must have been too naive to listen. In his autobiography *A Cricket Pro's Lot*, Fred Root tells a merry tale about the impact of the racing community on the Derbyshire players. In the 1920s Root went on to play for Worcestershire and England, but he had been born in Derbyshire and started his first-class career there, hence the schoolboys' delight when George Beet and Root played in the same side.

Jockeys and stablehands would mill around the Racecourse, Root relates, and sometimes join the cricketers in the nets. One day the Derbyshire pros gave a plausible fellow one pound each – half their week's wage in some cases – to place on some 'guaranteed' winners and fixed the time to meet him back at the nets after the races. He was never seen again.

Even today, more than half a century on, Taylor's legacy is a well-run ground. Touring teams have nothing to complain about during a three-day match against Derbyshire. The re-orientation of the square by 90 degrees has worked, as it has at Old Trafford. Outdoor nets are splendid; so too the indoor school with its various surfaces, where pace bowlers can fit in three-quarters of their run-up. If all is functional rather than scenic at Derby, annual relief comes at Chesterfield where Queen's Park continues to be glorious. I fondly remember Derbyshire playing at Buxton too, as did visiting teams, given the residential home for nurses next door.

***

In 2015 Derbyshire switched from an old-fashioned committee structure to a board composed of the great and good, from instability towards continuity. Coaches had come and gone, including Kim Barnett, who had not only scored the most centuries and runs for the county but captained them to that 1981 trophy. At one stage four head coaches had reigned in four years. But the appointment of a wise old bird from Zimbabwe, David Houghton, who had been round the county traps at Worcester and Middlesex, prompted longer-term planning; and Houghton's successor, Mickey Arthur, brought even more energy to reviving Derbyshire.

A new feature, born of financial prudence, is that Derbyshire's batting coach and bowling coach work with all age groups, from under-11s upwards through the academy ranks into the first team. And why not? Why change your mentor just because you are 18 and have joined the staff? A coach has to know his pupil thoroughly. The former fast bowler Steve Kirby had a plum job as MCC head coach, but in this context you can see why he transferred to Derby for his first county assignment.

'For years we talked about producing our own players but it's been lip-service,' Houghton said. 'We got into the first division in 2013 [Derbyshire's only season in Division One after the Championship was split into two divisions in 2000] with local players who had come through our youth development programme. Give them peace and stability then reap the rewards five to ten years down the line, that was my aim for the club.'

The county reached out to Repton, when a cricketing headmaster took charge, and Trent College, and Denstone. Houghton planned for all the county players and age-group teams to have a day out at each school, before Covid came, and then he returned to his native country to coach Zimbabwe.

Derbyshire is not synonymous with T20. In almost 20 years they have reached the quarter-finals only twice. The last occasion was in 2017, when they were drawn at home to Hampshire. Opening the bowling with the off breaks of Wayne Madsen, the old faithful who sustained Derbyshire's batting for at least a decade, would have been a good move against a traditional English opener; against the Pakistan all-rounder Shahid Afridi it was a disaster. Looking down from above, as a T20 player before his time, Charles Ollivierre might have put his hand up for the opening over to bowl quick yorkers instead.

Derbyshire's local league structure is sound, even if totals err on the low side. Their indoor school offers free use and free coaching to state schools, which is the sort of initiative that every county should have. Astroturf pitches have been installed in inner-city parks, which is important for Derby's Asian community.

But then there are the depredations – when counties which own Test match grounds, like Nottinghamshire and Surrey, come calling. Derbyshire had unearthed a very promising fast bowler from Stoke-on-Trent called James Taylor and invested in him and his elder brother Tom. Yes, the Taylors keep on coming – but going too. James Taylor made his first-class debut when he was 16 and dismissed the West Indian opening batsman Kraigg Brathwaite. He went through the Derbyshire academy, was given a two-year contract in 2017 ... and went off to the Oval, signed by Surrey.

There are financial compensations for Derbyshire, of course, if one of their former youngsters goes all the way into the England side, but he will not be around to inspire local youth or attract more Derbyshire members. This is the way of the world, the business world, but not consistent with cricket's traditional values, where the playing field should be level. Derbyshire finally found an opening batsman who could score 1,000 runs in a Championship season. It takes years of investment to produce one of those: in this case Ben Slater, born in Chesterfield. And the moment he 'made it' in 2018, Slater was signed by Nottinghamshire. All the hard work, none of the rewards.

Ross Whiteley was another who made his first-class debut for Derbyshire – where he could now have been one of their T20 stars – before preferring Worcestershire then Hampshire. Far-sightedly, Derbyshire awarded a four-year contract to the teenaged Matt Critchley, a wrist-spinner who could bat, and arranged for him to be mentored in Sydney by Stuart MacGill. After Critchley had scored exactly 1,000 runs in the first-class season of 2021 it was Essex that came calling.

Above and beyond the natural finery, Derbyshire is a county of resources. After a hiatus, they are making the most of them. Provided they do, they deserve to survive; and surely we owe it to Jane that they do. For, had she lived beyond the age of 41, she might have visited her favourite county again, and attended a village cricket match – somewhere near Bakewell, perhaps, while visiting Chatsworth – and fallen into conversation with the fine-leg fielder while walking round the boundary under her parasol, and accepted his offer of a drink after the game and, indeed, his subsequent proposal.

Durham

DURHAM, IN more senses than one, is cool. Its latitude lies only slightly south of Denmark and Moscow, yet it is also cool in the modern sense. It is the home of the cricketer of our age, Ben Stokes, who has energised Test cricket like nobody else has ever done save perhaps Sir Frank Worrell. It is the newest first-class county, after being promoted in 1992, and not unfashionable like some of those that lurk in the nether regions of the second division: in their first season Durham CCC generated more books than Derbyshire in their entire history. Having Lord Botham, as a player at the outset and now as its chairman, lends Durham a certain cool edginess.

His lordship has latterly lived on his estate near Scotch Corner, teaching his grandchildren rural pursuits. He is more proactive in Durham's administration than some might suppose, always shrewder than his image suggests. 'He's a very hands-on chairman of the board on the cricket side, and especially in the summer months,' says the club's CEO Tim Bostock. 'But at the same time he is very empowering in letting us get on with the business side.'

Durham was left out of the County Championship originally because it was too far north, even for the railways to reach: playing at Canterbury one day and Old Trafford the next was bad enough. And to this day, Durham seem distinct from the other 17 first-class counties in a couple of ways.

Suppose every county took to the field wearing plain shirts and face masks so all the players looked indistinguishable. Would you, if spectating or umpiring, be able to guess which county was which? Is there still a difference in style? Durham would probably be the easiest to distinguish. In the Championship they bowl less spin than any other county, their spinners taking about 10% of their opponents' wickets; and they usually have the smallest proportion of players from fee-paying schools (the further south a county, as a rule of thumb, the higher the proportion). So, an umpire might hear this second difference, the audible one of a regional accent, which binds together a largely home-grown team.

The broader and greener acres of England's North-East, where the air seems brisker, have always produced cricketers – but only in the last generation have they had a first-class i.e. a professional county to represent. Durham were the minor county champions nine times, which suggests the local mettle and high standard of its leagues. But to reach the top and represent England, Colin Milburn and Peter Willey were compelled to head south, both to Northampton.

It is true that a couple of England's Test captains have been born in the North-East: Andrew Stoddart, who shot himself during the First World War, and the late Bob Willis. But Bob was there only as a baby, when his father worked temporarily for the BBC in Sunderland, while Stoddart's father was a wine merchant, who found that having a customer base in Hampstead was more lucrative than Hartlepool or South Shields.

You have to wonder what England through the ages have missed. Would their attack have been so impotent after the two world wars if pace-bowling miners from Durham's collieries had been playing professionally around the land? Some of the greatest, most vivid spells of bowling for England have come from Steve Harmison and Mark

Wood, and Stokes himself. Graham Onions did the job for a while, too, and another fast-medium bowler of similar style, Matthew Potts, has joined in, which adds up to more than 500 Test wickets. Durham's pace bowlers have, in effect, bowled out England's opponents in both innings for over two years. Meanwhile, no pace bowler born in England south of Birmingham has taken 100 Test wickets in the last 40 years apart from Steven Finn. If only in pace bowling, there is a northern powerhouse.

It is therefore an understatement to say that Durham's promotion from the Minor Counties Championship was justified. In addition to producing these England pace bowlers and Paul Collingwood, they have won the County Championship three times and two limited-over titles in their 28 seasons. Based on the strength of their own leagues, they have quickly grown into fully paid-up brethren.

A still-burning question is whether Durham have been treated properly in return for all they have done for England. The penalties heaped upon them for financial irregularities were savage, like no other collective punishment seen in English cricket or the sport worldwide. For running up debts they were hit with a 48-point penalty in the Championship which plunged them in 2017 into the second division, where they remain, while points were deducted in the other competitions as well. Financial cuts had to be made and, as a consequence, Durham immediately lost the top three of their batting order in Mark Stoneman, Keaton Jennings and Scott Borthwick. To cap it all, after staging six Tests at their Riverside ground, they were forbidden to stage another ever again.

Understandably, the ECB wanted to make an example of Durham to discourage other counties from borrowing too much and getting into trouble. The point is that it was the ECB, or its predecessor the Test and County Cricket

Board, which told Durham in the first place that, in order to be promoted to first-class status, they had to build an international stadium. It made no sense, except if the North-East's economy was going to grow at 20% a year. Out-of-town cricket stadiums have yet to work really; and the nearest town to the Riverside is Chester-le-Street, where even pound shops have been closing, so the ground was never going to attract big local crowds on a regular basis. A ticket of £80 for a day at Lord's would still be exorbitant if sold for £40 at the Riverside.

The irony, of course, was that during the Covid lockdown the ECB was bailing out all 18 counties.

***

'My fondest memories in a way are of league cricket because of the education it gives you,' says Paul Collingwood, the first England captain to win a global trophy, out of their three to date. 'That is when you're playing for love of the game and that community feeling. I'd say that club cricket is 70–80% of the player. That's where you learn your competitiveness and basic skills – the rest is topped up when you play county and international cricket.'

Assuming Collingwood is right, we need to re-think our cricket structures if England's Test batting line-up is not to become ever more reliant on fee-paying schools and the mindset that is common to people from similar backgrounds. ECB development funding goes into academies and coaching: shouldn't more of it be going instead into making top leagues the nursery for budding professionals? No better education for boy cricketers than to play tough league cricket against men.

Collingwood was tough enough to become the first England batsman to hit a Test double-century in Australia for 78 years – although his 206 at Adelaide in 2006/07 ended in defeat as Andrew Flintoff, at least with the benefit of hindsight, declared half an hour too early. Yet he began as a bowler. The age-old reason: he was a younger brother and his older brother Peter wanted to bat. So this is what they did in their back garden and back street; and their father still coaches at Shotley Bridge CC.

'I think I got into the first team at 13, the sort of age when you're in awe of all the league legends and the overseas pros,' Collingwood recalled. 'Wasim Raja [one of Pakistan's finest left-handed batsmen] was once the pro at Shotley Bridge. Wasim Akram and Courtney Walsh used to be pros in Durham.'

Durham may have been cut off from the main body of English cricket by geography – too far north before motorways – but the other side of this coin is that the county is uniquely favoured: Durham's hours of daylight during the season are longer than for any other first-class county. Midweek 20-over cricket was the norm in Durham, both in league and cup competitions, long before 2003 when the counties caught on, to be swiftly followed by the rest of the world; and Collingwood remembers the 20-over games of his youth finishing at 10pm or 10.30pm.

'You had the excitement of thinking about the game all day at school, then three or four of you jumping into a car. I think I was about 16 at the time when I opened the bowling at Thornaby, after a 50-minute drive, arriving at five to six and going straight out. I swung the first ball back into this left-hander and this bloke hit me so far back over my head, it went miles – and he later bowled rockets.' It was Neil Johnson, a fine Test player for Zimbabwe.

A difference in this original form of 20-over cricket was that sometimes there was a limitation on the number of overs per bowler, and sometimes not. 'In one competition there was this pace bowler, Donald Brown – he worked in prisons, tough guy, and you couldn't get the ball off him.' So here was someone who bowled ten overs in a T20 game.

'I didn't become a batsman until I was about 17. I had a bad back – I suppose nowadays you'd say it was a stress fracture – and had to stop bowling for six months and worked on my batting. My brother Peter was a batsman from day one. He is four years older and a lot of people would say he was more talented. But being that much older he didn't have the opportunity to get a county contract [with Durham], that's how close it was.

'Me, at the age of 12 I told my school career's officer I wanted to play cricket for England. I kept an eye on Mike Roseberry and Simon Brown [two Durham lads who had made their way down south]. We had some friends from Shotley Bridge and one of them became a groundsman at Durham University with a house above the Racecourse, and I'd go and stay with him the night before a county game and help put the covers on and watch for free. At the end of the day I'd hit some throw-downs from my dad into the sponsors' boards. I guess I would have tried MCC Young Cricketers if Durham hadn't got first-class status.'

Collingwood made his move into England teams at the same time that Durham came good after an underwhelming first decade. He could obviously relate to the intense competitiveness of the Australians who played for Durham, like David Boon and Mike Hussey. In 2005, almost incredible to relate, Hussey was not wanted by Australia's Test team so he captained Durham instead. 'I think he got a double-hundred in his first game at Leicester when it was nipping about all over the place. We've had some great overseas [players] who have instilled their own steeliness.'

On that most epic of Test match days at the Oval in 2005 – at least until Stokes inspired the Headingley Test of 2019 – Collingwood brought his steeliness to bear. Time stood still that September morning as Australia's bowlers and nerves eroded England's top order in their second innings. Duncan Fletcher had ruminated long and hard as head coach before deciding that Simon Jones, after the leg injury that ended his England career, should be replaced, not by another pace bowler in James Anderson, but Collingwood. In his couple of Tests Colly had shown how he relished the battle and performed above his county self.

On the surface, Collingwood did little to merit his MBE, as Shane Warne was soon to jibe: scores of 7 and 10, and four wicketless overs. But there are lies, damned lies, statistics, and data: Collingwood bowled his quickest and had a slip catch dropped. At lunch on day five England were 127/5, Kevin Pietersen poking around on 35, Collingwood yet to score, with a first-innings lead of only six runs. It was in this dark hour that Michael Vaughan read his men and the situation brilliantly, telling KP to go for it; and thus the tide began to turn.

It is partnerships that count. Pietersen and Collingwood put on 60 in their completely contrasting styles. While KP hooked Brett Lee, Colly blocked as if he was the last man – or boy – in for Shotley Bridge. Colly soaked up 51 balls at the height of the battle in scoring his 10. When he was dismissed, and Geraint Jones soon followed, Ashley Giles partnered Pietersen in taking England to safety – and to the Ashes, after 16 years without.

A neat postscript is that Collingwood played for Shotley Bridge again in 2019. It was that grim weekend after England had jeopardised their World Cup chances by losing their qualifier against Sri Lanka at Headingley. Everyone went home. Collingwood had some guests from Australia, on a rather delayed reciprocal visit: he had stayed with Greg Knight in Melbourne in 2000/01 when Collingwood had been recognised as the city's Grade Cricketer of the Year.

'I got this call on Friday night – one of the players is injured, are you free? And I had registered at the start of the season. It so happened we were at home to Ashington and I was wondering if Woody or Harmy would turn up [i.e. Mark Wood or Steve Harmison, both from Ashington]. So there was Greg, and my brother Peter, and my kids watching me play for the first time, and I hadn't had a proper bat for years, but I go in and push the first couple of balls away – and I'm talking about not even medium pace.

'Then the devil on my left shoulder says I can hit his third ball back over his head, and I reckon it went 20 yards – caught at mid-off. Out third ball. But I did manage a hat-trick when I was bowling. I must have bowled five overs and I could not move for five weeks afterwards!'

'One thing makes my blood boil,' Collingwood says, when looking back on his life and times in Durham. 'When I was injured, I wanted to play a comeback game for my club, but I couldn't – another club would say it's not fair on us or whatever.

'What's the point of a club producing an England player if he can never play for them in future?'

This is not peculiar to Durham. When Marcus Trescothick was coming back from an injury, he was not allowed to play for his home club, Keynsham. This is not the way they do it in Australia: every international player has his state and his club, for whom he can play whenever he wants. The whole system is thereby strengthened, given backbone. Youngsters see role models in their nets. The Professional Cricketers' Association is full of members who feel rejected after their county has terminated their contract, and depressed. Former pros should be actively welcomed back to the club they played for, and ties strengthened, with all the benefits to mental health. It might just have made the difference for Colin Milburn.

And, while we are on this subject of the England cricketer's relationship with his club (with his county it's usually fine, plenty of money lubricating those wheels), something that makes my blood boil is the ECB's ingratitude. When a player plays 50 Tests for England, should not the club that produced him be given, say, £10,000 to spend on nets or some such facility which is named in his, or her, honour? I have visited Ashington, and Keynsham, and been appalled at the absence of official recognition.

Times have recently changed. Clubs that produce an England cricketer are now given a signed England shirt.

***

I remember Durham's first Championship game in 1992, against Leicestershire, at the university's Racecourse ground. On the eve of this inaugural game the cathedral city did not feel as though it was on the verge of a new epoch – and it was not. It took a dozen years of hard graft before Durham took off as a first-class county.

They had already played their opening Sunday League match at the Racecourse and beaten Lancashire in a thrilling finish. The team which their head coach Geoff Cook had assembled was good for runs, packed with experienced batting, but short on bowling. This soon changed when the Riverside opened in 1995: as at the new ground outside Southampton which was opened shortly afterwards, it was soon found that nothing can substitute for years and years of heavy rolling. The ball went up and down; no batsman was in; the confidence of every youngster, except Collingwood, withered on the vine.

The few runs chiselled out for Durham came from Jon Lewis, who defied gravity by moving from the south (Essex) to the north and scoring runs (northern batsmen have succeeded down south but very seldom the other way round); and from their overseas player, whoever had been carefully chosen. Having started in 1992 with only two local players in their side, Durham grew ever more until their own identity was defined. In September 2008, after Durham had defeated Kent at Canterbury, the team bus rolled out towards the motorway with their first Championship title to celebrate on the drive home.

Suppose the powers-that-be had never insisted in the first place on Durham building an international stadium in the middle of nowhere, if the outskirts of Chester-le-Street can be so-called: what would have happened if Durham had done what old-time Essex, Glamorgan, Kent and Yorkshire used to do and taken their games around the county? The town ground at Ropery Lane in Chester-le-Street is a real community club, alive when cricket is not being played and buzzing when it is; Durham have also played at Darlington and Gateshead Fell and South Northumberland, and if there is affluence anywhere in the North-East it is in Jesmond. Health and safety regulations make games at out-grounds ever more expensive to stage, but I wonder if Durham would have succeeded sooner if they had stayed with that model. They certainly would not have had so many points deducted and might still be in the first division.

***

For the last game of their 1959 tour of England the Indians visited Durham. They had already played 33 first-class games on their tour, including five Tests which had all been lost, so the tourists would not have been at their brightest. But it was still some innings when a 17-year-old schoolboy, who opened the batting, smacked them for 101: the Indian bowling was mostly spin, but class spin.

Colin Milburn was always a batsman, never a slogger, even though he was built like one. He combined the virtues of his father – a local league legend – with his ambition to be another Wally Hammond. Ollie made his second XI league debut for Burnopfield aged 11 and scored a fifty. At 13 he hit 145 in 17 overs. Milburn's opening partner in that match against the 1959 Indians still vividly recalls the occasion in front of a big crowd at Sunderland: it was Clive Leach, who had bowled left-arm spin for Warwickshire, before becoming a big businessman in the North-East and subsequently Durham's chairman.

'We won the toss and decided to bat but as I was padding up everyone was saying where's Ollie?' Leach remembered. 'He strolled in, and said hi everyone, and he was so cool and relaxed I thought he was over-reacting but that's the way he was. When we went out there he smacked it around, hitting the spinners over mid-on, and I felt like the learner at the other end. Imagine him nowadays in T20 – he would have been a wonderful player, and a wealthy man.'

England's answer to Chris Gayle?

Let us not forget the context of those times when Milburn made his century against the Indians. County cricket crowds were in sharp decline, along with scoring rates. No overseas stars. Coaches were regimental sergeant-majors who made youngsters block like they did. Milburn was rejected initially when he went for a trial with Northamptonshire, who only made an offer when Warwickshire tried to sign him.

In 1966, in any event, Milburn was selected to open for England against West Indies, when they were world champions in effect if not title. For the *Daily Telegraph*, after Milburn had scored 94 on his debut, EW Swanton wrote: 'He is brave with a fine eye and reflexes that belie his bulk.' In his second Test at Lord's Milburn made a century against Wes Hall and Charlie Griffith, Garfield Sobers and Lance Gibbs.

For the fifth Test of that series Milburn was dropped. West Indies had some of the most brilliant stroke-makers in

Sobers, Rohan Kanhai and Seymour Nurse and during the fourth Test at Headingley Milburn had been jeered by the crowd – for his boundary fielding – as West Indies clocked up 500. After losing the series, England's selectors needed a scapegoat, and it was Milburn. Why was he fielding on the boundary in the first place, when he was an excellent close catcher? Well, Colin Cowdrey was captain and he fancied slip. In the *Telegraph* the selectors' decision was endorsed: 'It is sad to see Milburn go, if only for the loss of his fighting spirit against the fast bowlers, but he really is a dreadful liability in the field.'

England's selectors, until the day when Brendon McCullum took over as head coach, never liked dashing opening batsmen. For Milburn, four more Tests, on and off, in the next couple of years, but mostly wilderness. Others were not so fussy. Western Australia signed him for the 1968/69 Sheffield Shield and he was a sensation. Sir Donald Bradman said of Milburn's 243 against Queensland in Brisbane: 'That was the greatest innings I've seen played by an Englishman in Australia.' And the Don had seen all of Hammond and Hutton.

You may know the painful rest. As England were touring Pakistan and needed a replacement, Milburn was flown in and scored 139 in the Karachi Test before rioting ended the tour. In May 1969 he continued in purple form with 158 against Leicestershire and participated in Northamptonshire's victory over the West Indians. Celebrating that night, he was driving when his car crashed near the county ground and he lost his left eye. India's Nawab of Pataudi, another right-hander, scored Test centuries with one eye but the good one was his left, Milburn's his right, and the surgeon said it would only function at 80%.

Milburn had two lifelong mates: Alan Hodgson, another Durham lad who emigrated to Northampton to bowl pace, and alcohol. Playing squash with Hodgson, Milburn found himself hitting the ball well, and his right eye improved more than the surgeon had prophesied. In 1973 he made a comeback and scored a fifty against Surrey and their quicker bowlers, the only half-century in that Championship match for Northamptonshire, who lost by an innings.

I watched part of this game at Guildford: not that innings itself but when Milburn had bowled earlier, at brisk medium (he took 99 first-class wickets), and cheerfully. But that was it: the sun had been shining brightly when he had rolled back the years, and while he was alright against pace, he could not pick up the flight of spinners. He was never to reach another fifty.

***

Although Durham have been a first-class county relatively briefly, some of the finest bowling spells of all time for England have been summoned up by their lads, in defiance of all the pain that goes with it. In the Headingley Test of 2019 Stokes ran in for effectively 24 consecutive overs, in what looked like an impossible attempt to drag the game back. How did he have the strength left to play the greatest Test innings for England?

Two of the finest spells by Durham and England bowlers occurred in the West Indies, the spiritual home of fast bowling. I will never forget the silence which overcame the crowd in Kingston, which is normally vocal, in 2004. It was a Sunday morning and Steve Harmison was running through the West Indian batting. This was not the script: it had always been England who collapsed against West Indies, especially in the Caribbean.

Harmison lolloped in with all of England's fielders behind the wicket expecting an edge and took seven wickets for 12. I never saw an England bowler I would less like to have faced. Such was Harmison's natural length that every ball that day threatened your ribcage. The Kingston crowd used the local term for what the batsmen were doing: they were playing the 'get-away-from-me' shot, fending off these rib-crackers. In historical context, I think it might have been a defining moment: the heart was torn out of West Indian Test cricket when Harmison reduced their heroes to mortals.

In February 2019, in St Lucia, Mark Wood unleashed the fastest spell recorded for England until that point, hitting 95mph. He had grown up at Ashington, where there is a downhill slope, and he followed in Harmison's footsteps alright. In fact, Wood bowled absolutely flat out, straining every sinew, which I am not sure Harmison always did, except once: in the last over of that 2005 Ashes series, the first over of Australia's second innings as the match was about to be drawn, when the nation was euphoric with relief.

Everything was in sync in St Lucia. Wood transformed himself into a human catapult and hurled himself down the pitch. I have never seen England slip fielders stand so far back – and yet with so little time to react.

***

It is, for me, the most poignant writing about cricket: *When The Eye Has Gone*, a play about Colin Milburn by Dougie Blaxland, alias James Graham-Brown. He was an all-rounder for Kent and Derbyshire but far more often 12th man; and he researched this one-man play by talking to Ollie's old mates, especially Alan Hodgson, who had smuggled beers into Northampton General Hospital when Ollie was recovering (if not psychologically) after the car accident and eye operation.

Comedy, in the first place, makes this play poignant. Ollie was full of jokes from the time he was an overweight lad and needed to self-deprecate in self-defence. Blaxland quotes Milburn's dad telling his son: 'The Golden Rule for cricket and life is never let anyone know that you're hurt; and the more it hurts the wider you smile.'

Thus, running through the play are the jokes that Milburn used to tell in self-deprecation, such as: 'That Colin Milburn is so fat that he went to London once in a red jumper and 30 passengers tried to board him.'

The play is set in the pub in Durham where Ollie used to drink after the bottom had fallen out of his world. After retiring from playing cricket in 1974 he had tried various jobs and radio commentary, where he was good – until he hit the bottle while on air. His staple was a triple gin and Coke, which his landlord named a Milburn. It was in those commentary days that I met him, when he sat at the back of the press box between stints; and I have not met a top former cricketer so genuinely far from being up himself.

In the course of the play Ollie talks us through his career from his childhood, amid the wisecracks, and about how all he wanted to do was play cricket; and the lack of self-pity after the accident; and how everyone wanted to know him when he was scoring runs, and nobody when he was not. This is not quite true: Botham, for one, lent him financial support in his final years, and was a pall bearer.

During the play, when warned he will drink himself to death, Milburn says: 'We are what we are and nothing on Earth is going to change us, and if you didn't laugh you'd bloody cry.'

Alone in this pub in Durham on the last day of his life, Milburn is in the Christian equivalent of Gethsemane. He knows, aged 48, his time has come. The setting is not so salubrious as a garden in Jerusalem, yet he has to enter.

Last orders. A final swig. Ollie drinks up his Milburn and says goodbye to the audience, before wandering into the pub car park, where he died one way or another of his own volition. The sound of the approaching, belated, ambulance is the end.

***

Durham had just arrived in Zimbabwe for their pre-season training in early 2020 when coronavirus forced them home. This was, or would have been, a nice initiative all round. Derbyshire went to Bulawayo, Durham to Harare, and Zimbabwe's two dozen best cricketers were going to play against both counties, fairly competitively. The trouble with most pre-season tours is you find decent facilities but no opposition.

Something else rather pleasing for Durham has come out of Zimbabwe. This is Brydon Carse, a strapping fast bowler who has represented England's white-ball team. His father James Carse bowled enthusiastically, if not very accurately, for Northamptonshire, after being born in Zimbabwe and moving to South Africa. Brydon Carse's mother also came from Zimbabwe, but he has British grandparents so he had only to spend four years qualifying for England.

Durham have bottomed out after the imposition of those hideous penalties. In 2022 they contributed Stokes, Wood and Potts to the England Test team, and Alex Lees who had been signed from Yorkshire: not the contribution of a backwater. The Riverside stadium is no white elephant: its conference rooms generate £600,000 a year, and the club is recording a profit after the debts had been running into millions. And maybe the chaps at Lord's knew something that we did not when they insisted on Durham building an international venue: the whole site, during the pandemic, was offered to the National Health Service.

Essex

ESSEX HAVE become the New Zealand of county cricket. In the parlance of boxing, they 'fight above their weight'. Not so abundantly endowed as many opponents, both Essex and New Zealand have thought, and planned, and maximised their resources.

One indication of how scantily resourced Essex used to be is that they were not one of the original members of the County Championship, unlike their neighbours in the south-east, Middlesex and Surrey, Kent and Sussex, who were elevated to first-class status before Essex joined in 1895. East Saxons took to cricket less readily than Middle and South Saxons.

Well into the 1970s Essex continued to be mid-table at best, fun and friendly opponents but never serious contenders. Starting in 1979, however, by means of strategic planning, notably in their choice of overseas players, Essex have won the County Championship eight times, more than any other team in this period, and the Bob Willis Trophy in the mini-Championship season of 2020; and, in addition, 11 limited-overs competitions. In modern times opponents endowed with a Test match ground – Lancashire, Nottinghamshire, Surrey, Warwickshire and Yorkshire (not Middlesex because MCC own Lord's) – have not been able to equal Essex, who from 1922 to 1966 had no ground of their own at all.

ESSEX

The last time I saw Essex win the Championship title was in 2019 (forgive me for wanting to forget that BWT final when the north wind blew through Lord's for five whole days). Most spectators at the County Ground in Taunton at the end of September in 2018 wanted Somerset to defeat Essex and thereby win the title for the first time. The axiom abides that Somerset is everyone's second-favourite county.

I was of the same persuasion – until Somerset's three spinners made the ball not simply talk but stand up and shout in Essex's faces. Sir Alastair Cook had to roll back the years to 2012 when he fended off India's spinners in Ahmedabad, Mumbai and Kolkata in order to nurse Essex through to the draw that secured them their eighth Championship, to go with the T20 title which Essex had won for the first time earlier the same month.

Essex's entire staff were present at Cyderabad to celebrate. It is no mean journey from Chelmsford to Taunton, yet the first-team players and coaching staff – who had driven by team bus – were joined by all their second-teamers and academy lads and backroom staff, who had gone by car and train (this was the last season pre-Covid). This hypothesis became apparent: that Essex offer a higher proportion of their population the chance to play cricket than any other first-class county, and their playing staff reflects the racial demographics of their community more closely than any other county.

Of Essex's playing staff, almost all are home-grown, and seven of their Championship-winning team were born in the same hospital, at Whipps Cross; 70% have come from local state schools and, in the fortnight before that Somerset game, nine of their first-teamers had represented their local clubs. When county players turn out for their clubs, the county's cricket is knitted together.

Essex were hit with a £50,000 fine for a racist comment made by their chairman John Faragher in a board meeting in 2017; and not everything by any means has been rosy in their garden, to judge by allegations made by some of their former non-white players. But outside their dressing room in the county at large, and in the wider context of race relations in Britain, to paraphrase Gilbert and Sullivan clumsily, Essex have come as close as any to being the model of a modern first-class county.

***

In Leyton, inside the renovated sports hall on what was Essex's county ground either side of the First World War, a man is sitting with a two-month-old toddler on his knee – while his wife plays cricket.

This is not the normal way round, in any society, indigenous British or south Asian.

It is a mother-and-toddler class run by Essex CCC. 'The local community came to us and said we've got about 15 mums with kids up to five years old who want to play cricket. Most of them have never played, but they have seen their families play it and they want to give it a go.' So says Arfan Akram, Essex's east London cricket coordinator.

'What we are trying to do is to create a safe environment which allows these mums to get out of the house. It's the most basic version of cricket. If they have a four- or five-year-old toddler with them, they start by playing catch with each other from a yard away, or else with another mum. Then they bowl under-arm, and use a plastic bat, and run round cones. They can cut in and out whenever they need to babysit. They can play for an hour and a half or five minutes, it's up to them,' Arfan says.

One day Essex got a call from an irate council about youngsters damaging daffodils in Barking Park and scaring mums with prams. Arfan went to see, and there were 40 or 50 lads with a bat and a tape-ball just wanting somewhere to play. As London is a 24-hour city, young men want to get out and play at various times of day and night: matches that may only last an hour, with six or eight players per side and four to six overs per team. Essex have grown it into a community tape-ball tournament staged at Leyton Orient FC that ends under floodlights.

In other words, Essex listen and respond; they do not impose from a distant office.

They are fortunate to have, in this renovated sports hall in Leyton, the first hub funded by the ECB's south Asian project, but maximising its use is another matter. When Bradford's Park Avenue ground was renovated, the charge was £10 per person per hour – in Bradford's poorest ward, where loads of kids are on school meals – until this cardinal error was rectified. Essex offer 20 hours a week of free community programmes, from mothers and toddlers to Afghan refugees (Afghans, I believe, are the community which is the keenest on playing cricket in Britain, and make up 90% in their refugee courses). If you want to hire one of the four nets, it is £15 per hour for several players to use so two or three quid each.

'This is the way I like to think of it. If a 53-year-old woman rings up and says I want to play cricket in Colchester on a Tuesday evening can we fix her up?' says Arfan. He grew up batting on the concrete that served for a garden in Walthamstow, or rather competing for the bat with his twin brother Adnan. He has played for Wanstead ever since and scored 110 for Cambridge University – when he was studying leisure and tourism management at Ruskin – in his second first-class game, against Kent who had four England Test bowlers in Martin Saggers, Amjad Khan, James Tredwell and Mark Ealham.

Essex have always produced a diverse range of cricketers: from England's two best opening batsmen of modern times, Cook and Graham Gooch; and England's two most defensive all-rounders, JWHT (normally translated as Johnny Won't Hit Today) Douglas and Trevor Bailey; to county cricket's finest comedian in Ray East; and, apart from Harold Larwood, three of England's fastest bowlers before the Second World War in Charles Kortright, Hopper Read and Ken Farnes. Such diversity, surely, will only continue to grow.

***

The most private place to receive a top-secret phone call was not the reception desk of the Meghdoot Hotel in Kanpur, where the England team were staying in early 1982.

'Phone call for Mr Gooch sahib!'

'Phone call, Graham!'

'Zap, it's for you.'

We had just returned to the Meghdoot after another interminable day in the most boring Test series England ever played, in India in 1981/82. The ground was hot and dusty, and you can imagine how polluted the rest of Kanpur was if the ground was called Green Park. India's captain, Sunil Gavaskar, having won the first Test, had decided that all of the next five Test matches would be the most excruciating bore draws, on the flattest pitches and with over-rates that were even slower. We are not talking 12 or 11 overs per hour, but down to nine an hour, which makes less than one ball per minute, even with two spinners bowling.

As Gooch huddled over the reception desk – no chance of the land line working audibly if he had taken the call on the extension in his room – he was trying to listen to Dr Ali Bacher, the boss of South African cricket. Bacher was proposing that Gooch should lead a team of disaffected England players to the apartheid republic; and there were a lot of disaffected players by the end of this tedious series.

A distinction should be made between the two England rebel tours to South Africa. The first was naughty, I would say; the second immoral. Gooch's players did not know what the penalties would be, and lots of English cricket teams had been touring South Africa with official approval until the Gleneagles Agreement. And, by going in the off-season, they were not going to miss any England fixtures. They did not expect such serious consequences as a three-year ban, whereas the 1989 side knew perfectly well they were helping the apartheid government just when they needed it most. (Not being holier than thou, if I had been an ageing cricketer, with a bad back, no other employment and a family to support, I too would probably have had my price.)

His leadership of this first England rebel party to South Africa is the only point I can advance against Graham Gooch. England could have used him, more than any other rebel, for the three years from 1982. On the other side of the equation: has anyone done more for English cricket, on and off the field, in so many capacities?

As a batsman, Gooch scored more competitive runs than anybody ever, over 60,000 – no wonder he got a bad back and adjusted his stance to standing upright. He was the bravest against West Indies' fast bowling, and against them at Headingley in 1991 I saw him play the finest Test innings for England, without much doubt, by a captain or anyone else, until Ben Stokes surpassed him on the same ground 28 years later.

As England captain, Gooch led his players into the modern era by training and going to bed early, instead of drinking and not going out at all, though the end of David Gower's career was an unnecessary fall-out. Since his retirement, Gooch has arguably put back even more, by throwing millions of balls at young Essex and England batsmen, mentoring Cook especially, and by raising funds – which Essex estimate at between £2–3m – for the foundation he launched. All done with those broad sloping shoulders, the same squeaky voice as WG Grace, and the moustache which made him look like the Mexican Zapata.

It cannot be a coincidence that the two fittest England cricketers of their era, and the two finest modern openers, came from Essex, Cook following in Gooch's footsteps on the treadmill. If you were in a taxi somewhere like downtown Auckland in the early 1990s, stuck in traffic, a lumbering figure would pound past along the pavement. Gooch scored the most competitive runs partly because he was physically ahead of the rest of the game. More recently, still on the go, he was doing charity food-drops during the Covid lockdown and delivering hot meals for NHS staff.

In pre-season training at Essex, Cook was always the champion of the bleep tests. Even at the age of 36 he preserved his record of never having been beaten in a bleep test for Essex or England, though if Cook had not retired from international cricket in 2018, Ben Stokes by now would probably be making him puff.

This is some contribution to English cricket. For a dozen years each, Gooch and Cook opened England's Test innings with immense bravery, stubbornness, phlegmatism and stamina, which enabled them to go on and on once they were set; not to forget supreme reflexes. Once Cook was badly bruised in the nets by Tymal Mills, the left-arm fast bowler originally from Essex, and Gooch damaged a finger or two when batting gloves were not what they are, but otherwise they had the reactions to cope with the world's fastest bowlers year after year, and at times in their illustrious England careers they wore down spinners too.

One difference though: they represented different catchment areas. Gooch was an east London boy, who grew up a few minutes' walk from the Leyton ground, often doing his extra physical training with West Ham United. Cook came from Essex's wider catchment area, which includes Cambridgeshire and East Anglia, and in his case Bedford.

By the 1930s Essex were nomadic, without headquarters, going round the county, playing their festival weeks at Brentwood, Colchester, Clacton, Romford and Ilford, Westcliff-on-Sea and Southend-on-Sea – and in some of these towns Essex would play at two different grounds. Other counties, too, took cricket to their communities but not so far into the 1960s as Essex.

Without any control over their grounds, until Chelmsford became their headquarters in the 1967 season, Essex had no say in their home pitches: a fundamental reason for their old 'inconsistency' which can be construed as a euphemism for lack of success. Another reason was their trait of having more than one captain during a season: in nine years, more than any other county, Essex had two official captains or more, amateurs of course. Usually, it was Tom Pearce's job as a wine merchant which had to be accommodated. For his players, it must have been a challenge to turn up at a club ground of a morning not knowing how the pitch would play, or under whom they would play.

Pearce was an international rugby referee in winter, while at the end of each summer he would assemble T.N. Pearce's XI for a first-class game at Scarborough against the touring team, giving everyone a pleasant wind-down after a long, hard summer. As he was also an England selector, he might not have had to do a lot of persuasion when inviting his players. When I was a child, we were told by Harold Macmillan that we had 'never had it so good'; and perhaps, if true, it was partly because life was so much simpler then than now. There was a straightforward duality when it came to choice, not a multiplicity. One chose either BBC or ITV. It was the AA or RAC; Oxford or Cambridge for the Boat Race; and either A.E.R. Gilligan's XI or T.N. Pearce's XI. I thought I preferred Gilligan's team, not that I ever saw either of them: they would play the touring team at Hastings. Did I prefer Gilligan's team because he had more initials? Hope not. But I suspect, if one had to be marooned on a desert island, Pearce would have been the friendlier companion.

In any event, what has made Essex into county champions, more frequently than any other county since 1979, has been their hard work in combing their three Es to maximise their resources: east London, the county of Essex, and East Anglia, one for each of their seaxes.

***

Having sold Leyton in 1922, it was not until 1966 that Essex bought Chelmsford, and like many of their decisions over the years, because they have never had much cash to splash, it was a shrewd investment.

After a hard week in the City, what better way to unwind on a Friday evening than a quick train to Chelmsford where the station is five minutes' walk from the county ground? So much is to be said for placing the cricket ground in the centre of a community, next to the market, and the river and the bus and train stations. If there is no hotel of international renown in Chelmsford for visiting teams (remember the Indians moved out in 2018), well, it is another way of making the most of home advantage.

A main cause of Essex's golden era has been that they have been the most astute in selecting overseas players: whether the exuberant Barbadian all-rounder Keith Boyce; Kenny McEwan of South Africa, as good as any batsman who never played Tests; Allan Border, bringing the same standards to his county as to captaining Australia; or Mark Waugh, most effortless of all-rounders. Doug Insole, who had been Essex's captain in the 1950s, was the *eminence grise* who researched these overseas players and came up with trumps every time, except for one Hugh Page. When Essex played at Castle Park in Colchester, my favourite Essex outground, I could imagine Insole back in the day when the Roman garrison staged their games and circuses on the same sward, making notes about that tall Nubian javelin-thrower, or the tough centurion swordsman from Galicia, as a future overseas player.

Their signings remain shrewd. Was Simon Harmer the most valuable of all Kolpaks? In addition to off-spinning Essex to their two most recent Championships – one haul was 83 wickets in 14 games at only 18 each – Harmer took over as T20 captain and made the winning hit in the 2019 final. Essex's overseas signings, strangely enough in recent years, have often been left-arm pace bowlers, such as Pakistan's Wahab Riaz or Mohammad Amir. Anything to do with creating rough outside the off stump for Harmer's benefit? And so what? All within the rules.

According to Arfan Akram, something else Essex acquired from Riaz and Amir was this nugget: both Pakistanis said they had played only tape-ball until their mid-teens, no hard-ball cricket at all. 'So you don't have to get into the system by the age of 12,' Arfan observes. And by having a team in the ECB City Cup, they used it as a safety net to catch talented 15- to 18-year-olds outside their academy system. Tape-ball cricket expands a talent base enormously.

* * *

Trevor Bailey had a dry humour, which he aired in books, newspapers and on *Test Match Special*; and he certainly 'bowled dry' for England in the 1950s, conceding 2.3 per over in Tests, whenever he was not blocking. (His strike-rate in Tests cannot be calculated because not all the scorebooks survive, and most of them were not detailed enough, but it cannot have exceeded 30 runs per 100 balls.) And, as Bailey played for Essex, his essay on his own county in *Championship Cricket* was the most insightful.

'When an Essex batsman is out of form he has to go a long way to find some nets, for none of our grounds boast these facilities,' Bailey wrote in 1961, before Chelmsford as the new headquarters came on stream. This deficiency would have been quite a handicap for Gooch and Cook if it had continued unrectified; and further explains Essex's inconsistency of old.

'Every time an Essex cricketer arrives at a home match he finds himself in a truly festival atmosphere,' Bailey added. 'The tents and marquees, the deckchairs and flags, the improvisation and the informality all help to produce a feeling of gaiety which seems out of place in more austere surroundings.' Such were the joys of the nomadic existence, to set against the travelling, because in effect the Essex players were playing every game away from home, or at least on the road, all season.

'No fewer than ten members of the Essex executive committee have played in first-class cricket. And most of the others have been active cricketers. To have committeemen who have a practical knowledge of the game which they administrate is obviously a great advantage ... It is true that not all counties can claim such an impressive committee batting order. This may well be one reason why the Essex captain is always granted far more freedom than is the lot of the majority of skippers.'

And, subsequently, why Essex's overseas signings have been so shrewd.

***

As captains, Gooch and Cook were competent and conscientious, but neither so astute as Keith Fletcher. He led them into their golden era of six Championships in 14 seasons, in addition to plenty of limited-overs trophies (until the early 1990s, when Warwickshire surpassed them). Fletcher was England's captain on that 1981/82 tour of India when his response to Gavaskar slowing down the game was to slow it down as much. The most aggressive of county captains, Fletcher went defensive on the international stage.

'Essex CCC is a family,' Mike Selvey wrote in 1992, having played against them for 20 years. 'They feed on togetherness, chumminess and familiarity from the chaps on the gate and in the car park, through the administration to the players. Of all the clubs in the land, Essex engender most affection among not only their own supporters but from players at other counties. Ask any which other county he would like to play for and Essex, rather than one of the big buck clubs, would probably be top of the list.'

Without such stalwarts as Fletcher and his predecessor as captain Brian 'Tonker' Taylor, Insole and Bailey, David Acfield and John Childs, Essex might not have survived their leanest years: in 1966 they were down to a playing staff of 11, one of them a reserve wicketkeeper. Ray East, their left-arm spinner, did much to lighten the strain with his humour. Apart from his own antics – like borrowing a bike to ride round the boundary when fielding deep at both ends, or pretending to be shot when a car back-fired – East was a cause of wit in others, as when buying a water-pistol for his room-mate John Lever, who walked out to bat in Scarborough and squirted the wicketkeeper (it was a festival, not Championship, match).

***

Dan Feist, Essex's cricket operations director, was selected to play for Surrey under-15s. He bowled economically – but never heard from them again. 'I was the only lad in the team not from a private school,' he remembers. He learned what it was like to be an outsider wanting to play cricket, and he has not forgotten.

Feist played for Merstham CC and wondered how his busy father found the time to do so much for the club, like mow the outfield. A Down's Syndrome boy came to them wanting to play and the club set up Merstham Magics, which at times had more than 30 people with similar conditions or cerebral palsy. 'If you're prepared to put that extra commitment in, you get so many rewards from it,' Feist says.

Early on in the Covid season of 2020 Feist had the idea – which the Essex players quickly espoused – that each of them should phone up to 100 of Essex's members to see if they were lonely during this lockdown and wanted to talk. 'Of our 5,000 members we have more than 1,000 who are in that danger area over the age of 70 and probably had to self-isolate,' Feist says. Unequivocally brilliant.

The young pace bowler Aaron Beard talked to a 97-year-old war veteran who had only two members of his regiment still alive. Another player found three members so keen to talk that those three calls took an hour and a half. Some of the players did food drops, working for a charity or out of a restaurant in east London owned by the father of one of their players. Essex's sponsors see the players doing good and offer their help. It is a virtuous circle.

Another of Feist's initiatives is to take the players back to the schools where they started – and thereby offer role models for the next generation. Doug Insole CBE, just before he died in 2017 aged 91, went back to his former school of Sir George Monoux, which had ceased to play cricket before Essex resuscitated their ground. Ravi Bopara went back to the primary school where the caretaker would turn a blind eye when he and his mates climbed back into the school playground out of hours to play cricket: he was moved to see the stumps still painted on the wall.

Ah, Ravi, forgive if I digress! There has been no more sumptuous shot in modern English cricket than Bopara's on-drive, not even Joe Root's back-foot stroke through the covers; I can understand why those who saw Peter May's on-drive wax so lyrical. Bopara says it was the only stroke which his first coach knew how to teach, and that coaching was what he missed most when young until, finally, his attempt to be the only state-school batsman in England's Test batting line-up fizzled out. I think it was the lack of self-esteem which stemmed from his coming from the poorest background of any England cricketer I know. How else could someone who scored three centuries in consecutive Tests against West Indies not go on to a major career? Especially when one of those Test centuries was at Lord's in May, when Fidel Edwards was swinging it at high speed, and Bopara had just flown in from the IPL that had been staged in South Africa. Conditioned by T20 hitting, Bopara stepped back outside leg stump to Edwards' outswingers – and still nailed them through the covers.

When Chris Silverwood was appointed Essex's head coach – taking them to the top of the second division in his first season, and top of the first in his second (2017) before leaving to coach England – he and Feist shared the same values of community engagement. Silverwood would take the trouble to go to a second XI game and talk to all the supporters. As for Feist, one of the benefits of lockdown was that he did not have to commute 36,000 miles a year from his Reigate home to Chelmsford.

As England's new Test philosophy has been defined by Brendon McCullum and Ben Stokes, it can only be a matter of time before Essex's stroke-player Dan Lawrence has a second chance. He was only 17 when he scored 161 against Surrey in his second first-class game. The son of the Chingford groundsman, Lawrence had to find his own way, often literally, when he would have to reach a ground by train as a lad. He has worked out his own style of batting, favouring the leg side, and of spin bowling as well. Too few of today's young batsmen can be bothered to bowl, so it marks Lawrence out, perhaps as Joe Root's successor at No.4?

Essex can also claim to have produced not only the most successful county team of recent decades but a former England captain who is now the best television commentator on cricket. Like Gooch, he came from east London, and grew up at the indoor school in Ilford where his father Joe coached – but without quite the same phlegmatism as Gooch. It is indeed this passion for the game that still burns, and bursts into his commentary, which singles out Nasser Hussain.

Glamorgan

OF ALL the grounds that have staged county cricket, where would you most like to watch a Championship match?

I will not opt for Lord's. Yes, for a Test match, but not for a Middlesex game. Too many parts of the ground are closed for county matches, except for the binge-drinking in a T20 game on a midweek evening.

What about a seaside ground, like Swansea or Scarborough, where after a day's play we can 'wear white flannel trousers and walk upon the beach' as TS Eliot phrased it? Or Folkestone or Eastbourne, if we are allowed an out-ground which used to stage Championship cricket, as for the purpose of this exercise I think we are.

Personally, I would prefer a ground up in the hills, but not Sedbergh, where Lancashire have started to play. The ghost of James Anderson would bestride the ground, grumpily: it is where he broke down before the Ashes of 2019, then returned to the England side without playing a game, only to break down again in the first hour at Edgbaston, leaving the stage to Justin Langer's Australians and their efficiency.

No, it has to be Abergavenny. It is there that I would most like to see a game of Championship cricket, if I am limited to one. It is no longer on Glamorgan's fixture list – whereas the out-grounds of Swansea, Colwyn Bay and Newport are – but it was a regular venue in the 1990s.

Abergavenny lies in Gwent, and Gwent combines the best of England and Wales: it does not have England's density of population, and pollution, or Wales's grim terraces and collieries where men were made to be moles. A Roman settlement, for its iron, it remains a market town, and if we are taking the train from Cardiff – which trundles on to Hereford, Leominster and Ludlow – it is not too long a walk from Abergavenny station to the prosaically named ground at Avenue Road.

Anything but prosaic are the surrounding sylvan hills: the Sugar Loaf, Great and Little Skirrid and the Blorenge, all pushing 2,000 feet, with the Black Mountains and Brecon Beacons beckoning beyond. If I am not covering the game, only watching, I shall walk up the Sugar Loaf at lunchtime. If the connectivity is any good, I will play the 'Lark Ascending' by Vaughan Williams on the way up, or if the sky is azure and the euphoria extreme – as it surely will be in these circumstances – then his 'Fantasia on a Theme' by Thomas Tallis.

Is it the clarity of the unpolluted light, or the greenness of the trees after so much winter rain, or the fact that man has not exploited nature ruthlessly here? In the valley below, on their bucolic and oddly shaped ground, the cricketers in white do not detract from this landscape and sense of well-being; they add to it, being the community at play.

Its odd shape spelt the ground's end as a Glamorgan venue, when six-hitting became too easy, and dangerous. At one point the boundary intrudes until you are standing almost at backward point. Why didn't MCC act 30 years earlier to curb the thickness of bats? Professional cricket would fit into more out-grounds if their cricket committee had done their duty a generation ago.

In 1995 Andrew Symonds – the body-building blaster who went on to represent Australia – hit 254 off 205 balls for Gloucestershire at Abergavenny with 16 sixes, which set a world record. Again six-hitting was too easy when Graeme Hick hit 252, before Glamorgan reached 493/6 in their second innings, which was insufficient to chase down their target.

Back in town, at the Prior Church of St Mary, we should find a moment for the finest piece of art that survives from Celtic Christianity in England and Wales – the wooden carving of the Jesse Tree and its astonishing face. Abergavenny was too remote, at the head of a valley, for this to be destroyed in the Reformation.

Glamorgan cricket used to play a similar role: it was different in kind from anything else in England. Especially after the Second World War, Glamorgan players were born in Wales, short and stocky, spoke Welsh in the field, fielded brilliantly and bowled a lot more spin than other counties. If their players seldom shone on the big stage when selected to represent England, Welsh nationalism fired them up against touring teams on turners at Swansea, where they defeated the Australian tourists of 1964 and 1968. The influx of too many players from the southern hemisphere has extinguished these traditions but, as a faint echo, their one Championship match scheduled for Swansea in 2020 was against Durham, the county least blessed with spinners.

***

It was only the gift of the gab, and smooth talking, which enabled Glamorgan to join the County Championship in 1921: nothing to do with MCC, or any predecessor of the ECB, you just had to persuade enough first-class counties to give you a game. Glamorgan arranged 18 fixtures, the fewest, yet sufficient.

Glamorgan assumed first-class status with a hefty financial deficit, barely any batsmen, and two opening bowlers who were aged 47 and 48. Their promotion 'was not justified by results' *Wisden* proclaimed. 'Looking at the season's work as a whole, it cannot be said that Glamorgan showed anything better than second-rate form.'

This judgement continued to apply through the 1920s. Amateurs were not good enough, professionals were too expensive. In 1929, such were the stability and continuity, they had six captains! One annual report spoke for the inaugural decade: 'In its first few seasons Glamorgan were like no other side; some will say it was not a side at all.'

Only when Glamorgan began to produce young professionals of their own did they justify their status. The first was called, as you might have predicted, Dai Davies – and his story is told in the special Glamorgan edition of the definitive book on the County Championship, *Summer's Crown*, by Stephen Chalke.

With the author's permission I summarise: Davies had finished his shift in the steelworks at Llanelli at 10pm one Friday night in 1923, only to be told his replacement had not turned up, so he kept working till 6am. At 11.30, after four hours' sleep, Davies was told a car was waiting outside his house to take him to Swansea to make his Glamorgan debut against Northamptonshire. Walking out at 12.45, he was told by his captain to bowl the next over and took a wicket in his first over, then a couple more; not bad after a 16-hour shift. Fortunately, the next day was Sunday, so Davies had time to sleep, and on Monday made 58 in his first innings, the highest score in the match for Glamorgan. They won by four wickets, while Davies won himself a three-year contract, and played on till 1939.

Glamorgan became ever more home-grown, and stronger, under the captaincy and secretaryship of Maurice Turnbull, who was killed in Normandy, then of Wilf Wooller. In the 1950s they fielded XIs who had all been born in Wales. Only Willie Jones, according to Glamorgan's archivist and scorer Andrew Hignell, was fluent in Welsh, but they all knew a bit. 'We did all our sledging in Welsh,' wrote Tony Lewis in his essay for the special Glamorgan edition of *Summer's Crown*.

If the county has a second language now, it is more likely to be Afrikaans. Five of Glamorgan's players were born in South Africa, including the new Steve Smith, Marnus Labuschagne. Whether Kolpaks or overseas signings or EU passport-holders, they are excellent value, and it speaks well of the culture created by Matthew Maynard, in his second term as head coach, that Labuschagne preferred Cardiff to much higher offers elsewhere. Yet, as these South Africans pound away, whether back of a length or 'in good areas', this is not Welsh cricket. And the mind might drift to a match at the Arms Park in Cardiff in 1935: Glamorgan v the South Africans, not Glamorgan including South Africans. It was when the tourists scored 401, then Dai Davies carried his bat for 75 out of Glamorgan's 142, who fell to 114/9 in their second innings with a while to go.

Then a Glamorgan batsman took charge, his name Cyril Smart, frozen in time as 'Slogger Smart'. He had come from Wiltshire, from the lovely village of Lacock, where lived Fox Talbot, who had taken the first photographs – unless we believe the French narrative that they got there first. Now the ground at Lacock is lovely in accordance with the village, which stages costume dramas if a scene is required with coaching inns and cobbles; and its rustic cricket was not going to produce a professional batsman, except that Smart's father was the cricket professional at Marlborough College. So, this is how 'Slogger Smart' learned to bat.

In the season of 1935 Smart was captured by the poet Danny Abse, then a wide-eyed schoolboy in Cardiff. Now we do not know which particular stroke it was that lodged in Abse's memory, but it could have been revealed in that match against the South Africans, when Smart hit 114 not out in a last-wicket stand of 131, and led Glamorgan to an honourable draw. Or it could have been the game against Hampshire that same season, when Smart lined up the off-spinner Gerry Hill and hit him for 6, 6, 4, 6, 6, 4 in one over: 32, to that point, was the most runs scored off a first-class over. Slogger Smart: a smart slogger.

> *1935. I watched Glamorgan play*
> *especially, Slogger Smart, free*
> *from the disgrace of fame, unrenowned,*
> *but the biggest hit with me.*

After the second verse, about how Smart would often hit the ball out of the Arms Park, Abse recalls this particular hit:

> *Once, hell for leather, it curled*
> *over the workman's crane*
> *in Westgate Street*
> *to crash, they said, through a discreet*
> *Angel Hotel windowpane*

That would have been a mighty hit. The hotel and street are still there, even if the Arms Park cricket ground had to make way for the Millennium Stadium.

Then Abse imagines Smart hitting the ball even further, in a 'rainbow arch' over the Angel Hotel – for a rainbow described the trajectory of a six in the olden days. The ball soars over the River Taff that flows alongside, upstream towards the Caerphilly Mountains. Perhaps it came to rest in Abergavenny, near the Sugar Loaf, except those green hills are now locked down, so nobody could fetch the ball back.

***

If Glamorgan largely justified its first-class status by the diversity it brought to our domestic scene – diversity of both players and places (and it had the ugliest of all county grounds in Margam next to the Port Talbot steelworks, as well as the loveliest in Abergavenny) – yet the Welsh county has also contributed to England's Test cricket. It is even worth hypothesising: would England have ever regained the Ashes since 1989 at all without the fire and brimstone of Simon Jones? In 2005 Jones was a steeplechaser, pawing the ground, ready to hurl himself at the highest fences. Australia's mental domination would have become ever more extreme, perhaps total, if England had not won in 2005.

When Duncan Fletcher was Glamorgan's coach, he heard about this mettlesome colt sent to Millfield. Jones early on would vary between a run-up that was too long and a run-up that was too short. Jones was happy experimenting with run-ups, grips and angles under Troy Cooley, the affable Tasmanian who was England's bowling coach. Cooley acted as big brother to Matthew Hoggard, Steve Harmison and Andrew Flintoff, calming their nerves on matchday, but all Jones needed was unleashing.

Jones was fired to concert pitch whenever he saw an Australian, following the appalling abuse he had received when lying on the Brisbane turf in 2002/03 after diving in the outfield and rupturing his right cruciate. Thence came the fire which singed Australia, whether he was up and at their batsmen or batting at No.11: Jones slogged 66 off 98 balls for only twice out in 2005, and but for his rollicking last-wicket stand with Flintoff at Edgbaston, would England have won by two runs? The brimstone had taken 18 wickets at only 21 runs each by the time Jones hobbled off in the fourth Test at Trent Bridge, never to return to international cricket.

Having been born in Swansea, it is unlikely that Jones – or his father Jeff, also a fast bowler for Glamorgan and England – would ever have played major cricket if Glamorgan had not been given first-class status. Simon batted left-hand and bowled right, the other way round from his father, but the careers of both were suddenly ended by the occupational hazard of injury.

Robert Croft bowled useful spells of off spin, especially in Sri Lanka in 2000/01, but Simon Jones is the only Glamorgan bowler to have taken 50 Test wickets for England. Tony Lewis did well as England's captain in India and Pakistan in 1972/73, losing two Tests, winning one, especially for someone who had never played Test cricket. He and Allan Watkins are the only Glamorgan players to have made a century for England, one for Lewis, two for Watkins. Overall, it has been the same with several counties in the West of England: their best cricketers, when selected for international duty, have not excelled before returning to quieter pastures. Except for Jones, that champion steeplechaser in 2005.

* * *

Never mind skill-sets however, or perfect techniques, what about the diversity: has any first-class county produced a more varied and colourful collection of cricketers than this Glamorgan XI?

1. Norman Biggs represented Glamorgan in 1893 before they gained first-class status, and Wales at rugby, then joined the West African Police and died in Nigeria in 1908 from a poisoned arrow. Was this an omen? During subsequent years of discord in the Glamorgan dressing room, most notably the 1980s, other players fell victim to poisoned shafts.

2. Royston Gabe-Jones remains the only 15-year-old to have played a Championship match in 1922 when, for the last game, Glamorgan were so short they roped in four debutants. Aged 15 years and nine months, the boy did alright, going in at seven, batting for an hour and a half, averting the follow-on and finishing 6 not out. He was at Blundell's at the time, later played rugby for Cardiff and became a businessman there, but never played for Glamorgan again. No allowance made for youth.

3. Fred Mathias. Won the Military Cross at the age of 20 for his reconnaissance work in the Royal Flying Corps during the First World War and is said to have skirmished with the Red Baron. So you could say he was one of the few students to have had a bird's-eye view of his subject when he read geography at Gonville and Caius. Availability seems to have been his great attribute as a cricketer: being a stockbroker in Cardiff, he was often available when Glamorgan were short. His first-class batting average was 12.

4. Hugh Vaughan-Thomas. Younger brother of the famous radio broadcaster in the Second World War, Wynford Vaughan-Thomas. Having become a teacher in Scotland, he became a major figure in developing landing-craft for D-Day, trialling them on Scottish beaches.

5. Tom Brierley. A wicketkeeper-batsman from Manchester Grammar, he achieved two extraordinary feats: one was scoring 116 for Glamorgan v Lancashire AND 116 for Lancashire v Glamorgan. The second was while eloping during the 1932 season, when he was supposed to be qualifying by residence for Glamorgan, to represent Canada (where he sometimes coached cricket) in the 1932 Olympics at Los Angeles in lacrosse.

6. Aubrey Morgan. From the family that owned a big department store in Cardiff, he became a high-flying diplomat in Washington during the Second World War and did enough for Anglo-American relations to be decorated by the USA.

7. Wilf Wooller. Only one person could lead this disparate lot: the man who played rugby for Wales the first time they beat England at Twickenham and the first time they beat the All Blacks, and who captained Glamorgan to their first Championship in 1948. The most dogged of all-rounders, if he was a bit cranky by then, he had been a Japanese POW.

8. Samuel Silkin QC, later Baron Silkin of Dulwich. He was trying to win a Blue when given a game for Glamorgan against Cambridge in 1938. He did not make the cut as a leg-spinner, but he did as Attorney-General from 1974 to 1979.

9. Gareth Edwards. Not the rugby player, this one played for England under-19s and one game as a spinner for Glamorgan in 1997 before becoming the long-term producer of *A Question of Sport*.

10. Jack Mercer. First to take 1,000 first-class wickets for Glamorgan, he had all the tricks as a medium-pacer and as a member of the Magic Circle. He spent two days in a bomb crater after being shell-shocked in the First World War.

11. Frank Ryan. As talented and maverick as another left-arm spinner educated in Bedford, Monty Panesar. Son of an Irish father who worked on the Indian railways, he joined the Royal Flying Corps, and impressed the Hon. Lionel Tennyson who captained Hampshire, but, prone to drink, qualified for Glamorgan instead. Reputed to have slept under the covers at a ground more than once when the worse for wear.

***

What is the next number in this sequence: 27, 21, 28 ... ? If you know, it is worth a bet on Glamorgan winning their fourth Championship. The first came in 1948, after 27 years, the second in 1969, the third in 1997.

That first title was achieved under Wilf Wooller, who developed a strategy which I would sum up as 'Mangle and Strangle'. In his biography of Wooller, *The Skipper*, Andrew Hignell records that in 1948 a mangle was carried round all the county's home grounds on the back of a lorry with a load of old blankets. Whenever it rained – and it rains twice as much in south Wales as eastern England, which is some handicap for Glamorgan to overcome – Wooller told everyone to mop up the field, put the blankets through the mangle, and mop again.

The strangle part of Wooller's strategy was to get opposing batsmen caught on the leg side. The preceding season, after looking round the country, Wooller concluded: 'There were few batsmen technically equipped as on-side players.' Then you could pack as many fielders on the leg side as you liked, and Wooller did, bowling right-arm inswing or off spin with a bevy of short legs. One of their old pros, Arnold Dyson, had learned in Yorkshire leagues the basic principles: stay low, never anticipate where the ball is going, just wait and react. The late Peter Walker became king of the leg trap, accepting more than 600 first-class catches, but Allan Watkins, Wooller himself and others were pretty hot, even without helmets. 'We are aware we cannot compete with Middlesex in batting or Derbyshire in bowling. But in fielding we give first to no side,' said Wooller after winning Glamorgan's first title.

In that first Championship-winning summer of 1948 Glamorgan hosted fixtures at Neath, Newport and Ebbw Vale – full value from their mangle – as well as Swansea and Cardiff. They played one trick by selecting Stan Trick, a left-arm spinner who took 22 wickets in his first two games; then an ace, by bringing back Johnnie Clay, their master off-spinner, aged 50, to seal the deal. When Clay rapped Hampshire's last man on the pads, who should be the umpire but Dai Davies, who is said to have impartially replied: 'That's out – and we've won the Championship!'

Their titles in 1969 and 1997 had much in common: not nearly so much spin as in 1948, although Don Shepherd and Robert Croft were excellent off-spinners, but solid batting line-ups, good pace bowling, and a valuable Pakistani. In 1969 it was Majid Khan who embellished the runs from Alan Jones (Glamorgan's all-time highest first-class run-scorer) and Tony Lewis. I was a lad at the pivotal game at Cheltenham: Gloucestershire were top of the table, powered by Mike Procter, bound for their first Championship of the modern era, until their batting collapsed for 73. Defeatism hummed around the ground. Majid strolled out, stroked 69, and Glamorgan not only won by an innings but knocked the stuffing out of their rivals.

Needing to win their last game at Taunton in 1997, Matthew Maynard was as princely as Majid when batting on a flier against Andy Caddick in filthy light; Hugh Morris too made a century in his last game before retiring to join the ECB; and a third batting stalwart, Steve James, hit the winning runs, although his favourite venue was Colwyn Bay, where he averaged 135. These three batsmen all hit fifty first-class hundreds, more or less.

This Glamorgan team had largely grown up together, by playing as the Academy team against men in the South Wales League. Waqar Younis was the Pakistani who complemented Steve Watkin when taking the new ball, and who made the old one reverse-swing at Sophia Gardens, while Duncan Fletcher master-minded. It augurs well for Glamorgan, and a return to their fundamentals, that James, Maynard and Morris became leading figures in the club's administration and coaching.

The Welsh language remains a unique resource for Glamorgan, a second language which no other county has. For decades Eddie Bevan reported in Welsh for BBC Radio; the website of Golwg360 provides daily match reports on Glamorgan's games in Welsh by Alun Rhys Chivers; and two cricket books have been published in Welsh.

***

The attempt to turn Sophia Gardens into a Test ground was misconceived, as the ECB have now admitted. Half the spectators for Test matches in Cardiff travelled from England, and another quarter from West Wales. Cardiff has simply never had the spectator base, at least since Glamorgan moved from the Arms Park in the city centre to Sophia Gardens in 1967, as they had to do, to make way for rugby and the Millennium Stadium.

Still, two Test memories in Cardiff will always survive: one of that last afternoon in 2009 when Ricky Ponting tried everything to dislodge England's tail after the last specialist batsman in Paul Collingwood had gone – tried everything, that is, except the most obvious ploy, which was to unleash Mitchell Johnson against Monty Panesar and James Anderson. To England's eternal gratitude, Ponting preferred the part-time off spin of Marcus North. This was as nerve-racking as any England last-wicket stand ever, and the crowd played their vocal part – as they did when Joe Root stroked the most sublime counter-attacking century in 2015 to put England's campaign to regain the Ashes on track.

As a venue for one-day and T20 internationals, though, Sophia Gardens serves delightfully. The walk from the station runs beside the Taff; the setting is rural within a city; and beyond the ground are more pitches in the park where south Asians play. Glamorgan, it should be said, are more likely to win their fourth Championship title when their links with their south Asian community are as strong as they have been with Northern Titans.

England, since their defeat at Cardiff in the Champions Trophy semi-final of 2017 at any rate, seem to feel at home there, where the range-hitting of the likes of Jason Roy and Jos Buttler has become a wonder to behold. The dimensions add a peculiar interest, the straight boundaries being so short, the square ones so long.

And if Dannie Abse's ghost walks upstream from the Arms Park to Sophia Gardens during an ODI, he will notice how the trajectory of balls hit for six has evolved. No longer the 'rainbow arch' but the trajectory of a tracer bullet, when Buttler clears his front leg and straight-drives the ball no higher than a few yards above the ground – not so high as the top of the sightscreen – before it skims into the Taff. Different times, different techniques, but still 'hell for leather', and a big hit with me.

Gloucestershire

GLOUCESTERSHIRE, LIKE Kent, celebrated – or would have celebrated – their 150th anniversary in 2020. The difference is that Kent rose to the front rank of counties because their club cricket was so strong. Gloucestershire were transformed into a first-class county by a single family.

In the first week of June 1870, Gloucestershire CCC began with a bang. What other noise would accompany the arrival of the boisterous Grace brothers from the unvarnished outskirts of Bristol? The three of them were spearheaded by the most famous sportsman there had ever been, William Gilbert Grace – and, some would say, there has ever been in Britain.

So no question who topped the bill for Gloucestershire's inaugural game against Surrey, even though one of the visitors, HH Stephenson, had captained one of the two English tours to Australia with all the mystique that involved. Still only 21, WG was averaging over 50 with the bat in first-class cricket – when pitches were so rough that a total of 100 gave you a fair chance of winning – and 13 with the ball.

Let us first adjourn to the tavern where Surrey's players are congregating on the eve of Gloucestershire's inaugural game. They are men of the world, and all except one are professional cricketers. I suspect they are more likely to have lodged near the docks and Temple Meads station – Brunel's railway from London to Bristol had made this fixture possible – than in genteel Clifton, where the three-day match was to be staged on the Downs.

'Listen up, lads,' says Surrey's team analyst in the tavern. 'This is Gloucester's first game so we haven't got much data. But basically, WG opens the batting with one of his brothers, then he opens the bowling with another brother, so nobody else gets much of a game. They haven't got any professionals either, just jazz-hat amateurs, so we should be done and dusted in a couple of days.'

And Surrey had four of the world's finest cricketers, including two who were to be selected for England's first Test in Australia seven years later. It would have been three, except their ace wicketkeeper Ed Pooley had been arrested for gambling earlier in the tour.

We know the sun came out after the 1pm start from the report in the *Western Daily Press* on the Clifton Flower Show which was taking place at the zoo, less than a mile from this match on Durdham Down: 'One was rejoiced to see that all the costly and elegant attire on which milliners and dressmakers have been engaged for weeks was not doomed to blush unseen,' their correspondent wrote, with equal floweriness. Some people appear to have attended both events, the cricket and the flower show: 'There were probably more than 3,000 present, including a good many ladies,' the *Bristol Times and Mirror* reported about the match, with several tents, 'one of them a very commodious one for the convenience of the ladies.' Gloucestershire's manhood was in full bloom on the cricket field, like the azaleas, for all their players were younger than 30.

Once the sun had emerged above Durdham Down the view would have been magnificent. The ground was right next to Avon Gorge, which would have looked, well, gorgeous: its cliffs boast a unique flora of yellows, whites and purples. Bristol's wealth was based on the tobacco and wine trades, so ships were still sailing up the Avon beneath Brunel's majestic Clifton suspension bridge. A pity this ground was never used for another county match: an Act of Parliament forbade any area of the Downs to be fenced in, or admission charged, and one can hardly imagine that WG would have played for very long for free. So Gloucestershire moved to Clifton College and, in 1889, to their own new headquarters at Nevil Road.

WG opened the batting for Gloucestershire with his elder brother Edward or 'EM', and top-scored with 26, batting 'very carefully' in their total of 106. All the bowling in this game was over-arm except for a few lobs by EM Grace and the round-arm off spin of Surrey's opening bowler James Southerton – which sounds sloggable on a true pitch but not on a rough one. The Durdham ground was used by Clifton Cricket Club and by Clifton Rugby Club. Lawnmowers had been invented up the road near Stroud in 1830, but one doubts whether much rolling of the pitch or outfield was done.

WG opened the bowling as well, of course, this time with his younger brother Fred, both medium-pace to judge by the reports, and very accurate. Of the first ten overs bowled by the brothers, nine were maidens. The over consisted of only four balls but even so this was pressure. The Grace brothers reduced Surrey to 82/8 by the end of day one.

Left-handed batsmen were rare in this era of Victorian conformity. No left-handed batsman was to make a Test century for England until 1912 (Frank Woolley). Yet their value was illustrated by Surrey's left-hander George Griffith who rallied the tail, hit an unbeaten 41, and took Surrey to 134, a first-innings lead of 28.

WG, interesting to note, was taken off by Gloucestershire's captain after Griffith hit him a couple of times. Nobody else would have dared, except his elder brother EM. In his obituary *Wisden* said that EM would have been the greatest cricketer but for WG, and he must have had some strength of character. Yet after Gloucestershire's inaugural match, WG took over from EM as captain – for the small matter of the next 28 years. In 1899 he fell out with Gloucestershire when he tried to play simultaneously for the new first-class side of London County (for £600 a year, decent wedge for an amateur). Therefore, WG played 359 first-class games for Gloucestershire, and was captain in 358.

Soon WG's force of personality was again manifest. He shared an opening stand with EM that cleared the arrears and was then given out, caught behind. He walked off and told the press reporters, and no doubt everyone else in earshot, that he had not hit it: 'According to the batsman's statement he did not touch the ball,' the *Western Daily Press* reported. It was Gloucestershire's umpire too that WG was undermining: each county supplied an umpire, and Charles Pullen, the Clifton club pro, stood for the home side.

For this inaugural game and for years afterwards the Gloucestershire team consisted of three Graces, a few other Bristol amateurs like 'Frizzie' Bush, who represented England at rugby, and a couple of chaps from Cheltenham. A young Irishman just out of Cheltenham College, Charles Filgate, took charge after WG had been given out: he hit 48 not out, including a five. No sixes in those days, or rather only all-run sixes: even when the ball was hit on to the roof of one of the tents, it only counted as four.

Surrey's old sweat Southerton had bowled throughout – 90 four-ball overs unchanged – for his 13 wickets. Surrey were set 140 to win. By the close of day two, the visitors had reached 30/1 against the bowling of WG and Fred Grace.

To illustrate how difficult batting could be before the heavy roller, Surrey batted for 101 overs in their second innings – and were dismissed for 88, so that Gloucestershire won their inaugural game by 51 runs. Harry Jupp, who would be in England's first Test team, opened and 'carried out his bat for 50, which occupied him nearly four hours' according to the *Morning Post*. It added: 'The wicket "kicked" a good deal towards the end of the game.'

Surrey had been getting close, reaching 76/6, when WG was taken off. Did that seal the end of EM's captaincy career? You can still hear mutterings, growing into grumblings, through the beard that was feared. But the switch worked and a slow left-arm spinner, Fenton Miles, mopped up while Fred Grace plugged away at the other end for 50 consecutive overs. Fred was only 19 and seems to have had the most attractive personality of all the Grace brothers, only to die of pneumonia less than a month after making his Test debut in 1880 alongside his two brothers.

In the return match against Surrey at the Oval, and now instated as captain, WG was back to his normal self, scoring 143, then bowling almost throughout as Gloucestershire won by an innings and plenty. He was so many streets ahead of his contemporaries – even more than Don Bradman was – in scoring three times as many runs as the next-best batsman, and taking twice as many wickets as the next-best bowler, that surely he has to be rated, still, the greatest cricketer.

Gloucestershire were up and running as a first-class county. Indeed they were *the* county of the 1870s, thanks to their Grace triumvirate (while their eldest brother became club secretary). *Wisden* stated Gloucestershire were 'the champion county' in 1874, 1876 and 1877, and shared the title with Nottinghamshire in 1873. Almost everyone in cricket agreed. It was left to newspapers and periodicals to work out their own method of scoring – fewest games lost or most games won – but, whatever the points system, Gloucestershire were the strongest shire.

Saying the County Championship did not start until 1890 is a convenient fiction, imposed after the event, to coincide with the first central organising body, a forerunner of the ECB. Unlike Northamptonshire and Somerset, Gloucestershire have won the Championship; and perhaps this very knowledge made them rest upon their laurels. They became used to having a world-class cricketer, and could afford to forget about grassroot structures; for, amazing to relate, starting with WG, Gloucestershire carried on producing great cricketers for a hundred years.

***

WG's successor as 'The Champion' was not one of his own sons – and certainly not the poor boy christened William Gilbert Grace junior, who pre-deceased him with appendicitis. He was Gilbert Jessop: the cricketer most suited to T20 who never played that format, but still the sensation of the Edwardian era.

The clue lies in Jessop's nickname: 'The Croucher'. Your elite cricketer has worked out a technique ahead of its time, and Jessop used at least two methods that were unique. One was that he lowered his eyes to the height of the stumps as the bowler delivered, and this crouching enabled him to get under the ball, to hit it out of the ground. His second idiosyncrasy was that he varied his grip on the handle (a long one) of his bat. If he sensed the ball would be full, he held his hands at the top of the blade to drive; if short, he gripped the bat lower down to cut or pull. Not very academic – he spent four years at Cambridge without gaining a degree – Jessop had a cricket brain. I keep a letter from his biographer, Gerald Brodribb, which says that Jessop designed and made his own batting gloves out of rubber garden hose stuck on an ordinary glove. ('Only once did he break a finger!')

Had Jessop had been playing now, in his prime, he could have been the biggest English cricketer yet in the Indian Premier League, bigger than Jos Buttler or Ben Stokes, for in addition to his hitting he was a fast bowler – he won his first Test cap in 1899 as a fast bowler. He had a penchant for bowling bouncers from round the wicket, another method a century ahead of its time, before Stuart Broad tried the ploy – and a 'gun fielder' at cover. In every role his pantherish physique enabled him to coil up then unleash. But mainly he was a hitter, and you only have to look at the black and white photographs – no film, alas – to appreciate that what Jessop was doing then, most white-ball batsmen do now.

Here Jessop runs down the pitch like Kevin Pietersen to drive with his back leg in the air like a flamingo. Here he swipes a full-length ball outside off stump over square leg; here he is slog-sweeping. As the 11th child of a Cheltenham doctor, he was brought up in a small garden, with the surgery windows on the off side, hence this leg-side repertoire. Jessop did learn to upper cut, from what we know, but he did not ramp, so he would have had to learn a trick or two before making his debut for Kanpur Kings or Lucknow Lancers or whoever; but he was still a century ahead of his time.

CB Fry, the first real analyst, observed that Jessop's power came from several sources: 'Precision in timing, an extraordinary freedom and quickness of arm-swing, aided and accelerated by a very full use of the wrists, and a knack of hurling every ounce of his body-weight into his strokes.'

The trouble is that scorers in Jessop's era recorded a batsman's innings in terms of minutes, and seldom added the number of balls. But we know he hit 61 off 24 balls for Gloucestershire v Somerset, and 72 off 29 against Warwickshire – in three-day Championship games, when no great need to hurry. In his two finest Test innings he scored 93 off 69 balls against South Africa in 1907 and 102 off 79 against Australia at the Oval in 1902, in 'Jessop's Match'. His Test average was not worthy but in this, the most famous innings for England before Ian Botham, Jessop later wrote that he was determined not to hit across the line against the brisk off breaks of Hugh Trumble.

Jessop reached 100 in less than an hour 15 times in first-class cricket, and 200 in exactly two hours against Sussex. Against the West Indians on their first tour of England in 1900, he hit 157 in one hour to their utter astonishment. The *Bristol Times and Mirror* reported: 'One of them [the West Indian fielders] would lie down and literally shake with laughter after a big hit.'

And he was robbed. Until 1910 the ball had to be hit out of the ground in England to count as six. Hundreds, or thousands, of Jessop's fours in his 26,000 first-class runs would have counted as six nowadays. But he might not have played much red-ball cricket, for Gloucestershire or anyone else, as he would have been raking it in for Hobart Hurricanes, Jamaica Tallawahs and Barisal Burners, as well as being the MVP in the IPL.

***

No county has been so influenced by its past as Gloucestershire, except perhaps the county that simultaneously celebrated their 150th anniversary, Kent. So often in British life, the Victorian past and its massive infrastructure dictate. No starting with a clean sheet.

Rather like an oil-rich country, Gloucestershire had little need to be proactive. They could sit back and wait for the next great batsman to come along. First WG Grace, then Gilbert Jessop, then Wally Hammond and, when he retired in 1947, along came Tom Graveney, though he had to leave for Worcestershire and acquire some steel in his soul before being fulfilled as a great batsman. Why bother creating pathways when you have such talent on tap in the county?

All that Gloucestershire's administrators had to do was ensure that 1) the pitches at Nevil Road turned and 2) the Cheltenham Festival was an annual success, keeping their members and other supporters content.

Of the 50 leading wicket-takers in first-class cricket of all time, five have been Gloucestershire spinners, one-tenth; while a sixth, WG, was his inimitable self, taking wickets with pace in his youth and non-turning off breaks in his dotage (plus plenty of chat to the batsman and just a scintilla of pressure on the umpire). The secret was simple: sand. Loads of sand was spread over the square at Nevil Road each spring, and the home spinners waxed.

None of these spinners did much for England: of their left-armers, George Dennett did not play a Test, Charlie Parker and Sam Cook one each; of their off-spinners, Tom Goddard and John Mortimore played a handful (and only David Allen had a fulfilled career). The pick was Parker, but man-handling Sir Pelham Warner in a lift, when he was the most influential man in English cricket, was not a great career move. If ever there was a bowler to pit against Don Bradman, it was surely Parker, a relentlessly accurate left-arm spinner turning the ball away from the right-hander, bowling a fullish length and teasing the batsman into off-driving on the front foot – a shot which Bradman was as loath to play as Steve Smith, being equally bottom-handed. But Parker was restricted to one Test (28 overs, 2-32), and to dismissing Bradman twice cheaply for Gloucestershire in 1930 – the game which ended in a tie – while the Don romped round the rest of Britain unimpeded.

No specialist fast bowler, however: Gloucestershire could not produce one of those. Hence, for all their great batsmen, and their spinners who took wickets by the thousand, they have never won the Championship since the 1870s, although they have come second six times. Indeed, WG, Jessop and Hammond had to do much of the pace bowling themselves, as well as bat, field and captain.

The county's second asset was their Cheltenham Festival. Back in 1876 at the College Ground WG had scored the first triple-century in the Championship, an unbeaten 318 against Yorkshire. One local newspaper suggested WG had placed a bet on himself doing so: if he had, this was not misplaced confidence, nor contrary to the laws of the day. He had scored 344 for MCC against Kent and 177 against Nottinghamshire in his two previous innings: just 839 first-class runs in ten days!

Ever since, the Cheltenham Festival has been a highlight of the social calendar. Wine flows in the tents, cider and beer in the temporary stands; the summer is customarily at its hottest when the festival is staged in the college holidays; and splendid is the view of the surrounding Cotswolds, where colonels and nabobs retired after making their fortune in India. If Gloucestershire have been having a poor season then win at Cheltenham, jolly good show! And it is much the same if they have been having a poor season then lose at Cheltenham. The occasion is the thing.

My father always claimed he had seen the most prolific week of any cricketer at first-class level: Wally Hammond's at Cheltenham in 1928. Against Surrey, in a game of otherwise lowish scores, Hammond scored 139 and 143, and took ten catches at slip – mostly off Parker – and dismissed Jack Hobbs for 96. Against Worcestershire (the game starting the next day) he bowled throughout, taking 15 wickets for 128, and scored 80 as Gloucestershire won by an innings.

My father was star-struck for life. He said the two greatest people who ever lived were Shakespeare and Hammond. He obtained an autograph – the latter's unfortunately – or rather he persuaded his twin sister to ask him; and Wally was far more inclined to respond to a female request.

A later Cheltenham Festival gave me an inkling of Hammond on the go. Zaheer Abbas – the only Asian batsman to make 100 first-class centuries – was batting for Gloucestershire against Essex's David Acfield, a fine off-spinner turning the ball down the slope. Zaheer, batting at the Chapel end, had the silkiest cover drive, maybe even wristier than Hammond's, and he kept cover-driving and piercing the field even when Acfield shifted his line ever further to leg side and speared the ball in at Zaheer's toes. The crowd, drunk already on their beverages and the setting's beauty, went delirious.

***

When you walked into Nevil Road until a couple of years ago, photographs of certain Gloucestershire cricketers were posted on either side of a passageway leading to the pavilion. No sign of the county's most successful captain, Mark Alleyne, who originally came from Barbados, or of Courtney Walsh, from Jamaica, who was great value as an overseas signing, taking over 800 Championship wickets at 20.01 runs each. When he and David Lawrence (not depicted either) were steaming in at hard and bouncy Cheltenham, batting was a lot easier in Tests on bland pitches. One overseas player who was accorded a photograph was Jonty Rhodes, of South Africa, who played one season.

Alleyne led Gloucestershire to two limited-overs trophies in 1999, and to all three in 2000. He, and the Kiwi coach John Bracewell, worked out their formula. The county had no star players – still don't, really, because they cannot afford one – but they had loads of all-rounders, including Alleyne, and fine teamwork. On a dry, grudging pitch at Nevil Road they would muster a total of sorts, then squeeze the life out of opponents with two off spinners and a battery of medium-pacers taking pace off the ball. Run down the pitch to counter them? Not with Jack Russell standing up.

Middlesex had been the home of Afro-Caribbean cricket, not least because it had Haringey Cricket College, which had nurtured Alleyne and more than a dozen other county players. Then it became Bristol, when Alleyne, Lawrence and Walsh were local heroes, and Bristol West Indians had their own ground and a pro from Barbados. Now it is nowhere, unless it is Hove.

***

The only drawback to this strategy of winning white-ball trophies was that Gloucestershire's Championship cricket was de-prioritised. They were demoted in 2005 and stayed in the second division until promoted at the end of September 2021. No great batsman or other star players, no big budget, no sand to be spread on pitches any more, just an arrangement whereby private school cricketers from Oxfordshire would join those from Gloucestershire. A difficult gig for Richard Dawson when he became head coach in early 2015, aged 34.

Yet Dawson worked wonders in the red- and white-ball formats to make the most of limited resources. Like so many coaches – England's former head coach Chris Silverwood, and the head coach who led Essex to the Championship and T20 titles in 2021 Anthony McGrath – Dawson was born and brought up in Yorkshire and played for the county. He had a few Tests for England, without cracking it at that level.

'He is very, very detailed with his tactics,' said the Gloucestershire all-rounder Benny Howell about Dawson. 'He doesn't sleep much because he spends so much time in going into detail – like at Cheltenham he worked out that so many runs went to the third man boundary in the Championship that we don't bother with a gully and always start with a third man. Yet he is old-school in that he keeps it simple for us, and he is always ready to throw balls at you in the nets.'

One of the county's initiatives to celebrate their 150th birthday was inviting 150 schools to visit Nevil Road, or the Cheltenham Festival, which might make the start of a future pathway. Another of Gloucestershire's initiatives during lockdown was to live-stream their games at Bristol with six cameras, covering every blade of grass, not the two which had been the national norm.

Nevil Road itself has never looked lovelier or, at least, the ground is the nearest it has been to handsome against the background of new apartments. Why an exposed field beside such Dickensian buildings as the Mueller Orphanage was ever chosen to be their headquarters is inexplicable – unless there is truth in the rumour that WG was a big friend of the developer. Was there something in it for WG when he declared the new Nevil Road to be 'one of the best grounds in the world'? Wouldn't put it past him.

Hampshire

NO FIRST-CLASS county has been so dependent on patrons as Hampshire. From within its borders the county has produced astonishingly few cricketers of note, especially when compared to neighbours like Surrey and Sussex. Without patrons, therefore, Hampshire would have resembled its neighbours to the west, Dorset and Wiltshire, and might never have risen to first-class status.

These patrons began with the Earl of Tankerville and Sir Horatio Mann, continued with the Honourable Lionel Tennyson, grandson of the poet, and carry on today in the person of Rod Bransgrove. Their purses have enabled Hampshire to import cricketers from other counties and countries, and thereby win the relatively large number of 14 trophies. The trend is as strong now as it ever was.

A second feature of Hampshire cricket has been the sociable nature of their captains, often Old Etonians whose exploits have been given more space in *Tatler* than *The Cricketer*. In all the annals of cricket, it is hard to think of anyone who has played harder – off the field – than Tennyson, Colin Ingleby-Mackenzie and Shane Warne.

Most stories about this triumvirate of Hampshire captains have the same theme: after a day's play in the provinces, they drive to a party in Chelsea, carouse and dance with society girls till dawn, and are then chauffeured back to their game.

The only difference in these narratives lies in whether or not they have time for a nap before the resumption of play; and Tennyson and Ingleby-Mackenzie probably consumed less pizza.

Whether this sociable disposition of their captains has made Hampshire more watchable is a matter for debate. Tennyson would keep the same pair of medium-pacers on all day; Ingleby-Mackenzie wrung hundreds of maiden overs per season out of the dour Derek Shackleton; and Hampshire, overall, have drawn a higher proportion of Championship games than most counties.

On the other hand, in the seaside setting of the United Services ground in Portsmouth or Dean Park in Bournemouth – fresh air mixed with the munching of sandwiches in deckchairs and the burr of John Arlott's commentary – the impression was often given that Hampshire's captain was about to make a sporting declaration, and that their cricket was the most carefree of all the counties.

A third theme runs through Hampshire's cricket, or at any rate bookends their history:

There is a green hill far away
Without a city wall

We may remember this hymn – and the music teacher saying that 'without' in this case means 'outside', not the normal sense of lacking something. In any event, the words will serve to describe the location of Hampshire's first ground and their last or current one: Broadhalfpenny Down in Hambledon – the so-called 'cradle of cricket' – and the Ageas Bowl in Botley on the outskirts of Southampton.

The two grounds have much in common: their grand views over Hampshire's hills sweeping away to the south coast and grand matches involving not only Hampshire but the England team; and some grand cricketers, albeit ones who have learned their cricket outside the shire. All of this, thanks largely to patrons and their purses.

And being on a 'green hill far away without a city wall', the Ageas Bowl came up trumps when England in 2020 had to stage six Test matches in bio-secure environments and behind closed doors. Southampton staged three, Old Trafford three, and there was no doubt that the former was preferable: its hotel was superior; the players could get out and breathe on the golf course; and there is a No.2 ground, which only Hampshire has, where other members of the squads could practise.

In general I am against out-of-town cricket stadia, because spectators are effectively limited to car-owners. But in a generation or two, given the rate of population growth along the south coast, the Ageas Bowl will surely be surrounded by conurbation; and during the Covid lockdown we were all immensely grateful for its wide open spaces and infrastructure. If Broadhalfpenny Down was the cradle of cricket, the Ageas Bowl was the ventilator.

***

The Bat and Ball Inn was a most hospitable hostelry when matches were played on Broadhalfpenny Down in the 1770s. John Nyren has immortalised the vigour of the punch that was served – not the watered-down stuff dished up after the Napoleonic Wars that had devastated the English economy – but alcohol that packed a punch: 'Not your modern cat-lap milk punch, but good unsophisticated John Bull stuff that would make a cat speak! Sixpence a bottle!'

The author was simultaneously extolling the virtues of his father, Richard Nyren, as landlord of the Bat and Ball Inn, but still: those victuals and viands, the hog roasts, the claret and punch, must all have been pretty tasty to keep the gentry and aristocracy sated when they played at Hambledon, before they adjourned to London and made MCC, from the 1790s, the leading club in the land.

Much learned discussion – a euphemism for acrimonious debate – has gone into establishing why Hambledon suddenly became the strongest cricket club in England in the 1770s, and why it just as suddenly relapsed. My interpretation is that in the case of Hambledon at any rate, history is made by great men: in this case, Richard Nyren. He was everything to Hambledon: the captain, a fine left-handed batsman, a useful bowler, and the club secretary as well as the landlord of the local inn.

Nyren held the purse strings, coaxing annual subscriptions out of wealthy patrons and doling out not only prize money to the players but expenses. For this was surely the unique selling point of the Hambledon club: mileage. Most players were men of yeoman substance – farmers, or shoemakers, while John Small made cricket bats and balls – and they topped up their income not only with match fees (up to five guineas for a win, three for a loss) but with expenses. Unfortunately, the accounts from the club's heyday do not survive to tell us how many pence per mile they got, but this mileage surely made all the difference in setting Hambledon apart. Some of their players had to ride ten miles or more to practice sessions, for only a couple lived in Hambledon. A few even came from Surrey and Sussex, setting the trend for Hampshire's signings to follow.

Hambledon is an utterly extraordinary phenomenon when you consider it: that gentry and even aristocracy were content to play under the captaincy of Nyren, a landlord, in the 18th century. But if a cricket match was being played for 500 or 1,000 guineas, you had to have your best man as the captain, whether or not he was a commoner. George Trevelyan might well have been right in his hypothesis that if French aristocrats, simultaneously, had been playing cricket on their estates with their workers, instead of being courtiers in Versailles, they would not have had their chateaux burned.

When the Hambledonians abandoned their exposed hilltop ground and moved down the road to Windmill Down in the village of Hambledon, Richard Nyren relocated to the George Inn, where again he held all the strings into the 1790s. Once he stopped – and his son does not seem to have been exaggerating – Hambledon lost its 'head and right arm'.

* * *

It was a time of emergency. National morale was damaged. The country desired a leader to rouse everyone with the call of up and at 'em. An Old Etonian was just the ticket.

Sounds familiar?

The leader in this case was the Honourable Lionel Tennyson, the time 1921. The previous winter, in their first series since the Great War, England had been wiped out 5-0 in Australia, the first of only three Ashes whitewashes (the other two in all too recent memory).

After the Great War the Australians, for the first time in Test cricket, had selected two fast bowlers, not the normal one. There was no hiding place except square leg, when Jack Gregory and Ted McDonald ran in and thudded short balls into English batsmen who had no thigh pads, no chest guards, no helmets, and had not faced quick bowling since 1914.

England's selectors have seldom turned their attention towards Hampshire, but they did in 1921 when England went 2-0 down in this five-Test series, making it seven defeats in a row since the First World War, and all by hideously large margins. Out went the dogged and doughty but uninspiring captain Johnny Douglas, who had led England to all seven defeats. In came Tennyson as the new captain to rally the troops.

This Tennyson was not synonymous with poetry so much as swashbuckling. After Eton, where he was a fast and furious bowler, he had gone to Cambridge but, like his father and grandfather, did nothing so vulgar as obtain a degree. After Cambridge came the Coldstream Guards and London nightlife on an epic scale. Tennyson might have given Colin Ingleby-Mackenzie and Shane Warne a run for their money except that he blew all of his on racehorses. In little more than one week in 1911 he lost £12,000 in gambling on horses – not £12,000 by the values of today, but of then, which might be a million pounds now.

Any judgement we make about Tennyson ought to factor in his experiences in the Great War, when he rose to major. He lost both of his brothers while he himself was injured three times and reported killed. For a fortnight he and his men were stuck in a trench knee-deep in water, but with barely any water to drink. They were freezing cold, under heavy German fire and equipped with little ammunition. The supply of PPE in those days was not too hot either.

So, no wonder Tennyson hit the nightlife so hard when the war was over. Even while on leave he committed adultery with a woman of high society – she was Clare, the only daughter of Lord Glenconner, whose aunt married Asquith, the former prime minister – and Tennyson did not contest it in the divorce proceedings. Clare was a beauty who could do *The Times* crossword in ten minutes and bathed in milk for her skin, according to Alan Edwards' biography of Tennyson, *Regency Buck*; and she was rather insecure. Clare and Tennyson married two days after her divorce came through but his main solace during the Great War seems to have been drinking heavily and playing cricket behind the lines, before marching back to the front.

A couple of Australian fast bowlers were never going to daunt Tennyson in 1921 when he got a phone call at 1am in his London club to say he would be playing for England at Lord's later that morning. He placed a £50 bet on his making 50 and, for once, went to bed. Australia's leg-spinner Arthur Mailey did trouble him though, because Tennyson was a firm-footed driver. Mailey dismissed him for 5 in his first innings and, when Tennyson had scored 9 second time round, he edged Mailey to the keeper, who dropped it. So he was lucky too, and deserved a little.

Tennyson went on to a rousing unbeaten 74 before England lost the second Test and was made captain for the rest of the series when Douglas was deposed. In the third Test at Leeds he immediately went over the top in leading his troops by posting himself at silly point for Charlie Macartney, the Australian batsman who brilliantly bridged the gap between Victor Trumper and Don Bradman. In stopping a drive, Tennyson split the webbing between thumb and forefinger on his left hand and had to have three stitches, which would not have been so deftly inserted then as now.

England collapsed after Australia had scored 407. To demoralise the nation further, Jack Hobbs – the best batsman – went down with appendicitis. He could not bat and was out for the rest of the summer. At 165/7 Tennyson strode out with his left hand encased in a little wire basket to protect the injury, and holding a harrow bat in his right hand. Tennyson was not just bluff and bluster: he had thought to buy the smaller bat in a sports shop that morning with a view to batting one-handed.

Tennyson proceeded to set the standard for one-handed batsmen in Tests and the next two of note were both Hampshire players: in 1984 Paul Terry and – more successfully – Malcolm Marshall. Tennyson smacked 63 in only 85 minutes to avert the follow-on by two runs.

'His return to the pavilion was greeted with cheers befitting a Cup Final hero,' Edwards wrote. 'It was an innings that captured the imagination of the whole nation and entered cricket folklore.' England lost the third Test, but they had the better of the next two draws under the leonine Lionel.

Tennyson never captained England again, only Hampshire and minor touring teams abroad, when he escaped Clare and the English winter. Frank Mann, of Middlesex and the brewing family, was a much safer pair of hands: there were no wild indiscretions in South Africa in England's next Test series. Tennyson was what England needed in a brief, reviving dose, not the long term.

This assessment came from HLV Day, a lieutenant in the Royal Artillery who played under Tennyson for Hampshire and also for England at rugby: 'Lionel's leadership was based on unhesitating obedience … the choice of his team, its strategy and tactics, if any, were his affair.' Only two words – 'if any' – but they are rather devastating. And yet Day was playing in 1922 when Tennyson pulled off the biggest turnaround ever in the Championship: Warwickshire 223; Hampshire 15 and, following on, 521; Warwickshire 158 all out. Hampshire, after being dismissed in only 53 balls (Phil Mead 6 not out, the highest score, at No.4), won by 155 runs.

Tennyson, however, came cheap to Hampshire, being an amateur funded by Clare. And he was in effect a patron because he subsidised the club. 'Give me a tenner,' he said when the Hampshire secretary popped into the changing room and was told by Tennyson that his hotel bill in Bournemouth had amounted to £67. So he stayed as captain until 1933, when journalism called: it was the *News of the World* which this Old Etonian signed for to cover the 1934 Ashes. Tennyson's successor was another Old Etonian, this time with four initials – William Geoffrey Lowndes Frith Lowndes – not a plebeian two or three.

Tennyson's *de facto* family was his Hampshire team. It consisted of Alec Kennedy and Jack Newman, the pair who did most if not all of Hampshire's bowling; Mead and George Brown; and Walter Livsey who, deft at glovework, doubled as Hampshire's wicketkeeper and Tennyson's valet. Not his actual children. Both he and his wife were 'poor parents', according to Edwards; their children had to be brought up by one of Lionel's relatives. Still, Tennyson is not the only cricketer who has found a surrogate family in his cricket team and, in the words of his own war diary, he was forced to live with sights 'too horrible and dreadful' to forget.

***

Not much doubt about Hampshire's All-Time XI, except perhaps for one position, the No.5 batsman. Both CB Fry and David Gower moved to Hampshire for the later stages of their career when arguably past their peak, Fry from Sussex, Gower from Leicestershire. Fry averaged 57 for Hampshire, but English bowling was weak after the First World War. Or else Robin Smith, a superlative player of fast bowling:

> Barry Richards
> Gordon Greenidge
> Roy Marshall
> Phil Mead
> CB Fry or David Gower or Robin Smith
> George Brown
> Alec Kennedy
> Malcolm Marshall
> Shane Warne
> Derek Shackleton
> Andy Roberts

An amazing team, and especially in bowling, because George Brown was an excellent swing bowler as well as wicketkeeper-batsman. Yet not a single one of them was born in Hampshire.

The entrance to the Ageas Bowl is cleverly named Marshall Drive, because it commemorates both of their Barbadian Marshalls, who were unrelated. Roy Marshall qualified by residence for Hampshire after a few Tests for West Indies in the early 1950s, and from my reading of the game was the first to drive sixes over extra cover on a regular basis. Malcolm Marshall remains the most complete fast bowler there has been.

Gordon Greenidge came from Reading rather than Barbados; Andy Roberts from Antigua, Shane Warne from Australia. George Brown walked from his home in Oxford to have a trial in Southampton and join the staff. Alec Kennedy, who pioneered the leg-cutter to go with his inswinger, was born in Edinburgh before being raised in Hampshire.

Derek Shackleton came from Todmorden, and originally bowled leg breaks. This is tantamount to hearing that the pope was a stripper when a lad because Shackleton grew up to personify parsimony, and was more likely to buy a drink than risk conceding a run. In the 1948 pre-season nets Hampshire's chairman announced that everyone had to try bowling pace because they were short of quick bowlers. You can't say it was the worst idea because Shackleton went on to take 100-plus first-class wickets in 20 consecutive seasons, an all-time record, with the metronomic accuracy of Mohammad Abbas. Trevor Bailey defined Shack's bowling in *Championship Cricket*: 'In the air he tends to deviate the ball into the batsman, but he does a little both ways off the pitch.' In all, Kennedy and Shackleton have taken the seventh- and eighth-most first-class wickets, not far short of 3,000 each.

We think Australia's Steve Smith has mannerisms and obsessions. The left-handed Phil Mead would tug the peak of his cap four times, tap his bat in the crease four times, then take four shuffling steps to assume his stance. As he scored more than 55,000 first-class runs, and was not a quick scorer, Mead must have gone through his routine about 150,000 times.

Nobody has scored more Championship runs in a career than Mead's 46,268 and nobody has scored more Championship runs in a season than Mead's 2,843 in 1928. The question is why he did not represent England more than 17 times. Obviously, there was competition and the fact that Jack Hobbs joined Surrey at the same time as Mead did made for one place fewer at the Oval – which was why he moved to Northlands Road in Southampton – as well as one fewer in the England team.

Was there something in the fact that Mead skipped Hampshire's game at Old Trafford in 1928, officially through 'tiredness'? The Hampshire committee was not entirely sympathetic; they only awarded him half-pay for that game. Lancashire had the great fast bowler Ted McDonald, signed after the Australian tour of 1921. Mead, moreover, did not live up to his English form on his two tours of Australia.

* * *

So why has Hampshire not produced more England players? Basically, if you do not count a couple of chaps who toured South Africa in the 1890s, when nobody counted those fixtures as a Test match until long afterwards, and a couple of one-cap and one-day selections the first real England cricketers born in Hampshire were the off-spinner Shaun Udal and Chris Tremlett, who was a serious bowler in the Ashes of 2010/11.

The infertility of this soil is strange when you consider that Winchester College has produced a couple of top-class cricketers and could have been a nursery for local talent. But Douglas Jardine chose to play for Surrey and England, the Nawab of Pataudi for Sussex and India. (It is always worth remembering that Pataudi scored three consecutive first-class centuries for Oxford, two of them against Yorkshire, immediately before he lost an eye in a car accident; he could have been one of the all-timers.)

Wykehamists have preferred to do other things than play cricket for Hampshire, like make a pile in the City. William Ward was a good enough batsman to make the highest score then recorded, 278 for MCC v Norfolk in 1820; he used to practise with a narrow bat, almost 200 years before England hit on the idea again, and he became rich enough to buy the lease of Lord's. Rishi Sunak goes unrecorded in *Wisden*'s averages for Winchester College. He might have been too busy being head boy.

***

Hampshire has had one hot spot which has produced cricketers. Not Hambledon, not Southampton, not Winchester College, not in Hampshire's borders at all, but Cowley Marsh in Oxford. It makes a fascinating example of how cricketers in England are nurtured. As a hot spot, Cowley Marsh came close to being a southern version of Lascelles Hall, the West Riding village that once produced half of Yorkshire's side.

Cowley Marsh used to have 12 cricket grounds – not just 12 separate squares but a dozen grounds, each with its own pavilion. Some belonged to Oxford colleges, some to local teams. Either way, this enormous nursery needed plenty of manpower before the First World War. So cricket was the way to make a living, not only as a player but as a coach or groundsman. Thus local standards rose, and the county for these products to play for was Hampshire, not least because they did not have sufficient players of their own.

By the mid-1950s, four of Hampshire's six leading all-time run-scorers had originated from Cowley Marsh. First was Alec Bowell, a batsman and cover-point; and he probably recommended Hampshire to take a look at George Brown, whose biography is sub-titled *England's Most Complete All-round Cricketer*. Brown not only kept wicket for England, using his own motorcycle gloves, but took 600 first-class wickets as a bowler, and scored 25,000 runs. Brown also played what might have been the first scoop, as Warwickshire's captain Bob Wyatt described it: 'Our fast bowler Howell was bowling and George Brown hit a short ball in a remarkable way, over the wicketkeeper's head and full pitch over the back sightscreen for six.' Brown's biographer, Michael Stimpson, claims it as the first recorded scoop and, from this description, I am inclined to agree.

John Arlott, still the finest of all radio commentators, wrote of Brown's trial in Southampton: 'It was said – and he never denied it – that he walked the entire sixty-odd miles with a tin trunk holding his cricket gear, clothes and belongings on his shoulder – and without the fare back.' Brown was a prankster, but it might be true.

Brown, in turn, brought from Cowley Marsh both Johnny Arnold – a double international who played one game for England as a cricketer and footballer – and 'Lofty' Herman, a pace bowler who took more than 1,000 wickets. Charlie Rogers, a bowler and groundsman at Cowley Marsh, had five sons who all became professional cricketers; and a son of one of those sons, Neville Rogers, scored more than 15,000 runs.

However, at the same time that these lads played and practised cricket at Cowley Marsh, there was a bicycle shop in Oxford, run by a man called William Morris. He grew to become a car manufacturer, and Lord Nuffield. The dozen cricket grounds at Cowley Marsh were submerged beneath his car plants.

***

The side that won Hampshire's first Championship, eventually, in 1961 was assembled by Desmond Eager, father of the famous photographer Patrick. He passed the captaincy on to Colin Ingleby-Mackenzie, who led the county to the top. When Hampshire won the Championship for the second and last time in 1973 who should be first through the dressing-room door with champagne but Ingleby-Mackenzie? The ghost of Tennyson no doubt entered next, followed by that of his valet Livsey, carrying a crate of champers on ice.

***

It was such a good plan, virtually foolproof. The new Southampton ground is as much the creation of one man as Derby was the work of W.T. Taylor, and Leicester the work of Mike Turner, and Northampton of Ken Turner, and Worcester of Paul Foley. Rod Bransgrove made his millions in pharmaceuticals; when the Ageas Bowl was selected to stage the first World Test Championship final, in June 2021, it was some return on his investment.

As today's patron, Bransgrove has used his purse to assemble the best all-round pace attack in county cricket, and the Somerset groundsman Simon Lee was brought in to produce result pitches: no more Cyderabad in Taunton but Seamerabad in Southampton. Kyle Abbott is as challenging as a fast-medium new-ball bowler can be, and largely with an old one he took 17 wickets in a game against Somerset, who had been in pole position for the Championship until Abbott rearranged their poles. Mohammad Abbas is perhaps a yard quicker than Shackleton but equally accurate; Keith Barker became ever more threatening after leaving Warwickshire by swinging the new ball in to right-handers from round the wicket, like George Hirst before the First World War. In 2020 Hampshire dug deep to sign Nathan Lyon to complement their pace attack, only Covid made the deal fall through.

Hampshire nearly won their third Championship in 2021 – one more wicket in the final game at Liverpool would have made the difference – and again in 2022. Their batting, under James Vince, could not quite match their bowling. But money can buy most things in life, including Championship titles.

Kent

LIKE A new ship in Chatham dockyard, Kent's 150th celebrations were launched in style on 4 March 2020 in the nave of Canterbury Cathedral. Attended by 800 people, it was a lovely occasion by all accounts, although none that I have seen pointed out the irony in the choice of setting.

A roll of honour, mentioning all the great and good cricketers who have represented Kent, was sung as a psalm by the choir. And the county's past, present and future deserve to be celebrated. 'Thou art good Kent.' Verily spoke the Bard in *King Lear*.

The thanksgiving service in Canterbury Cathedral was not tainted with anything so vulgar as statistics, but a few will support the contention that the cricket fields of Kent have been as fertile as those of any other shire. The two essentials for cricket are sunshine and space, and the south-east is the driest region of England, while Kent spreads all of 80 miles from Dover to London, without any massive conurbations or mountains in between – just the towns, suburbs and villages which can accommodate a cricket field.

The top all-time achievers in first-class cricket are bound to be those who played in the Championship in the period between 1890 and 1990, when a player could enjoy 30 or more three-day games a season. Given these parameters, no county – no first-class team in the world – can match Kent in all departments.

Of the 27 leading run-scorers in first-class cricket, three came from Kent in Frank Woolley, Colin Cowdrey (Lord Cowdrey eventually), and Les Ames. Of the 30 leading wicket-takers, five came from Kent in Tich Freeman, Colin Blythe, Derek Underwood, Doug Wright and Woolley again. Of the 20 leading wicketkeepers, four came from Kent in Alan Knott, Fred Huish, Godfrey Evans and Ames again. To boot, the only fielder to have caught 1,000 catches is Woolley.

The style has matched the statistics. Running through the annals of Kent is a yearning to be the most dashing, or gallant, or cavalier of all the counties – even more so than Hampshire, whose swashbuckling captains have usually had a dour medium-pacer to give them control. This is not to say that Underwood would float the ball up outside off stump and say hit me, for Kent has had its leavening of earthy professionals. But that yearning has always existed, and it led to a schism, one which evoked a famous scene in Canterbury Cathedral.

Kent have enjoyed two golden ages – at the end of the Edwardian era, when they won the Championship four times, and the 1970s, when they won it twice along with various limited-overs trophies. In both of these eras they had batsmen who would charge like knights in shining armour, whether Mr KL Hutchings (as the scorecards termed him, not 'Ken') and Frank Woolley, or Asif Iqbal and Colin Cowdrey.

Dashing batsmanship has been difficult on the slow seamers at Canterbury in more recent years, which transformed Darren Stevens, at wobbling medium pace, into a juggernaut after he had taken six first-class wickets at 67 for Leicestershire. Yet the spirit is still willing: for Hutchings read the dashing Sam Billings, the present club captain.

As proof of their morale under Billings, when captain and wicketkeeper, Kent's fielding is as sharp as that of any side in the land.

As part of Kent's campaign to maximise their resources, under the title of Raising Standards, Adrian Llong, the groundsman who produced belters at Beckenham, transferred to the St Lawrence ground. The subliminal message behind the slogan is now taking effect: Kent's batsmen are again lowering their visors, raising their standards, and charging down the pitch to cover-drive, notably Zak Crawley.

Staying in Division One of the Championship, while winning the T20 Blast in 2021 and the 50-over competition in 2022, is proof that Kent are making much of their resources. Their director of cricket, Paul Downton, kept wicket for Kent in his youth before accepting that he was not going to displace the incumbent. This was Alan Knott who, in the eyes of many selectors, would be the wicketkeeper-batsman for England's All-time Test XI; he might even keep Adam Gilchrist out of the World's All-time XI if the match against Mars were to be staged on an uncovered pitch (not that rain could be expected in the away fixture).

Kent's premier league structure seems sound: ten clubs, five of them inside the M25, so their portion of south-east London is not ignored. While Kent's men have won the County Championship six times, Kent's women have won it eight times since 2006. Charlotte Edwards did nothing except advance the reputation of the county's batsmanship, and Tammy Beaumont follows in her wake. Kent's commitment to their development of women's cricket is apparent, according to Downton, 'in the way the county delivers a similar age-group development programme to both boys and girls, the growth in women's sections in club cricket, and in a women-only introductory league playing indoor soft-ball cricket.'

'The county is very proud of the success of the Kent women's team, particularly in recent years,' added Downton. 'As part of our 150th celebrations, we retrospectively awarded county caps to 45 Kent women going back to our first match in 1937.'

***

The ancient landscape of county cricket has altered remarkably little. Once there was a hierarchy called 'the Big Six'; now it consists of counties which have Test match grounds. The northern shires of Lancashire, Nottinghamshire and Yorkshire have been present in both hierarchies; so too Middlesex (although MCC of course own Lord's) and Surrey. Since the First World War, Warwickshire have replaced Kent as one of the six main counties, Edgbaston being more of an international venue than Canterbury.

Kent owed their primacy, in the original Big Six, to Lord Harris. Rob Key was a fine captain of Kent, before becoming England's director of cricket, but their most influential captain has to be Lord Harris. He was the *eminence grise* of English cricket: no eminence, indeed, has been grisier. After Eton and Oxford, he captained not only Kent but England in the inaugural Test in England in 1880. Not even WG Grace himself was going to displace Lord Harris.

Harris established his authority in two ways in which we still feel his influence. The first was that he went a long way to curb throwing. He told Lancashire that Kent would honour their fixture against them at Canterbury in 1885 and would prepare the ground and send umpires out to the middle, but Kent would not put an XI into the field unless Lancashire excluded their two bowlers widely suspected of throwing. The Red Rose wilted and backed down.

The second way in which Lord Harris shaped county cricket was that, being kindly paternalistic, he conceded that a professional who could not get into his county team had the right to switch to another county and thereby earn a living. But he deplored the county that actively lured an established player away from another county. The same attitude prevails to this day, although the two-year residential qualification has gone.

Who else chaired the meeting in 1909 which launched the ICC, or Imperial Cricket Conference as it originally was, consisting of England, Australia and South Africa, but Lord Harris?

A bit of a stickler, Harris was not the finest Governor of the Bombay Presidency which the Raj sent to India – he would carry on playing cricket in Poona while riots raged in Bombay – yet there is still a major schools tournament played in Mumbai for the Harris Shield.

Harris was so keen on promoting the sport worldwide – or rather within the empire – that when the ICC expanded from the original three countries to include India, New Zealand and West Indies, who should again chair the meeting in 1926? I don't suppose he would have approved of the new supermarket at St Lawrence, as part of the ground development which saved Kent's finances, but maybe he would have grudgingly accepted it. Or he might even have become the chairman of Sainsbury's. After all, another player on the Kent staff, Ian MacLaurin, went on to be the chairman of Tesco.

***

Kent's soil has nurtured some of England's finest cricketers without a doubt. However, they have tended to be viewed through rose-coloured spectacles. The batsman who excels in the Garden of England acquires a more lustrous reputation than his counterpart at Cardiff or Derby.

The first line of that roll of honour which was sung like a psalm in Canterbury Cathedral listed the 'Lion of Kent'.

Alfred Mynn, by my reading, was the first cricketer who could walk into the England dressing room of today and look the players in the eye physically. Mynn was positively Flintoffian, a giant by the standards of the early Victorian era, according to the description by Fuller Pilch (the only other player to be mentioned in that psalm's first line): 'Six feet two, and near upon eighteen stone, all bone and muscle.' Mynn was also blessed with enormous hands so that he caught flies and bowled leg-cutters: 'You remember when the ground was a little hard, how Alfred would drop her short, and the ball would cut right across from the on to the off and hum like a top.'

Of all the Kent cricketers to have been lionised, however, Frank Woolley ranks first, above Mynn or either of the Colins, Blythe and Cowdrey; and he must have been one of the most beautiful of all batsmen, being slightly taller than David Gower yet otherwise similar. Both of them gave the impression that they stroked the ball, when their wristwork hit it fiercely hard.

Of all critics, Sir Neville Cardus rhapsodised about Woolley the most eloquently, especially when he batted against Ted McDonald, the fast bowler of Australia then Lancashire. 'It must have been thrilling to see Spofforth bowling at Grace, Lockwood bowling at Ranjitsinhji. But let us be just to our own day's glories; McDonald bowling at Woolley was a sight not less grand than any ever seen on a cricket field; the mirrors of the cricketers' heaven will reflect it forever.'

'He knows not the meaning of crisis; cricket is always the carefree meadow game with a beautiful name when Woolley plays,' Cardus added. And does therein lie the rub? Woolley averaged 36 in Tests, and only 33 against Australia when England needed him most (Hobbs, his direct contemporary, averaged 54 against Australia). For certain Woolley was up with the pace of the fastest bowlers, as was Jack Hobbs and very few others. But he was bowled 30 times in his 91 Test innings, a very high proportion for any batsman of any period. In Test matches he was bowled 13 times in single figures alone, which suggests a penchant for strokeplay early in his innings that left a gap between bat and pad. (Crawley, in his first 50 Test innings, was dismissed in single figures in precisely half of them, usually caught.)

Raymond Robertson-Glasgow was more judicious in his appreciation of Woolley, after bowling to him for Somerset: 'Frank Woolley was easy to watch, difficult to bowl to, and impossible to write about. When you bowled to him there weren't enough fielders; when you wrote about him there weren't enough words ... The only policy was to keep pitching the ball up, and hope. He could never be properly described as being "set" since he did not go through the habitual processes of becoming set ... He jumped to his meridian.'

Cardus was so taken with the Kentish style of cricket because it came at the opposite extreme to the Lancastrian. Thus: 'Cricket is always a game for Kent, rarely a penitential labour.' Cardus defines a true Kent captain as 'keen, chivalrous, and always in love with the game'. After Lancashire's away match in 1926 – 'the Dover field is tucked away in hills along which Lear must have wandered on his way to the cliffs' – Cardus wrote: 'To my dying day I shall remember gratefully these afternoons in Kent, afternoons full of the air and peaceful sunshine of England.'

Robertson-Glasgow was less romantic, more critical. 'Myself, I preferred to watch him [Woolley] or play against him on some ground not in Kent. Praise and pride in home-grown skill are natural and right; but at Canterbury, in the later years, these had degenerated into a blind adulation that applauded his strokes with a very tiresome lack of discrimination.' Here was another warning: this yearning for cavalier style could get out of hand.

***

When I traced the lineage of Kent wicketkeepers in *Cricket: the Game of Life*, I called it 'cricket's longest-running tradition' and have subsequently seen no reason to revise it. Every first-class county has produced some excellent keepers and whole seasons have elapsed at Canterbury without a supreme exponent. But starting in 1744 with the first wicketkeeper of note and continuing until Geraint Jones – albeit he came from Queensland – and Billings, Kent have produced more outstanding stumpers than any other team in the world.

Their pioneer went by the surname of Kips, or sometimes Kipps, his first name unrecorded. He kept wicket for Kent in their immortal match at the Honourable Artillery Ground in 1744 – immortal in that it inspired the first extant match report, in verse. We know from a prosaic footnote in James Love's poem that 'Kips is particularly remarkable for handing [sic] the ball at the wicket, and knocking up the stumps instantly, if the Batsman is not extremely cautious.' And from an incomplete scorecard of this match between Kent and the Rest of England, we know that Kips did not concede a bye – rare in a two-innings match then or at any other time – and made a stumping. So, Kent is the county of hops and Kips.

The first well-known wicketkeeper to round-arm bowling, not least Mynn's, was Ned Wenman from Benendon. But he did not throw himself around like a modern. If the ball was heading down leg side, it kept on going down leg side until it reached the long stop, which was a specialist position. As Lord Harris described Wenman in *A Few Short Runs*: he 'used gloves, I believe, little thicker than lined dogskin, and did not pretend to take every ball'.

Fuller Pilch remembered: 'Just think of Ned Wenman behind a wicket: was there ever a better? He didn't stop every ball, or every other ball perhaps, for he left his long-stop to do his own work. "What's the good of Mr Walter Mynn for long-stop if I am to do all his work and knock my hands to pieces? No, let him do his work, and I will do mine."

Long-stop was no sinecure on grounds unrolled. Lord Harris himself took pride in recalling that it used to be his specialist position, and that twice in one season he had run out a batsman at the far end, that is the non-striker's. Wicketkeeping gloves seem to have been invented during Wenman's 30-year career; being skilled at manual labour, as a carpenter, he made his own pair.

Another feature of Kent's keepers is that most have been good batsmen, as they should have been. Hours of watching the ball intently, and moving quickly, will condition the youngster to bat as well as keep. So many of England's batsmen nowadays have kept wicket in their youth, from Jos Buttler and Jonny Bairstow to Rory Burns and Ollie Pope.

Not surprisingly, the first wicketkeeper to score a Test fifty came from Kent: Edward Tylecote, who achieved it in the 12th of all Tests. So too the first keeper to score a Test hundred: Harry Wood, in the 37th. The trouble is that Lord Harris let Wood go: a Dartford boy who had trials with Kent, Wood left to play for Surrey after Harris decided he preferred Tylecote. Only Tylecote soon became too busy teaching mathematics and collecting butterflies for county cricket.

Never mind. Soon enough Fred Huish came along to become the first – and only – keeper to make 100 dismissals in a first-class season before the First World War; and there he still is, sixth in the all-time list of keepers with the most first-class dismissals. Old Fred still holds the world record for most stumpings in a first-class match – nine against Surrey in 1911 – and comes second only to another Kent keeper for most stumpings in a career: 377 to Les Ames's 418.

'Role models,' says Paul Downton, when asked to explain this Kent tradition, and undoubtedly this is a major factor. He kept wicket because his father George kept wicket, brilliantly too: he was an amateur who did not want to play for a living but still played ten games for Kent when Godfrey Evans was representing England.

But there must also be some environmental reason, or circumstance, which I reckon is this: Kent have had some of the finest spinners who have turned the ball away from the bat. Of their five who have taken 2,000 first-class wickets, all of them turned it away from the right-hander: Colin Blythe, Frank Woolley and Derek Underwood were left-armers, Tich Freeman and Doug Wright leg- or wrist-spinners. You have to be a top-class keeper to catch all those outside edges and effect all those stumpings, especially on uncovered pitches. When Huish set his world record in the game against Surrey with nine stumpings, Kent used three bowlers, all of them spinners who turned their stock ball away from the right-hander.

These five spinners, in addition, bowled many overs at Canterbury from the pavilion end and therefore had the local advantage of turning the ball down the steepest slope at an English county ground along with Lord's. In addition, Kent have always played more games at out-grounds than most counties – latterly Beckenham and Tunbridge Wells – with their more natural pitches which are inclined to break up for spinners. Tich Freeman took more than 100 first-class wickets at eight separate grounds in Kent.

All elite cricketers are ahead of their time in some way, which is what makes them elite. I wish Fred Huish had written a book, like his contemporary keepers Arthur Lilley and Herbert Strudwick, but no. One trick which we like to think of as modern was practised by old Fred. When the ball ran loose on the leg side, and the Australian batsmen tried a single during Kent's game against the tourists in 1902, Huish kicked the ball on to the stumps at the bowler's end for a run-out.

Les Ames raised the bar so high as a wicketkeeper-batsman that it is only in the last couple of decades that the game in England has caught up. Ames averaged 40 with the bat, and Matt Prior alone has matched that. The only people to have done the wicketkeeper's double of 1,000 runs and 100 wickets in a first-class season are Ames, three times, and John Murray of Middlesex, once.

Ames, it has to be said, conceded more than his share of byes – about 16 per Test – because, like Wenman, he was no fan of diving down the leg side and dirtying his flannels (professionals had to pay for their own laundry). Godfrey Evans altered the parameters in one fell and famous swoop. In the 1954/55 Test at Melbourne, when Frank Tyson was bowling downwind, and like it, the left-handed Neil Harvey glanced down the leg side and Evans, in leaping and catching him right-handed, raised the roof and the bar. No more long stops!

Alan Knott did not attend the thanksgiving in Canterbury Cathedral: retiring to Cyprus indicated how much he valued his privacy. While in the lineage of Kent wicketkeepers, as the finest of them, he was still an original, being so intensely dedicated to his obsession. His last hour or more before bedtime was devoted to organising all his kit for the morrow. He did not wear soft gloves but hammered a dent in the middle of them for hour after hour, into which the ball would lodge. Knott has the advantage of very long fingers: indeed he joined the Kent staff as much for his off spin.

As flexible as a porpoise, and wary of his diet ahead of his time, Knott raised the standard in the amount of ground he could cover. Whereas Evans had gone for that Ashes-winning catch down leg side, Knott leaped for everything outside off or leg. The crowning glory came when he kept to Derek Underwood on a wet pitch. They did not exchange signals: Knott read the cues astutely enough as Underwood ran in, feet splayed, to know whether it would be the spinner that turned and bounced or the arm-ball which detonated leg stump out of the ground. Apparently Ames, when watching a game while he was Kent's manager, would sigh and remember his liaisons with Freeman.

***

Cardus identified the two traditions, or cultures, within Kent cricket as the realistic and idealistic. Usually, they have combined in the dressing room. In the 1980s, however, instead of being a creative tension it exploded into schism, if we may borrow an ecclesiastical term from Canterbury Cathedral.

Christopher Cowdrey represented this idealistic tradition. He came with all the qualifications: born of the imperial purple as the son of Colin; the godson of Peter May, the former England captain; and Tonbridge School. Dashing, up-and-at-'em officer class, in the cavalry of course.

Chris Tavare represented the realistic tradition. Sevenoaks School – not so grand as Tonbridge – and Oxford, but nothing flamboyant. When selected for England, Tavare put on a hair shirt and blocked, but he was a Test cricketer of substance whereas, for Cowdrey, his handful of Tests were a bit of a breeze. To a northern outsider, this rivalry must have looked like the difference between posh and ultra-posh, yet it split the county. Who should captain? The old pros, Knott and Underwood, backed Tavare; the committee, outright 'rah', backed Cowdrey.

One should not push this parallel too far ... yet the setting in both cases was Canterbury.

In 1984, 714 years after Thomas a Becket was murdered by King Henry II's knights beside the stairs leading to the cathedral crypt, Tavare was dispatched after doing his duty – indeed *for* doing his duty. Tavare too had something of a saintly disposition; and Becket was found to have worn a hair shirt under his robes. Tavare at least survived his experience, but left for Somerset, to join his best Oxonian friend Vic Marks.

'Many considered it unfortunate that at the end of a second successive season of marked improvement in Kent's fortunes the decision was made to sack Tavare,' *Wisden* proclaimed. 'He had done much to restore Kent's prowess in all forms of cricket and scarcely deserved, on the evidence of his two seasons in command, to lose his job. He is succeeded by Christopher Cowdrey, so the captaincy changes hands for the sixth time since 1972 when Cowdrey's father, Colin, who had reigned peacefully for 15 years, was succeeded by Mike Denness. Changing the captaincy again may not necessarily put Kent back on the winning path.'

You can say that again. Having been the county side of the 1970s, Kent did not win another trophy in the 20th century in spite of having some serious cricketers like Mark Benson and Steve Marsh, the late Graham Dilley and Richard Ellison, and overseas players like Carl Hooper. Indeed, from the date of that schism in 1984 they won a total of two limited-overs trophies before 2021.

Today the blood has dried and been erased. The thanksgiving ceremony took place without reference to the murder in the cathedral or at the St Lawrence ground. Henry indeed was Kent's hero in their promotion into the first division at the end of the 2018 season, albeit Matt from New Zealand, not the king. Everyone pulls together now under Billings, who combines the idealistic and realistic traditions. Verily, Kent, thou art good.

Lancashire

IT HAS taken more than 150 years for the Red Rose to approach full bloom. If it is not quite there, Lancashire are coming ever closer to maximising their vast potential, just like their Old Trafford ground.

Only Lord's, back in the summer of the triangular tournament in 1912, had hosted three Test matches in one summer before Old Trafford did so in 2020 (not to mention six one-day internationals). Thereby Lancashire's headquarters leapfrogged over Yorkshire's at Headingley and took fifth place in the list of grounds worldwide which have staged the most Tests.

There have been three previous periods when the Red Rose has budded promisingly: in the late 1920s when they won the County Championship four times in six seasons, and in the early 1970s, and again in the 1990s, when they were frequently limited-overs champions. But only now is the whole of Lancashire pulling together, taking with it cricket in the north-west.

Lancashire alone can rival Surrey for wealth: they, indeed, make more money from non-cricket activities than any other county. But then there has always been money in Manchester: where there's muck, there's brass. In 2019, the only year when England has staged a World Cup and a five-Test Ashes series, Lancashire had a record turnover of

£34m and made a record profit of £5m. At their very own Old Trafford, Lancashire CCC have usually been the poor relations of Manchester United, but not when the World Cup qualifying match between India and Pakistan was staged. The number of millionaires who wanted to see, and be seen, made a Man U match look like a kids' kickaround in the park. On the morning of that qualifier, tickets were being touted for a thousand pounds. So many private jets flew in from India, America and the Gulf that Manchester Airport could not accommodate them all and had to divert some to Liverpool.

I would like every county ground to be multi-purpose, and therefore alive all year round, drawing people into gyms, sports shops and cafes under the stands. Lancashire have progressed further down this route than any other county. The combined turnover of the Hilton Garden Hotel, with 150 bedrooms inside the ground and run by Lancashire, and the red-roofed Point – which can accommodate 1,200 people for conferences, meetings or weddings – was almost £10m a year before the hotel was extended.

The ground's redevelopment is just about working architecturally, although judgement cannot be conclusive until the 9,000-seater temporary stand is replaced by something permanent. Adding a tier to the old pavilion, and blending it with the top of the Point, has renovated the Victorian structure and given the ground its own identity, in red. Like Lancashire CCC, the pavilion has seen many ups and downs over the years but finally grown into a synthesis of ancient and modern.

When Old Trafford's cricket ground stages a concert, it can host 50,000 spectators and generate a profit of a quarter of a million pounds. The ample car parking facilities bring in another £300,000 year-round, especially lucrative when Manchester United play at home. Lancashire used to have a

No.2 ground, or nursery, on the site where the nets and some of their car parking spaces are.

About £34m is some turnover for any cricket club, and some turn-round as well. 'In 2010 we were within ten bob of going bust,' said Paul Allott when he was Lancashire's director of cricket. Or, as the chief executive Daniel Gidney explains (not that he worked at the club before the crisis): 'There was a perfect storm, in that we had the global recession in 2008, and our loss of Test match status [when the square was turned round], and our £60m redevelopment of the ground was opposed by another developer, which cost us a million pounds in legal fees.' The court found, fortunately, in Lancashire's favour.

But no, it was not for lack of money in times past that the Red Rose failed to bloom.

***

To understand what Lancashire was like when the county club was formed in 1864 – and one reason why it took so long to proceed from square one to approaching their fulfilment – no place is better to start than 'Cranford'.

Elizabeth Gaskell's novel captures Manchester a decade earlier, in the 1850s. Before the heroine finds herself a rich mill-owner to marry, she leads us through the cobbled streets of the Industrial Revolution at its most brutalising. English factory-workers exist in abject grime and poverty and Irish workers – brought in to under-cut the wages of the English workers – live in even worse conditions. Nobody in such a society is going to have any time or wherewithal to watch or play cricket, except the mill-owning elite.

So when Lancashire CCC was formed, in the mid-Victorian splendour of the Queen's Hotel in central Manchester in 1864, it was a gentlemen's club: not an organisation dedicated to spreading the sport among all classes around the county, or to winning matches, but a gentlemen's club.

'There are cheap jokes about Manchester's weather; "Cottonopolis" is a jibe, and there are slums and smoke enough, but Manchester is the home of the *Manchester Guardian*, of the Hallé concerts, of a repertory company which made its influence felt throughout the country ... in addition to producing some of the great political figures of the 19th century,' wrote Dudley Carew in *To The Wicket*. 'There are clubs in Manchester where the talk is wittier and better informed than in the corresponding clubs in London. Old Trafford is the expression of this comfortable, cultured tradition.'

In seven of Lancashire's first eight games, no professionals were selected to represent this gentlemen's club and, when they were, they soon realised their station in life. According to Stephen Chalke in his definitive work on the County Championship *Summer's Crown*, Lancashire's professionals 'were kept in place, being allocated a "cow shed" in which to change and eat their own packed lunches'.

The man who did most to shape Lancashire CCC was a cotton mill-owner's son who was also MP for Blackburn, Albert Hornby, and his son was to rule Old Trafford for almost as long. When the myth of the Ashes was generated at the Oval in 1882, and Australia won by seven runs, Hornby was England's captain – and therefore the man responsible for the strategy of not playing shots, simply blocking, as England failed to chase down their target of only 85. He was captain again when England played their first Test in England away from the Oval, at Old Trafford in 1884. But then the host county's committee selected the England team, not MCC or independent selectors, so they would choose Hornby, wouldn't they? He did not rise to this occasion, becoming the first batsman to be stumped in both innings of a Test, for 0 and 4.

At county level Hornby could bat. He scored the first seven centuries for Lancashire, and led them to their first Championship titles in 1881 and 1897. He also became the first man to captain England at cricket and rugby, which was a little strange – strange because he was so little. When he was in the Harrow first XI he weighed less than six stone while holding his bat; and his nickname was 'Monkey', which might have been inspired by the parting of his hair down the middle as well as by his size and simian agility. Lancashire's professionals did not address him as 'Monkey' but 'the Boss'.

It seems amazing now that one so slight should have played full-back for England, but that was before All Black forwards had to be tackled. Hornby was in England's XV for the first rugby international, against Ireland in 1877, and was captain when they lost in Manchester to Scotland in 1882, so in neither sport was his captaincy successful. 'Small, truculent, bellicose, adventurous, rash and a poor runner between wickets,' was Christopher Martin-Jenkins' verdict on Hornby, which was scathing by the author's standards. Hornby, however, did inspire the poet Francis Thompson to write his immortal lines on Hornby and Richard Barlow batting together, when 'the run-makers flicker to and fro, to and fro'.

A century after their foundation, in the early 1960s, Lancashire were scarcely less hierarchical, or feudal. David Lloyd, in his entertaining autobiography, says that the place where junior professionals changed was called 'the Dogs' Home': no great improvement on a cowshed. He recalls 'an *Upstairs, Downstairs* divide, in which the young players were expected to be cringingly subordinate to their seniors'.

Club members – gentlemen, in name – could still stroll down to the nets and have the professionals bowl at them, gently. The county was still captained by an amateur. In 1962 an Old Reptonian was appointed, Joe Blackledge, who had never played first-class cricket before, after the captaincy had been advertised in *The Times*. Appearances and class distinctions were what mattered, results secondary. A structure of committees and sub-committees aggravated matters: the general committee sacked two senior players, whereupon the members sacked the committee. Before 1960, before any radical changes in the structure of Championship cricket, Lancashire seldom finished outside the top six in the table; from 1961 to 1969, as the tectonic plates shifted, they finished once in a single-digit place.

When I entered the Old Trafford press box – of which there have been at least four in my time – frequent references were made to the seating area in front of the Victorian pavilion where Lancashire's members sat. The tabloid term for it was 'the Pit of Hate' and it was not undue hyperbole because there was nowhere in English cricket to rival it for verbal abuse except Headingley (which, according to the late Malcolm Marshall, was the only ground in England where West Indians were racially abused). But that was the Headingley terraces; this was the Lancashire membership baying for blood, and often of its own players. Cyril Washbrook could provoke booing as much as anybody when he was Lancashire's captain in the 1950s. I think the cause was that the members still felt they belonged to a gentlemen's club and therefore retained the right to abuse any employee. This toxicity fed into the committee structure, where nobody was ready to toe a line and everyone felt entitled to say what he (definitely he) wanted, irrespective of the club's best interests. The general committee, in turn, made life difficult for the captain and players. Trevor Bailey noted how one captain received a telegram from the committee telling him who should open the bowling!

***

Everyone was pulling in different directions. League cricket, moreover, was always threatening to siphon off those Lancashire players who wanted to play less than six days a week, and for more money. Great days extended through the 1950s when Lancashire League clubs employed the very finest West Indian cricketers, from the Three Ws and Garfield Sobers to Wes Hall and Sonny Ramadhin. Why go to Old Trafford, to get bored and rained on and watch a draw (and Lancashire have drawn more Championship matches than any other county) when you could watch world-class players down the road and a definite result in one day?

Lancashire lost the world's best-ever bowler – you could still argue – to league cricket. Syd Barnes, who bowled quick leg spin mixed with off breaks, and took 189 Test wickets at 16 each, played two seasons for Lancashire at the start of the 20th century then spent the rest of his career in leagues, where he could earn more money and prolong his career. His accountant must surely have approved when Barnes was still rated the best bowler in England at the age of 56.

The impact of league cricket on Lancashire was summed up by Hon. Terence Prittie when he filled in as the *Manchester Guardian*'s cricket correspondent in 1946 and observed: 'The financial lures of the Lancashire and Central Lancashire Leagues had hit the county very hard. Eddie Paynter had left them,' (after averaging 59 for England), along with another England batsman, Norman Oldfield. 'Lancashire's troubles did not end there. Farrimond, their international wicketkeeper, and Nutter, who should have been an England all-rounder of the near future, migrated to the Leagues too.' All-rounders fared especially well in league cricket, because a collection would be made for anyone who scored a fifty or took five wickets. Given crowds of two or three thousand spectators ready to enjoy their

Saturday afternoons off, that was a lot of threepenny bits to supplement a salary.

Lancashire's response to this crisis in 1946? Appoint an amateur captain who had never played county cricket before, of course. John Fallows, as their captain and a specialist batsman in 1946, averaged 8.14, before retiring.

**

Still, there was enough brass to enable Lancashire to become the first county to win a hat-trick of titles in two different formats, by bringing in overseas players. The first was Ted McDonald, who spearheaded Lancashire's three consecutive Championship wins from 1926 to 1928. He was paid £500 a year, then the biggest salary in county cricket, more than Jack Hobbs at Surrey and perhaps almost as much as WG Grace used to rake in as an amateur.

Jimmy Anderson, Brian Statham, and McDonald, who was born in Tasmania: Lancashire has been home to three of the finest pace bowlers. Extreme flexibility is something they had in common: so athletic that they could warm up with a fag, a pint and a stretch while others slaved in the nets, and so fit they were all at their best in their thirties, not twenties. Of this trio, Anderson swung it the most, while Statham and McDonald tended to seam the ball in to right-handers. Anderson and Statham seldom bowled a bad ball, being remorselessly accurate, but don't think McDonald was the least or slowest of them just because he played so long ago.

We have the word of Sir Neville Cardus that McDonald, for the first ball of Kent's second innings against Lancashire at Old Trafford in 1928, bowled a short ball that flew over the batsman and keeper: it 'crashed halfway along the pitch and then hurled itself high over the heads of the batsman and Duckworth. Whence does McDonald draw his terrible strength and velocity? His run to the wicket is so easy, so silent.' Anybody who can run in, without warming up as bowlers do now, and bounce his first ball over the batsman and keeper is sharp.

Mike Procter, Bruce Dooland, Clive Lloyd, Ken McEwan, Viv Richards, Simon Harmer? Economists can probably calculate who was the most valuable – the most rewarding – of all overseas players; but it could well be McDonald. He won the Championship – the only format which then existed – four times for Lancashire in his six and a half seasons. In all he took 1,053 first-class wickets at 20 runs each when Old Trafford was a belter.

Having toured England with Australia in 1921, and terrified English batsmen, McDonald had signed for Nelson for £500 a year plus bonuses. In 1925 Lancashire lured him for the same salary, and a house, and the promise of a benefit after only five years (it made £1,947 in 1929, equal to about £100,000 in 2023 – less than the largest benefits of Yorkshire players, and less than the £2,906 of Charlie Hallows the year before, but not bad for an overseas). He needed the money to pay his gambling debts in horse racing. As a league pro, McDonald had learned to bowl off-cutters as well as flat out, and delivered well over 1,000 overs per year for Lancashire.

So Lancashire were the champion county when they harnessed McDonald's pace to their strong, but very defensive, batting line-up. For truth be told, or at least if Cardus is to be believed, never did any county bat so dourly. Other critics agreed: 'There was a time in the twenties when the cricket they played set a deplorable standard other counties were all too willing to copy,' Carew wrote, as a cricket correspondent for *The Times*. 'Time and again it seemed that Lancashire, with Hallows and Watson to start them off, went into the field with the negative intention of not losing the match.' This dourness applied in the Roses match above all. Eight consecutive Championship matches between Yorkshire and Lancashire in four years in the late 1920s were drawn; over half of Roses matches in all.

'Day after day columns of indignation, coloured with all of "Cricketer's" charm and dramatic indignation, spilled themselves over the *Manchester Guardian*. Lancashire was denounced with the fire and wit of Disraeli,' Carew wrote of Cardus. But the wittiest, and subtlest, criticism which Cardus levelled at Lancashire's batsmen is to be found in his *Autobiography*, that flawless work of prose (I have never spotted a comma out of place).

Cardus was married during the 1921 cricket season during one of Lancashire's home matches. 'I went as usual to Old Trafford, stayed for a while and saw Hallows and Makepeace come forth to bat. As usual they opened with care. Then I had to leave, had to take a taxi to Manchester, there to be joined in wedlock at a registry office. Then I – that is, we – returned to Old Trafford. While I had been away from the match and had committed the most responsible and irrevocable act in mortal man's life, Lancashire had increased their total by exactly seventeen – Makepeace 5, Hallows 11, and one leg-bye.'

Lancashire's scoring rate was so low because their batsmen preferred to camp on the back foot, whereas Frank Woolley was sailing into his cover-drives and slog-sweeps, as the pull-drive used to be called. At a *Wisden* dinner I met Robert Runcie after he had retired as Archbishop of Canterbury, and he had watched Lancashire's batting when a lad growing up in Crosby. 'George Headley modelled his batting on Ernest Tyldesley,' he told me. 'When Tyldesley toured the West Indies with MCC, Headley saw him playing against Jamaica.' We cannot question the veracity of this statement from such an elevated source and we know that Headley, when possible, played off the back foot. But Johnny Tyldesley, Ernest's elder half-brother, played off the front foot when he was England's first regular No. 3 batsman in the Edwardian era and, so dashing, that he was not a poor man's Trumper.

Yet the dullest cricket inspired the most luminous cricket prose. 'In a representative Lancashire and Yorkshire match of 1924–1934, runs were severely discountenanced,' Cardus wrote. 'No fours before lunch, on principle, was the unannounced policy; and as few as possible after. But fours or no fours, runs or no runs, the games touched greatness because of the North of England character that was exposed in every action, every movement, all day.'

Lancashire v Yorkshire in the era of Herbert Sutcliffe and Emmott Robinson, Wilfred Rhodes and George Macaulay, Charlie Hallows and Harry Makepeace, Ernest Tyldesley and Ted McDonald: so far away in terms of time, and tempo, yet so near in one respect. The Roses match in the Championship has, for many recent years, been played behind virtually closed doors, but the 20-over Roses match still packs in a full house, just like a century ago. The consumption of alcohol might have escalated, ever so slightly, but singing – which used to be a feature of cricket at Old Trafford in the late Victorian and Edwardian eras, not least when it was raining and spectators sang to keep their spirits up – carries on.

The T20 Roses match of 2018 at Old Trafford, in front of a capacity crowd, was as entertaining as any cricket match of such a length could be after rain had reduced it to 14 overs a side. Lancashire scored 176/2, Liam Livingstone hitting 79 off 37 balls; Yorkshire replied with 175/4, losing by one run. Had Cardus nipped out to get married during that game, he would have missed rather more than 17 runs. Sometimes that many were scored in one over.

***

It was the signing of Clive Lloyd of West Indies and Farokh Engineer of India, that sparked the first hat-trick of titles in a limited-overs format: the Gillette Cups of 1970–72, under the captaincy of Jack Bond. Lancashire had already come close to a limited-overs hat-trick by winning the first two Sunday Leagues in 1969 and 1970.

If we remember Lloyd, or 'Hubert', as an electrifying left-handed batsman, he was even more electrifying as a fielder in the covers before his knees went. I recall watching him in the Oval Test of 1973, when he would lie dormant like a leopard in the long grass before swooping, and his victim halfway down the pitch would panic as if electrified. Lloyd was taken to Lancastrian hearts (attitudes had changed since the 1930s when the West Indian Learie Constantine was rejected by some committeemen as McDonald's successor), and knighted in the New Year honours list of 2020.

Engineer was ahead of his time in being a wicketkeeper who could not simply bat but open the batting and hit, having an all-rounder's licence. He brought flash and panache to a defensive era of the Indian as well as Lancastrian game. He was part of the last flowering of Parsi cricket in the early 1960s, when their tiny community supplied four regular members of the Indian Test team: Polly Umrigar, Rusi Surti, Nari Contractor and Engineer.

'The start of the Sunday League offered a challenge that was right up our street,' wrote the other Lloyd, David, who opened the batting with Engineer. 'Most of us had come through the leagues and were accustomed to playing overs cricket in a single afternoon. While certain other counties floundered in the environment, or failed to identify its potential, we took to it immediately.' Lancasheer la, la, la, Lancasheer la, la, la!

The only drawback perhaps was that Lancashire specialised in the limited-overs formats to such an extent that they took their eye off the red ball. They went on to win eight one-day trophies in the 1990s; but the Championship – last won outright in 1934, shared in 1950 – remained as elusive as ever. It was not until 2011, when Old Trafford was closed for renovation, and Lancashire played their home games at Liverpool and other out-grounds with result pitches, that all the petals of the Red Rose began to flower. Once they won the T20 trophy in 2015, Lancashire had the full set.

***

The first known person of note in English cricket to die of coronavirus was David Hodgkiss, Lancashire's chairman. He had attended the last big sporting event before the first lockdown, the Cheltenham Festival, where he is thought to have caught it. Hodgkiss was 71. 'He was a top bloke and the effect of his demise will be felt for a long time to come,' said Allott.

Or maybe Hodgkiss's legacy had already become apparent. 'He was a wonderful man, who used to open the batting for Cockermouth,' said Daniel Gidney. 'Whether you were a pot-washer in the catering department or an opening batsman in the first team, he had the same smile for everyone.'

Players seldom have a good, and truthful, word for their administrators, but Hodgkiss inspired these two tributes from players past and present. 'I knew him extremely well,' Engineer said. 'He was the best and most popular chairman LCCC ever had.' And Matt Parkinson, the leg-spinner whom England were trialling, and who received his Lancashire cap from Hodgkiss, tweeted: 'A great man who always had time for everyone and loved the red rose. Will remember his capping speech for a long time.'

This is a world away from Lancashire's hierarchical system which held them back for so long. Hodgkiss deserves to be remembered as the man who chaired the club – no more committees, just a small board of great and good – as they finally emerged as the northern powerhouse which their resources had equipped them to become many years before.

Lancashire have long had a friendly relationship with Cheshire and they have extended it to Cumbria too. The tension with all their many leagues has disappeared, along with the Central Lancashire League itself. David Lloyd, once he joined Lancashire, was no longer permitted to play for his home club of Accrington. Nowadays Old Trafford hosts a two-day fixture between Lancashire second XI and a team of the best league players. This forms part of a pyramid leading to the top, as in every Australian state, whereas the shape of cricket in Lancashire used to be that of a blancmange.

'We are aiming to get cricket into 1,000 state schools in the north-west for boys and girls,' said Gidney. Lancashire already produce 10% of all county cricketers: in other words, 10% of current players were either born in Lancashire or came through pathways within the county. Yes, this is near fulfilment. Finally, the Red Rose is fully flowering.

Leicestershire

I ATTENDED Leicestershire's four-day match against Derbyshire in the Bob Willis Trophy in 2020 during lockdown and enjoyed it immensely as a taste of normality. The city of Leicester had been suffering from a particularly high rate of coronavirus and rules were even more stringent at Grace Road than most county grounds. A Leicestershire second XI player had left his kit in the dressing room but was not allowed to re-enter the ground to collect it until the following day. Lunch was somewhat functional for the players: they sat in the indoor school, one per table, as if it had been exam-time. Yet the game went on, providing entertainment on live stream for people stuck at home, and that was the thing.

It would only be slightly irreverent to observe that the number of spectators at Grace Road for this match – nil – was little less than normal. Any of Leicestershire's home games in the Championship over the last decade has offered plenty of scope for someone who wanted to practise social distancing. In 2019, the previous season, 8,994 spectators had attended Leicestershire's seven home Championship matches, fewer than 1,300 per game, fewer than 400 per day. If there is a nip in the air, most non-members will cluster inside The Meet, which could pass for a converted aircraft hangar but for the lingering whiff of bacon butties.

Eight times in 13 Championship seasons (excluding the BWT mini-season) Leicestershire have finished bottom of the second division, and along the way they needed a bail-out from the ECB. The pattern seemed set in stone: if a promising youngster appeared, he was bound to be snaffled by Nottinghamshire, who also nicked Leicestershire's overseas pro Mohammad Abbas, or some other predator. Stuart Broad, James Taylor, Harry Gurney, Greg Smith and Zak Chappell all left Grace Road for Trent Bridge and not necessarily fame and fortune. Young county cricketers are too keen to listen to their agent and to switch counties before they know their own game, thus heaping make-or-break pressure on themselves. There is a system for compensation, of course, and Leicestershire were receiving six figures annually when Broad, Taylor and Gurney were in England squads, but the effect was still demoralising. No county has endured a bleaker decade in the Championship apart from Northamptonshire in the 1930s.

***

Paul Nixon comes from Carlisle, and Cumbrian cricketers are the toughest we have, born of windswept farms and declining shipyards. England ought to have mined this shaft more. Nixon was followed south by Mike Burns, who tried his hand at everything at Somerset from batting and bowling to keeping wicket and captaincy. Then there is Liam Livingstone and Ben Stokes. Not many softies in that quartet.

England called up Nixon as a keeper-batsman in January 2007, to much surprise as he was 36, with a World Cup to follow after Australia had finished whipping England. But somebody had to replace Geraint Jones, who had been broken on that tour by the psychological warfare ('Queensland's third-best wicketkeeper'). Nixon had never been hailed as the sleekest glove-man, and the moment he set foot on the Sydney Cricket Ground a fast and bouncing white ball burst through his upturned gloves and sped to the boundary.

This must have hurt in more than the physical sense. Self-doubt must have assailed Nixon: wasn't he too old, or simply not good enough, for this international job? Many England players on that tour had wilted while Australia beat them 5-0 in the Ashes, then walloped them even more emphatically in the T20 international that followed. Australia piled up 221 from their 20 overs (James Anderson 4-0-64-1).

Nixon was not overwhelmed, however, as too many team-mates were. While England's batting was collapsing in the T20I in the face of that record total, he helped himself to a nice little 31, unbeaten, settling into Australian conditions, steering the team away from rock bottom, to fight another day. The survivors somehow turned England's tour around to win the ODI triangular series against Australia and New Zealand and it was no fault of Nixon's – just the general incompetence of their 50-over game – that England did not qualify for the Super Eight stage of the subsequent World Cup in the West Indies.

So Nixon has salvaged wreckage before, and he was bursting to do it again as Leicestershire's director of cricket. His county are not bottom and bankrupt in his book, oh no. 'We are going on the greatest journey cricket has ever seen, from the bottom to the top,' he announced. His objective had simplicity on its side, if nothing else. But then he starts taking you with him.

'We are the most successful T20 county,' Nixon proclaims. What do you mean? 'We have won the T20 title more often than any other county.' Well, yes, this is true: Leicestershire were quick off the mark when the format was introduced, powered by Nixon himself as keeper-batsman, and they won the final in 2004, 2006 and 2011. 'For a club of our size to do that, that's magnificent,' he says, not unfairly.

'Who was the first to score 1,000 T20 runs?' Nixon asks. Sorry, can't think. 'Darren Maddy,' says Nixon. Oh yes, good old Dazza, who blocked in a few Tests for England then evolved so rapidly at Grace Road that he was recalled for the first T20 World Cup. 'And who was the second person to score 1,000 T20 runs?' Pause. We should have guessed. 'Paul Nixon,' says Paul Nixon.

'We are the hardest-working team in the country,' says Nixon, gathering ever more steam. The Midlands is not the optimal region for a first-class county in some respects: the traditional county of Leicestershire is bordered by four other first-class counties, with populations of lowish density, competing for spectators and sponsors, so they have no hinterland of minor counties from which to draw. Nixon, however, is making the most of their situation, as you would expect.

Nothing fancy like pre-season tours of Dubai or Barbados. Instead, Leicestershire use the Academy at Loughborough, or whatever the ECB's latest name for it is, with all the gizmos. Nixon decided to stage 'semi-matches' in the indoor school, piling on the pressure by turning up the volume of crowd noise which can be pumped into the hall, and making the incoming batsman wait on the viewing balcony and trot down the steps for his innings.

And miracles do happen, at least in T20, provided you believe. Sam Hain was propelling Warwickshire towards a target of 190 at Grace Road when Leicestershire's captain Colin Ackermann came on with his occasional off-spin, and in his four overs took seven wickets for 18, the best figures ever recorded in a T20 match of any standing: seven wickets in 24 balls! Suddenly, somehow, becoming a top county again in some format no longer seems impossible.

Nixon cut his teeth as a T20 coach at Jamaica Tallawahs, after retiring as a player and before returning to Grace Road as coach. (It is usually a massive mistake to go directly from being a player to a coach at the same club.) 'I learned about systems there, and smart risk, and about being consistent as a bloke when you are coach, and how to put on some bravado when necessary even if it is an act.'

Long before it became fashionable for sportsmen to establish their own academy, Nixon set up his own sports foundation 'for 25 kids in Leicester who didn't enjoy school', where they did vocational courses as well as sport. Contemporary cricket, especially the T20 format, has seen too many psychologists and consultants selling snake-oil, but Nixon has put down roots and has substance. If Leicestershire go under as a first-class, Championship-playing county, it will not be for lack of hard work and enthusiasm on his part.

Nixon is not the only hard man to have coached Leicestershire. When they joined the Championship in 1895 their coach was the former Yorkshire left-arm pace bowler Tom Emmett, who by my reading was the first exponent of reverse swing. The ball was not polished in those days, by convention not law, so it would have soon aged, and on a hot day one side at least would have become very scuffed. Emmett sometimes bowled a ball which pitched on leg stump and hit the top of off, and called it 'the Sostenutor'; and as he bowled it with a roundish arm, I reckon it could have been a reverse-swinger away from the right-hander.

Anyway, that is by the by, or as Emmett's flummoxed wicketkeeper might have said, 'by the bye'. In the nets at Grace Road, Emmett used to stand beside the bowler's stumps and cheerfully say: 'Call that bowling? Why, I've two lasses at home who can bowl better than thee.' Remind of you a later Yorkshireman, who came to be knighted, and his mum?

***

It was at Grace Road that cricket changed forever more. After the umpire had called 'play!' at 11.30am on 2 May 1962, the sport would never be the same again.

The occasion was the opening of the Midlands Knockout One-day competition. It had been devised by the young Leicestershire secretary, Mike Turner, who had joined the county staff as a leg-spinner. He played a few games before it was realised that his acumen could be better applied off the field, and he was trained up by the secretary Charles Palmer to be his successor.

A limited-overs competition! A county cricket match played in one day so that spectators could see the result! It was a brilliant concept, because the whole sport needed energising. By the early 1960s, basically, only West Indians played strokes; run-rates and over-rates were plummeting, crowds evaporating, the game stifled by orthodoxy and the fear of getting out.

In 1961 the Australian Test all-rounder, Colin McCool, who then played for Somerset, had written: 'I think that the MCC coaching scheme is monstrous ... the basic aim seems to be to teach batsmen to do everything except hit the ball. In 1960 the South Africans visited England and produced a brand of cricket as exhilarating as a glass of muddy water. Everybody moaned about the dullness of it all [but] they were just getting a taste of English cricket as played by someone else.' Trust an Aussie to tell it straight.

Necessity – to save Leicestershire from bankruptcy – was the mother of Turner's invention. His county was only kept going through the 1950s by their supporters' association and the temporary fix of football pools, which Warwickshire, Northamptonshire and a few other indigent shires had tried.

Incredible as it seems now, each innings back in 1962 consisted of 65 overs per side, with a maximum of 15 overs per bowler, and play was scheduled to finish at 7.30pm. Given 65 overs nowadays, some batting sides would be targeting 500. Leicestershire, batting first against Derbyshire, reached 250/5 and won: according to the *Daily Telegraph*, a target of 251 off 65 overs constituted 'an awesome task'.

In the other game or 'semi-final' of the Midlands Knock-out competition at Trent Bridge, Northamptonshire scored 168/9 from their 65 overs: they were not bowled out yet they could barely manage two and a half runs per over. Northamptonshire still defeated Nottinghamshire comfortably and went on to beat Leicestershire in the final a week later.

The ball, eventually to be turned white, had been set in motion. It was this experiment which directly led to the nationwide Gillette Cup in the following season of 1963. Until this point in the game's evolution, bowlers had attacked the batsman. Henceforth, the batsman would come more and more to attack bowlers.

Give credit not only to Mike Turner, for saving the professional game's finances and future, but Ron Roberts too. He was the *Daily Telegraph*'s correspondent at this epoch-making match and recognised it as being so: 'If this cricket appears too contrived for the purist, one must concede that there is an art in its application. Moreover, it can contribute to a sharper approach to three-day matches, and an appreciation of how much more can be done in them. In time it could tap a source of public interest hitherto unrevealed.'

Prophetic or what?

***

Everything has to be right for a small county to win something so sustained as the County Championship. The right decision-makers off the field, as well as the right captain and players, have to be in place. You can't be doing with a chairman who has never played himself but thinks he knows everything about the game. At a big county like Yorkshire it did not matter how antiquated their committee structure was: there were so many good players, and a few great ones, they would still win the Championship. But at most counties everyone has to be pulling together to win a title.

Everyone pulled together at Grace Road in the mid-1970s, and in the late 1990s, on both occasions under the direction of Yorkshire exiles. You can make a whole team out of Yorkshiremen who have migrated to Leicester (don't forget Dickie Bird), and almost a whole team of Lancastrians. It is inevitable that a county with a small population will have to import players from other counties and countries to survive; less so that it will lose so many of its own cricketers.

Ray Illingworth masterminded Leicestershire's first trophies, but then he was English cricket's mastermind. Leicestershire under Illingworth won the first Benson and Hedges Cup in 1972 and again in 1975; two Sunday Leagues; and their first County Championship in 1975. Yorkshire were left kicking themselves, and their committee, for failing to respond to Illingworth's reasonable request for a contract lasting longer than one season at a time.

Two features of Leicestershire's first title stand out. The first was that only one player was born in Leicestershire: Graham Cross, also a footballer, and not a regular. Yet only Illingworth, and their overseas player Graham McKenzie, could be called major signings; the rest were the result of shrewd recycling.

The second feature was that spinners, not seamers, took the majority of wickets: two left-armers and two off-spinners (Illy himself and Jack Birkenshaw) took over 30 wickets each. More than anyone, Illingworth knew how to get the best out of a cricketer – as England captain, he harnessed characters as diverse as Geoffrey Boycott and John Snow – but there was more to his shrewdness.

Illingworth got the Grace Road groundsmen to leave grass in the middle of the pitch – for the benefit of his three seamers – and shave the ends for his four spinners, including himself of course. This was creative groundsmanship. But Lord's – in the shape of the old Test and County Cricket Board – took a dim view. Really dim, in fact. Subsequently spinners have become ever more marginalised in Championship cricket. The norm at many counties is to play four seamers and a batsman who bowls some medium-pace or else a few darts. Monochrome cricket.

The strategist when Leicestershire won the title in 1996 and 1998 was Illingworth's fellow off-spinner from Yorkshire, Birkenshaw, one of the unheralded brains of English cricket and spin bowling. A piece of administration far ahead of its time helped him.

'I just tried to deliver what Jack wanted,' said Paul Haywood, the former Leicestershire player who was the chairman of their cricket committee then. So Birkenshaw was given control of the playing budget, as head coach, 'with no interference'. Unprecedented. The advantage in being a small organisation is that it can move quickly. Nowadays, counties which have a director of cricket let him spend the playing budget; this was the coach, a generation ago.

'It took Jack four or five years to get his squad together,' Haywood remembered and, as Birkenshaw shopped around, he found some bargains. 'He brought in Vince Wells from Kent, Aftab Habib from Middlesex, David Millns from Notts and Alan Mullally who had had trials at Hampshire – inspirational signings who hadn't performed at other counties – and Phil Simmons from Trinidad, who was the glue as vice-captain. He could bat, he could bowl, he could field at slip, he could read situations and individuals.'

And Simmons took over as captain when James Whitaker was injured.

In those three seasons, 1996 to 1998, Leicestershire won two Championships, and lost two games. In 1996 they used only 13 players, the fewest by any Championship-winning county. In 1998 they went through the Championship season unbeaten, as no county had done for a quarter of a century, with Paul Nixon again the chunterer-in-chief behind the stumps. What is surprising is not so much that Leicestershire are bottom of the table nowadays as that they were top of the red-ball table little more than 20 years ago.

***

For roughly the first third of their existence, and their last third, Leicestershire have been based at Grace Road; in between they were based at Aylestone Road in the centre of Leicester, next to the football and rugby grounds. And if you think that Grace Road is something of a misnomer for its wide expanses, and a setting which does not attract rave reviews, what about the sledging which has been aimed at Aylestone Road?

Dudley Carew in his book about the 17 first-class counties in 1946, *To The Wicket*, wrote: 'It is difficult, even with the best will in the world, to get up much enthusiasm over cricket in the Midlands ... The Midland landscape is entirely without those flourishes of romantic unexpectedness which elsewhere make England for so small an island so rich and diverse in scenery.'

Then the arrow was specifically fired at Aylestone Road, which was owned by the Electricity Board, and its 'deplorable ugliness ... without any redeeming feature. On one side it is bordered by broad, squat monstrosities which look like overgrown oast-houses and belong in spirit to the set of some futurist, nightmare film of industrialism. Cinders are a prominent part of the landscape and, when the wind is in the right direction, the mingling of cinder-dust and smoke from the monsters which appear to manufacture chemicals makes witches' brew of the atmosphere.'

Those of us who did not watch cricket before 1960 have, I suppose, forgotten how often cricket was played in heavily polluted air.

Leicestershire gave up Grace Road in 1901, because it was too far out of the city centre to attract viable crowds. They played at Aylestone Road, then returned to Grace Road after the Second World War, taking The Meet with them. They have never played anywhere else for long; and it might have helped now if they had, and still did, to spread more roots around their county.

They have played at three grounds in each of Coalville, Hinckley and Loughborough, but never more than 20 matches, except at Ashby-de-la-Zouch. A record of sorts was set there for a big hit when Leicestershire's Jack Firth hit a six into a goods train passing behind the sightscreen, and the ball ended up 18 miles away in Leicester.

The best nets in England: like their proximity to Loughborough, this is another of Leicestershire's assets, though they are out of sight and out of mind, unless you walk behind The Meet and down an alleyway outside the ground. Before their construction in the early 1990s, these nets used to be tennis courts, so they are flat, as flat as can be, absolute belters, with their own dedicated groundsman. This is why touring sides have been happy to start their tour at Grace Road. No point going to one of those counties – half of them – which have their nets on the ground itself, and which cannot therefore be used during hours of play.

The Meet is so-called because of Leicestershire's connection to fox hunting, yet one cannot imagine a huntsman dressed in crimson, keen on a stirrup-cup before giving chase, going anywhere near the place. Or if one did arrive and proclaim 'a bumper of hot toddy, my good woman!', he would no doubt be told, 'Sorry, duck, we've only got bacon butties left.'

But it is a friendly place upstairs, with home-made cakes for tea, old chairs and a second-hand cricket bookstall. If a curious Frenchman wanted to know what Championship cricket has been like for the last 150 years, he would gain an accurate impression if you took him to The Meet, if you bought him tea, and if you watched together as a pace bowler ran down the slope towards the flower baskets in front of the pavilion, and you talked to a stranger seated nearby about anything from Gogol to googlies.

* * *

'I really believe the second division was the beginning of the club's decline,' said Jon Agnew MBE, the BBC's cricket correspondent, who bowled up and down the slope at Grace Road throughout the 1980s.

Not since 2003 have Leicestershire been in the first division. Sponsors and spectators have drifted away and, unlike Kent and Sussex who have often defied gravity – by staying in the first division, even though they do not have the resources of counties with a Test match ground – Leicestershire have to compete with a big football club and a big rugby club in the same city.

'I think the county's future depends on establishing closer links with the city's south Asian community,' Agnew added. He cited the brief tenure as chair of the club by Mehmooda Duke: the first Muslim and first female chair of a first-class county.

According to the 2011 census, the population of Leicester was divided 50-50 between white British and other communities, of which by far the largest was Asians from

India with 28%. This figure includes Indians who emigrated directly from India, largely Gujarat, AND those who arrived via East Africa from the 1970s, prompted by the expulsions by Idi Amin from Uganda.

At this stage I have to declare an interest. The second city after London to participate in the *Wisden* City Cup, which became the ECB City Cup, and which I founded for 16- to 21-year-old lads who could not access mainstream clubs, was Leicester. We had some fantastic fun, dividing the city into four teams and playing T20 games on a midweek evening.

A game was staged one evening at Banks CC – one of those excellent cricket grounds which banks used to run, so their employees could play on Saturday afternoons in the 1950s, only half a mile from Grace Road, but small by today's standards. A crowd of about 150 turned up and one of the Asian players on Leicestershire's staff led the warm-up training. Raj, who managed the Banks ground, belted out IPL-style music in between overs and there was some powerful six-hitting and skilful spin bowling before a close finish, then a delicious halal dinner for the teams. 'The best thing that's happened to cricket in Leicester,' Raj kindly commented.

Only ... so many sixes were hit that we lost 13 balls. Thirteen balls lost, in 40 overs of play, even though tree-high netting shielded the main road on one side of the ground; and the neighbours complained. The council stopped us playing there. Another deterrent: Leicestershire CCC were not very interested. It was a good box for the Leicestershire Cricket Board, in charge of development, to tick. But integrate the county club and the city's south Asian population (this was a decade ago), what's the point of that? The ECB would still dish out the development money, even if it was kept for the boys.

'We've tried and tried to get the south Asian community involved in the club,' various Leicestershire officials have said over the years. I wonder, though, if they have tried in the right ways.

Essex offer a subsidised course at Leyton for mothers who fancy a bit of cricket, and toddlers. This is one way to get people involved in your county club, starting young. Leicestershire stage wedding receptions in the Charles Palmer suite in the pavilion. But when their indoor school was being designed, did the club tell the architects to consult with Leicester's south Asian community, with a view to staging their wedding receptions, equipped perhaps with a dance floor and sound system for Bollywood hits?

Leicestershire had devised their own local solution to involve schoolboys: the district system, in which the city was divided into five districts that played each other at under-age level. This has been abolished in the last decade.

Looking at Grace Road from the south Asian community's point of view, why would you want to get involved after decades of rejection or at best indifference? When the ECB Leicestershire Premier League was strong – and Kibworth were twice the National Club champions – Asian clubs were not allowed to join. The city of Leicester had about 30 Asian cricket teams, who hired grounds from the council, but the league criteria stated that clubs had to have their own ground, sightscreens and covers. To an extent this was justifiable, to maintain standards. But how do you expect an aspiring Asian club to raise the millions of pounds required to buy inner-city land and build their own ground? Of course, you don't expect them to.

Personally, I believe Leicestershire could have made more of an effort, sooner, to connect with their south Asian community – for example, by putting up a team of their younger players to meet a south Asian XI, home and away, on one of their council-owned grounds as well as Grace Road. Connecting, and integrating, not existing side by side like oil and water.

After all, the captains of England's indoor cricket teams, male and female, Anish and Niki Patel, were brought up in Leicester. The city's south Asian community produced a decent off-spinner in Jigar Naik: not the lithest in the field but he averaged over 20 with the bat and had a strong off break. In 2010 he took 35 first-class wickets at 17 each. Here was someone, not to build your whole strategy around but part of it, and another way to bring south Asian supporters into the ground. What happened subsequently? 'In four years we did not play a specialist spinner in Championship games at home,' Naik says. Illy would not have allowed that.

***

Stalwarts. Leicestershire always had stalwarts to keep them going, at least until the 21st century. Stalwarts who stopped the county sinking to the depths of Northamptonshire in the 1930s or Glamorgan in the late 1980s. Stalwarts like Les Berry and Maurice Hallam who, as opening batsmen, scored 55,000 first-class runs between them without a solitary England cap. Stalwarts who sometimes went on to become the club coach and drilled the same solid, unpretentious values into their charges.

Ewart Astill and George Geary were the most famous pair of stalwarts Leicestershire had: all-rounders who took 2,000 first-class wickets and made the best part of 20,000 runs or more, right up there with Alec Kennedy and Jack Newman of Hampshire, if not quite the equal of Yorkshire's George Hirst and Wilfred Rhodes. In 1935 Astill became the first professional county captain of the 20th century (Berry came second in 1946). But there were stalwart professionals before Astill and Geary who kept the club going and, very occasionally, caught the eye of England's selectors.

Albert Knight was a professional cricketer who wrote a book which was published, and if there were any who did so before him – who actually wrote it – I cannot think of one off hand. Numerous professionals in the 19th century drank prodigiously and, without any wage to keep them through the winter, died young. Knight, a steady batsman, had been educated at Wyggeston Grammar School and became a Methodist preacher.

His book, published in 1906, lives up to its title of *The Complete Cricketer* for he deals in detail with every department. What is outstanding is his eulogy of Victor Trumper and his innings of 185 against England in 1903/04, a series in which Knight played three of the five Tests, including a match-winning innings of 70 not out. It is also remarkable that Knight identified the two best bowlers in the world as non-white: the Aborigine 'Jack' Marsh, whom he had played against on that tour, and Krom Hendricks, the South African left-armer who was forbidden by Cecil Rhodes to tour England in 1894. I doubt whether a book at the same period by an England amateur would have ventured the same radical opinions.

Astill came from the same non-drinking tradition as Knight, starting as an off-spinner with the Temperance Cricket Club. 'There was an enviable ease in his bowling, with the lolloping run and the tireless wheel of the arm. He could spin the ball acutely from the off, even on true surfaces,' wrote Raymond Robertson-Glasgow. But – and it took a bowler to recognise it – 'though he had facility, accuracy, cunning, he somehow lacked that enmity, that *fervida vis animi*, which is the bowler's crowning gift.' Gordon Parsons, running up the slope at Grace Road with steam coming out of his ears, would have shown him how.

'Geary's bowling was always good; sometimes it was great when, on a pitch to suit, he got that big hand to cut the ball from leg, at something more than medium pace, and made it fly from the readiest bat to wicketkeeper or slips. On those days he was nearly a Sydney Barnes and could beat the world': such was Robertson-Glasgow's testimony from close at hand.

***

Too many modern umpires for my liking resemble night-club bouncers, close-shaven and cool, taciturn and tough. The funniest of all umpires was Alex Skelding, another Leicestershire stalwart. We felt aggrieved in 2020 when we missed two-thirds of a summer of cricket. What would it be like to miss four years, in your mid-twenties, as a pace bowler, which Skelding did in the First World War?

Skelding lost his chance of an England cap, but not his sense of humour. While a player he observed: 'Bowling is more often a headache than a headline.' Skelding was one of the first bowlers to wear glasses and said: 'I can't see without 'em, and on hot days I can't see with 'em as I'm bowling with steam in my eyes; so I do it on hearing only, and appeal twice an over.'

***

Overall, you feel that Leicestershire have bottomed out. Some good decision-makers are now in place, with Paul Nixon as cheerleader. The fact that the city council gave them a loan of £1.75m over ten years, in return for a seat on the board, gives them an anchor which other precarious counties lack. Their T20 games can be attended by up to 500 spectators of Asian origin and they often have an Afghan to cheer. They have two Community Talent Champions who scour grassroots cricket in Leicester, and have brought about

15 players so far to the county's attention that they would otherwise have missed.

By some irony, too, the current has been reversed: a player has transferred from Nottingham to Leicester, and a wrist-spinner too. In only his third championship game, when aged 18 years and one month, Rehan Ahmed not only took five wickets in an innings but scored a century against Derbyshire, at a faster rate than one run a ball, to save the match.

As he had stood out in the Under-19 50-over World Cup earlier in the year, Rehan was clearly going to be identified as Adil Rashid's successor in England's white-ball future: what was startling was that he was drafted into the Test party for Pakistan, and looked entirely at home on his debut in Karachi. He had been told of his selection the night before, and his opening spell was nervy: he said he had not been able to sleep, and maybe for once the timing of Ben Stokes and Brendon McCullum was wrong, in that he should have been informed at breakfast on the morning of the match. Otherwise it was a dream. Rehan's stock ball from childhood had been the googly, and this started working first, but then his leg break began to turn. Far from just flushing out the tail, which has been the summit of expectation for some England wrist-spinners, some of his seven wickets came with corkers; and the spinner who takes wickets out of nowhere, when the ball is soft and old, is gold.

This piece of talent identification and development, almost on its own, justifies Leicestershire's first-class status. Rehan brought a talented off-spin-bowling brother with him, to be coached by Naik. One day soon, even in a Championship game perhaps, there might be difficulties if social distancing has to be enforced again at Grace Road.

Middlesex

FROM WG Grace's golden summer of 1895 until Jonny Bairstow's dazzling batting in 2022, surely it is the case that no cricketer brought more joy to the British public than Denis Compton in 1947. While Len Hutton was busy being orthodox up North, Compton's strokeplay raised the nation's morale, because he banished all thoughts of austerity.

A banquet was served to the tens of thousands who flocked to Lord's to sun themselves after the vicious, and almost fuel-less, winter of 1946/47. When Compton hooked pace bowlers then ran down the pitch to spinners, not only was there honey and jam again for tea, but cakes and sandwiches for all, no rationing of anything in fact, for hour after life-reaffirming hour.

I never saw Compton play – except in the press box – but will always remember John Woodcock, doyen of *The Times*, being asked who his favourite cricketer was. It was more than a smile as he summoned up the memories of summers and winters spent watching one of a kind. A little clearing of the throat, a luminousness that radiated from deep within, then: 'Oh, it has to be Denis.'

In that summer in which he helped to lay many a ghost, Compton scored 2,033 runs at an average of 96 for Middlesex in the Championship and 753 runs at 94 for England in the five Tests against South Africa. In all first-class cricket, he scored 3,816 runs and 18 centuries, records which we can agree will last forever.

His lifelong friend simultaneously batted at No.3 for Middlesex and England. Bill Edrich hit – Edrich hit while Compton stroked – 3,539 runs with an average of 80 compared to Compton's 90. But the more important statistic, though it can never be quantified, is this Middlesex pair made many people enjoy life again.

Compton was forced to recall his vintage summer when he authored a lengthy preface for *The History of Middlesex CCC* (I would not presume to say 'wrote': he was always far too occupied in enjoying the good things of life in the press box before dictating a bit of copy). He remembered receiving 'a national hero-sized post-bag of hundreds of letters a day' and how, as a Brylcreem Boy, he had his 'face plastered across every advertising hoarding in the country ... For I was the one who started the whole sponsorship business in cricket.'

'Basically, I was a back-foot player, but this was where I found a new delight in disturbing a bowler's rhythm by advancing three or four yards down the pitch to hit the ball to any part of the field I wanted,' Compton added. 'On one occasion I slipped on my backside four yards down the track, I still managed to get the ball on to the middle of the bat and steer it down to fine-leg for four.' You can imagine a grin as cheeky as Joe Root's greeted that boundary.

Compton said that Middlesex's game plan was to post at least 350 on the board by 5pm so they had time to bowl the opposition out twice in three days. In all too many four-day Championship games the aim has seemed to be 280/4 by the close of day one, attrition in lieu of entertainment.

Eventually the years, and knee injuries when playing football on the wing for Arsenal, caught up with Compton and ended his on-field career. As the cricket correspondent of the *Sunday Express* he became a leading critic in the school of modern players not being so good as they used to be in his day; he riled Ian Botham in particular, when Botham was his spiritual successor. Nevertheless, nobody in English cricket, not even Stokes in 2019 or Bairstow in 2022, has so warmed the nation's heart as Compton in his golden summer of '47, because he did it after wartime.

Edrich had been a senior officer in the RAF, awarded the DFC, and decided to switch from professional to amateur with a view to captaining England after Wally Hammond, who had made the same career move. I suspect Edrich's record – by night rather than day – ruled him out of the England captaincy. Like Hon. Lionel Tennyson, who led England in 1921, Edrich was too intent on living life to the full after a world war to be risked as an England captain on tour. You get the flavour of what Denis and Bill were like off the field from one of my favourite jests: 'Bill was the best man at Compo's third wedding, and third man at his best wedding.'

It was just as well, in any event, that Middlesex played all their matches at Lord's in 1947. Had their home ground been Southgate or Uxbridge, Compton could never have lifted to quite the same extent Britain's morale.

***

Middlesex, however, have not always played at Lord's. Back in the 1730s, the team of that name would play on any flat piece of field, before the first grounds were dedicated to cricket. Who were their main rivals? Well, nothing has changed there: Surrey, then as now. Cricketers north of the river are always going to feel rivalry with those south of the Thames.

Although Middlesex as a county was abolished for local government purposes in 1972, the county cricket club was sufficiently established to survive, and indeed to enter its most prosperous period under Michael Brearley. Simply by virtue of being situated in north London, near to ports and airports, Middlesex has long been the first county to attract cricketers from overseas who land in England.

For a start, the original Middlesex teams were sponsored by the heir to King George II. Frederick, Prince of Wales, had been brought up in Hanover after his father had departed to England to consolidate his power. Without his parents, and socially isolated, Frederick found solace in cricket and the bats that were sent to him in Hanover. You can see today in the palace grounds, away from the formal gardens, a lovely paddock made for cricket after the clearing of trees.

Once Frederick had finished his schooling in Germany and moved to England to re-join his parents, he tried to be more English than English, in opposition to his father who was more German than German. Hence Frederick's love of the new English sport of cricket, and his patronage of Middlesex. He is recorded as having given their cricketers a guinea apiece after one game against Surrey.

Frederick's mother called him 'the greatest ass and the greatest liar' but the queen herself was not exactly well adjusted. Anyway, I have a soft spot for Fred, because he had a soft spot for Flora Macdonald, and pleaded for clemency to his younger brother, the Duke of Cumberland, or 'Butcher Cumberland' as he was known after the Battle of Culloden. Flora was spared when Bonnie Prince Charlie's men were taken from the Tower to be hanged, drawn and quartered on Kennington Common next to what is now the Oval.

**

Middlesex were briefly based at Southgate when the Walkers, a brewing family, built their fine ground which still has excellent pitches. By the early 1870s they were based at Prince's, which was briefly the most fashionable cricket ground in London, ahead of the Honourable Artillery Club ground, let alone Lord's and the Oval.

Prince's was in Knightsbridge, next to what became Harrods. If one were a member of the Guards, one took one's lady friends to Prince's, to go roller-skating if they were daring, or play lawn tennis or watch cricket. The name helped to advertise the venue and raise subscriptions, although the ground was the creation of two brothers by the surname of Prince, not aristocrats.

By 1876 it was apparent that this prime piece of real estate in Knightsbridge was not going to last long as a cricket ground. Prince's was sold, and Middlesex accepted the offer by Marylebone Cricket Club to play their home matches at Lord's; for Middlesex to pay all the expenses and keep all the gate money, and for Middlesex members to be allowed into the pavilion for free.

At one time, when gatemen were at their snottiest, Middlesex players did not have the right to walk upon the field at Lord's except when playing in a game: they had to walk round the ground to practise in the Nursery and were not allowed in the pavilion if Middlesex were not playing. Nowadays, however, MCC and Middlesex co-habit happily. Or rather it is a *menage a trois* because after The Hundred began London Spirit moved in.

It is hard to see how Lord's and MCC would have survived without Middlesex, and vice versa. *Lillywhite's Annual* declared that Lord's 'benefited greatly' by the arrival of Middlesex and 'the addition of a few county matches to the Marylebone programme will certainly strengthen it in a point where it has been undeniably weak of late years ... There had been for some time to the outside world an air of monotony and apathy about the cricket at Lord's.'

No wonder: Lord's was the original terror track, surprising as that may seem to those who have known it for the blandest pitches in England this century (six successive Tests from 2006 ended in draws). When Nottinghamshire were batting against MCC a ball kicked off a pebble and hit George Summers on the cheek, killing him, aged 25, on 19 June 1870. Necessity being the mother of invention, the next man in wrapped a towel around his head for some protection: thus Richard Daft pioneered the original piece of protective headgear more than 150 years ago.

'Lord's was a heavy clay and badly drained, and the outfielding was always rough and treacherous': this was written by an MCC member who batted for Middlesex, Edward Rutter. He added: 'The [MCC] Committee were deplorably lethargic and out of date.' Yes, MCC needed invigorating by Middlesex. A 'happy marriage', so the Middlesex and England captain Sir Pelham Warner called it (unlike his own).

Middlesex CCC have therefore been unique: the only first-class county without a home of their own, at least until they developed Radlett, yet performing on the grandest stage of all. 'We are a small club,' their former pace bowler and president Mike Selvey said. 'Everyone thinks we are a big club but we are a small club.' This is true. Their club office, in the hut at the back of the Lord's pavilion, is often so crammed with kit and boxes that it is hard to find a spare chair.

Pros and cons have arisen. Any cricketer who comes to London and excels in a few games of club cricket is going to be sounded out for Middlesex second XI, with a contract to follow if all goes well.

Conversely, Middlesex have less incentive to nurture players in their own league cricket; and the local pathways dried up, no longer producing a Patsy Hendren or Mike Gatting or Mark Ramprakash. It is not that the Lord will provide, but that Lord's will attract players from all over the world to Middlesex. And whereas cricketers in the north or west of England may have been out of sight and out of the selectors' minds in the days before data analysis, performances at Lord's have always been noticed. No coincidence that more England captains have played for Middlesex – including the four who won the Ashes in Australia, the Sirs Pelham Warner and Andrew Strauss, and the Mikes Brearley and Gatting – than any other county.

***

Who has taken most first-class wickets on a single ground?

Very surprising as it may seem nowadays, the answer is a Middlesex spinner. Since John Emburey and Phil Edmonds and Phil Tufnell, Middlesex have seldom bowled spin. Take their first-class bowling averages for 2019 and every one of their top six bowlers is classified by *Wisden* as RFM.

The answer is Jack Hearne, who took 1,739 first-class wickets at Lord's at 16 runs each with brisk off spin. He was the lord of Lord's. The ground's grandee, Sir Pelham Warner, not only captain of Middlesex and England but founding editor of *The Cricketer*, deigned to devote a single paragraph to Hearne – a professional – in his *History of Lord's*, a paragraph of four and a bit lines. Warner did not even tell us which end Hearne preferred (presumably the pavilion end) but his praise was lavish, if brief: 'His beautiful method was a model for all time, his rhythm in action, lovely swing, and control of pace and length being as near perfection as any bowling could be.'

As Middlesex's senior pro before the First World War, Hearne reinforced the culture of hierarchy and deference which assumed an extreme form at Lord's (as when the PA announced: 'For Mr. F.J. Titmus on the scorecard, please read Titmus (F.J.).' For Middlesex's away games, the pros would gather at their boarding house – nothing like the amateurs'

Spectators watching county cricket at Queen's Park, Chesterfield. Derbyshire first played here in 1898.

Paul Collingwood acknowledges the Riverside crowd after playing his last innings for Durham against Middlesex in 2018.

Trevor Bailey hits out during Essex's match against the South Africans at Castle Park, Colchester in 1965.

County cricket at St Helen's, Swansea in the 1980s. The sweeping terraces remain to this day.

The dour but effective Derek Shackleton, who took 100 wickets or more for Hampshire in 20 consecutive seasons.

Ted McDonald bowling for the Australians at Aylestone Road, Leicestershire's old home, in 1921.

One of Kent's many great wicketkeepers, Alan Knott, demonstrates his technique at Canterbury in 1969.

Brian Statham at Old Trafford in 1965. A Lancashire and England great who bowled with unrelenting accuracy.

Denis Compton demonstrates his technique at Lord's in 1951. No cricketer brought more joy to the public than Compton in 1947.

The last football match at the County Ground in Northampton was staged in 1994 before cricket took over exclusively.

Floodlight cricket at Trent Bridge as England meet Australia in a one-day international in 2009.

Spectators at the Recreation Ground in Bath watch Somerset play Worcestershire in 2005.

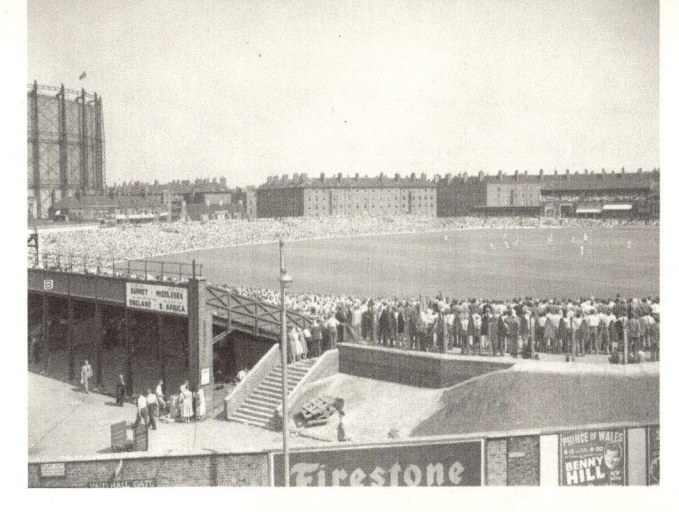

The Oval in 1955 where a packed house watched England meet South Africa.

Sussex play Yorkshire at Arundel in 2014. The ground can hold around 8,000 spectators with its high banks offering fine vantage points.

A packed Edgbaston watches England versus West Indies in 1957.

The scorebook of Gloucestershire's inaugural match in 1870 v Surrey. Note that WG Grace opened not only the batting but also the bowling. He was taken off in both innings by his brother EM, who never captained the county again.
Photo: Elliot Lake, GCCC Heritage Trust.

Gloucestershire & Surrey — On June 2nd 3rd & 4th 1870

SECOND INNINGS.

No. of in	Names of the Batsmen	Score	How Out	Bowler's Name	No. of Runs	Total No. of Runs
	Grace, W. G.	1133122121431	c. Pooley	Southerton	25	
	Grace, E. M.	1234412	c & b	Vince	18	
	Matthews, T. G.	2111	c. Mayo	Southerton	7	
	Townsend, F.	223212143	c. Pooley	Southerton	20	
	Grace, G. F.	13321121	c. Griffith	Southerton	15	
	Filgate, C. R.	1412451251511121214111 3	Not	Out	48	
	Halford, I.	2	H. Wicket	Southerton	2	
	Mills, I.	2	c. Pooley	Southerton	2	
	Bush, A. I.	214241	c. Humphrey	Southerton	14	
	Miles, R. F.	32111	bowled	Southerton	8	
	Macpherson	1111	bowled	Southerton	5	
	Byes	2				2
	Leg Byes	1				1
	Wides					
	No Balls					
					Total	167
					Grand Total	

| the Fall y Wicket | 1 34 | 2 45 | 3 53 | 4 74 | 5 93 | 6 95 | 7 105 | 8 134 | 9 157 | 10 167 |

Wide Balls	Bowler's Name	Bowlers overs and runs obtained from them
	Southerton	
	Street	
	Vince	

Total No. of Wide Balls	Bowlers	Total No. of Balls	Total No. of Runs	No. of Maiden overs	No. of Wickets	Bowlers	Total No. of Balls	Total No. of Runs	No. of Maiden overs
	Southerton	202	67	20	9				
	Street	72	38	2	0				
	Vince	124	58	14	1				

SERVATIONS.

A hotel was built a few years ago but not much else has changed at New Road. Here, Worcestershire meet Surrey in 2014.

Fred Trueman bowls a bouncer to Geoff Pullar at Bramall Lane, Sheffield in the 1959 Roses match.

hotel – and Hearne would sit at the head of the table, carve the joint and hand round portions in order of seniority. Junior pros had to stand until the seniors had chosen where they wanted to sit. This insight into Middlesex cricket before the Great War has been handed down to us by Harry Lee in *Forty Years of English Cricket*.

'The rank and file were told what to do and what not to do,' according to Lee. 'They were not asked to think; and indeed, if some of them had been so asked, they would have been hard put to it to comply.' In other words, the complete opposite of the structure which Michael Brearley introduced in the 1970s, when every player was encouraged to offer ideas.

Another bowler to take more than 1,000 first-class wickets on a single ground was another Middlesex and England off-spinner, Fred Titmus, whose career spanned five decades. He varied his off breaks with a swinger off his index finger that would start its flight by heading down the leg side. 'Don't sweep Fred' was the first piece of advice given to Graham Gooch when he played against Middlesex.

***

As London has offered so many opportunities for work and play, and Lord's has been the grandest stage for any cricketer, a wider range of people have represented Middlesex than any other county. From all over the British Empire they came, and from all over the Commonwealth they still come, if only to play in the T20 Blast.

So many Australians, South Africans and Indians used to play for Middlesex that when the first global organisation was formed in 1920, the county was nicknamed the League of Nations. In 1895 a Parsi doctor, Mehallasha Pavri, was given a Championship game as an amateur; and soon afterwards Ahsan ul-Haq, from Jullunder, who was studying to be a lawyer. Ahsan ul-Haq gave it a smack alright: in fact he belonged to the Afridi clan, which has produced Shahid of that ilk. Class was the key factor of course. Ahsan ul-Haq, who played for Hampstead, and Pavri were amateurs; heaven knows the vocabulary if they had gone to the Grace Gates and applied for a job on the MCC groundstaff.

***

It must have been a bit tough to survive years of fighting in the trenches in the First World War, then die of Spanish flu a week after the Armistice: but this was the fate of Major Reggie Schwarz. Born in Kent of Silesian parentage, he attended Christ's College, Cambridge, played rugby three times for England as a half-back and a few games for Middlesex as a batsman. He then became secretary to the millionaire Sir Abe Bailey in South Africa. Schwarz was therefore a key figure in the founding of the ICC – Imperial Cricket Conference as it was initially – in 1909, as Bailey's idea, and before then he exported the first 'mystery ball' from Lord's to South Africa.

Bernard Bosanquet had played for Middlesex as an orthodox batsman after leaving Oxford and, from 1897, had experimented with his googly or 'the Bosie' as Australians named it in his honour. In 1900 Bosanquet unveiled his invention in a first-class match and thereafter a batsman had to watch the bowler's wrist and fingers to predict the direction in which the ball would turn. Australians could not fathom it and Bosanquet had two match-winning Test spells against them, mixing up his leg breaks and googlies at – crucially – decent pace.

When playing together for Middlesex, Schwarz picked Bosanquet's brains. Schwarz, however, could only bowl googlies – which was enough in those days when a batsman barely used his pads (they were certainly not his first line of defence). Schwarz topped the South Africans' bowling averages on their 1904 and 1907 tours of England and before the First World War he bowled 18 of his 46 right-handed victims in Test cricket, more than one-third, a very high proportion.

As a consequence of the googly, batsmen began to close the gap between their bat and front pad. Stemming from this change in technique, lbw became a far more frequent form of dismissal. In first-class cricket in 1870, one dismissal in 40 was lbw and, of Schwarz's 55 Test victims, one was lbw. By 1923, however, in first-class cricket in England, one dismissal in eight was lbw. Nowadays this proportion has increased to one dismissal in five. The DRS system and ball-tracking in international cricket have favoured the bowler, giving him a second chance to appeal, and shown umpires that the ball was going to hit the stumps more often than they had previously thought.

* * *

Australians have been playing for Middlesex almost as long as Middlesex have been playing at Lord's, as the forerunners of Steve Eskinazi. One of the first was Albert Trott who hit a ball on the pavilion roof, and who remains the only bowler to take four wickets in four balls and a hat-trick in the same first-class innings: Somerset's batsmen in 1907 cannot have been very good starters.

Another Australian was a century ahead of his time as cricket's first agent and international entrepreneur. Frank Tarrant was skilled enough at batting and left-arm spin bowling to have played for Australia, but he preferred Middlesex, where he developed influential contacts. He knew his horses too, being Aussie. So during the First World War and thereafter he worked in India for maharajahs, notably those of Patiala and Cooch-Behar, supplying them with cricketers, coaches – Jack Hearne and Lee among others – and racehorses. Had Tarrant been operating now, his clients would be well represented in the Indian Premier League.

* * *

When Middlesex's all-time XI takes the field – the match has to be against Surrey, and Frederick's ghost should be able to throw in some decent prize money – no doubt about the captain. Sorry Sir Pelham, though he led Middlesex to the Championship title in 1920, and no, not Frank Mann nor George Mann, although both of them captained Middlesex to the title, the only case of father and son doing so in Championship history. Sorry Mike Gatting and Sir Andrew Strauss too. It has to be Michael Brearley.

When Brearley took over in 1972, having finished with universities in the UK and USA, he had to contend with an old guard. Peter Parfitt, John Murray and Fred Titmus all had England careers of note and they made a formidable triumvirate in the field. Titmus wheeled away, tightly, from the pavilion end, Murray brought his gloves together in a magic circle behind the stumps and Parfitt stood at slip, often standing taller for the fourth ball of an over as Titmus would drop one slightly shorter and tempt the batsman to cut. Seldom has cricket been so polished.

To judge by his appearance ... no, never judge Brearley by appearance. He might dress like the postgraduate he was, but do not be misled. He broke Ian Botham in like a wild horse, through the exertion of his will. He saw off the Middlesex old guard before fashioning his own team, which by 1981 consisted of 11 internationals, the first time in county history that had happened: nine had represented England, alongside Jeff Thomson of Australia and Wayne Daniel of West Indies to ginger up the attack. Like Ray Illingworth, to whom he can be most closely compared as a captain, Brearley always wanted a full hand of bowlers, including a couple of spinners.

Brearley thought inside and outside boxes. Take the 1977 derby against Surrey. No play was possible on the first two days except for five overs, yet Middlesex still won by nine wickets on the third and last. They dismissed Surrey for 49, then Brearley declared after one ball of Middlesex's first innings (forfeiting was not allowed), dismissed Surrey a second time for 89 and knocked off the runs, led by Brearley himself.

Such ingenuity gave the impression that underneath Brearley's floppy sun hat rabbits were concealed, and proliferating. He plucked out another in 1982 when he brought Titmus back, aged 49, and 33 years after his Middlesex debut in 1949, to conjure up three last wickets.

It was all too much for Middlesex's opponents as the county won the Championship four times (once shared) under Brearley's command and two one-day trophies. And it was too much for England's opponents as well. The one occasion when I saw him bereft of rabbits was in Australia in 1979/80: he was, for once, short of firepower. It was the series when Bob Willis took three wickets in the three Tests and Botham had to do almost everything on his own. There was nothing Brearley could do to stop a stronger side winning, but give him a game between two well-matched sides and his captaincy would tip the balance.

John Emburey and Phil Edmonds were Brearley's spinners for Middlesex and often for England too. Before them, and Titmus, leg-spinners such as 'Young Jack' Hearne and Jim Sims and Ian Peebles and Walter Robins would wheel away at Lord's, never mind Trott and Tarrant and old Jack Hearne. Where have all these spinners gone, and why?

Plenty of spin bowling is done in the Middlesex League. Half of the 18 first-team games consist of 120 overs in a day, when spinners can bowl at least 20 of them; the other half of 50 overs, with the normal limitation of ten. But not since Phil Tufnell have Middlesex produced a spinner in their grand tradition.

The dearth might be explained by conditions at Lord's: the square used to be played on most days of the season, if not a Middlesex or MCC game then one of those long-standing fixtures like Eton v Harrow. The groundsman had no time to prepare or over-prepare, and pitches were far more natural. In addition to all his thousands of runs at Lord's, Compton took 308 first-class wickets there, bowling his mix of left-arm spinners.

It is not only spin that became conspicuously absent from Middlesex cricket; so too the Afro-Caribbean community. Middlesex offered the Windrush generation a chance to play and by the 1980s five members of their side were Afro-Caribbean. By the early 1990s the England team relied on Afro-Caribbean fast bowlers. Not anymore.

Several factors were involved in the disappearance of Haringey Cricket College, which produced about 20 first-class cricketers (and it was a college, giving students an education, not merely a club). Essentially, when the ECB was founded and took control of all cricket in England and Wales, it assumed responsibility for Haringey CC – and decided not to fund it. It would have been good if Middlesex, or MCC, or both, had moved in and taken over Haringey once the ECB had let it die.

Instead, to diversify, Middlesex have launched a partnership with Sachin Tendulkar, who has an apartment in St John's Wood. They are not allowed to stage pop concerts or weddings or conferences at Lord's, so they have to use their intellectual capital or cricket knowledge. Middlesex set up their first such academy in Mumbai with 200 children.

Under the directorship of Angus Fraser, Middlesex have also looked far closer to home for their players, by nourishing youngsters in their own leagues, including spinners. Luke Hollman came from the North Middlesex club and is state-school educated, which is becoming the exception at some counties rather than the rule. The refugee boy from Sri Lanka, Thilan Walallawita, was also unearthed in local leagues. The pair of them appear to be receiving more support than Ravi Patel, the left-arm spinner who was selected for England Lions before withering on the Middlesex vine.

Middle Saxons no longer exist. The county is no longer a physical entity and Lord's is not theirs, although they are gradually building a home of their own at Radlett. Middlesex CCC muddles along, like other areas of English life that have grown up rather eccentrically, like a tree between the pavement stones of a city street. And it sometimes blossoms.

Northamptonshire

HOW CAN anyone interested in cricket not have a soft spot for Northamptonshire?

Nobody can feel threatened by a county that has the smallest population of the 18 first-class counties as defined by the traditional boundaries; that has never won the Championship title; that at one period went 99 consecutive games without winning, losing 61 of them and drawing 38; and that has been dismissed for the grand total of 12. It was in 1907, only two years after they had been promoted, and remains the lowest total ever in Championship cricket. (When Oxford University scored a dozen in the mid-Victorian era they batted with only ten men.)

Derbyshire alone have won fewer trophies in their existence, four. Even Durham, who have barely started, have won as many trophies as Northamptonshire's five.

Counties that have won the fewest trophies:

Derbyshire	4
Durham	5
Northamptonshire	5
Glamorgan	6

Yet Northamptonshire have added abundantly to the gaiety of the nation's cricket, whether losing or winning. England's last two world-class spinners grew up at Wantage Road in

Northampton, Graeme Swann and Monty Panesar, before touring India in 2012/13 and out-performing India's spinners in their own backyard.

Two of the most exciting batsmen ever to represent England — and exciting batsmen were not plentiful in the land before limited-overs cricket — played for Northamptonshire, before being struck by tragedy.

Fred Bakewell, after averaging 45 in his first six Tests for England, and scoring 241* against Derbyshire, was being driven home by a team-mate in a sports car without a roof, around midnight, on a hill on the A50. His team-mate, Reggie Northway, was found dead in a ditch, and there was no evidence he had been drinking to excess. Bakewell — who had come from an approved school and whose life needed cricket — broke his right arm in so many places that he never played again.

Colin Milburn was the same age, 27, when he had his car accident in Northampton, after averaging 46 in his first nine Tests for England. Again it was midnight, but this time there had been a party, as Northamptonshire had just defeated the West Indian tourists of 1969. Milburn had been drinking, before driving his car into a lorry, breaking the windscreen and losing his left eye.

Lancashire did not like the look of the fastest bowler England had produced to that point, Frank Tyson, but Northamptonshire gave him a go, and soon Tyson developed his massive shoulders, became 'The Typhoon', and in 1954/55 achieved that once-in-a-generation feat of winning the Ashes in Australia.

Northamptonshire recently unearthed another England outright-fast bowler in Olly Stone, from Norfolk, before Warwickshire snaffled him, then Nottinghamshire, as those counties which own Test grounds tend to do. Given such a small population, Northamptonshire have done wonders in discovering future England cricketers in highways and byways, especially the North-East.

Even in the last decade, either side of running up debts of more than £4m, Northamptonshire managed to win the T20 title in 2013 and 2016. They did not look the physically fittest team of sportsmen to grace this planet, several of them being ample of girth, yet they had the mettle to win.

So it was just as well, when the club was struggling in the 1930s, that they somehow found the money to keep going, rather than dropping down into the Minor Counties Championship as was urged, for they would surely never have returned. Northamptonshire have been a sort of spice, not so basic as salt, but coriander, or cinnamon, without which English cricket would have lost some of its savour.

***

Whitsun Bank Holiday Monday was not an occasion for nationwide celebration – events in the Sudetenland were making a second world war inevitable – but Wantage Road was a happy place on the evening of 30 May 1939.

Northamptonshire had just won their first Championship match for four years 'amid scenes of great jubilation', according to the *Daily Telegraph*. After playing 99 games which had ended in a draw or, more often, defeat, the county had finally won at the 100th attempt. It was against Leicestershire, the Midlands' other penniless first-class county, but never mind.

Four years, without winning a Championship game: soul-destroying or what? Yet the home captain Robert Nelson told the jubilant crowd of 6,352 paying spectators: 'I want to pay tribute to the team who have struggled through a trying period without losing heart, and who have kept cheerful in all circumstances.'

Northamptonshire had just hit upon a pair of bowlers with a bit of pace, who had reduced Leicestershire to 8/5 on the opening morning and dismissed them for 134. Batting had never been Northamptonshire's strong point, from the moment they had been promoted in 1905, but a youngster called Dennis Brookes scored 187, going on to become the county's all-time top run-scorer and play one Test for England. The home side might have felt confident, for once, after Nelson declared at 510/8.

As defeatist humour has been a feature of English sport, it might have surfaced when Leicestershire batted a second time.

As the *Daily Telegraph* reported: 'When the second ball of the opening over in Leicester's second innings knocked Berry's leg stump out of the ground there was a roar of cheering, but the crowd had not heard the umpire's shout of "No ball." Buswell was the bowler, and Berry hit the next ball out of the ground for six.' Les Berry was in the process of becoming Leicestershire's top all-time run-scorer. Northamptonshire's self-doubts must have resurfaced: a huge lead but was victory going to elude them for the 100th consecutive time?

But Northamptonshire, always forced to shop for bargains, had introduced a couple of New Zealand Test players. One was a leg-spinner, Bill Merritt, who played when not making more money on Saturdays in the Lancashire League. Northamptonshire finished the job, on Merritt, who took six wickets in 10.7 overs (yes, 1939 was the one season when English cricket used the eight-ball over). This victory saved them from finishing bottom of the table for the sixth season in a row; Leicestershire finished last instead, not that anybody was noticing as the last round of games were cancelled.

Nelson was an up-and-at 'em leader, who had only taken over the side the year before, in 1938. He must have been referring to Northamptonshire during his captaincy specifically when he said the side 'kept cheerful in all circumstances'.

Stephen Chalke, indefatigable researcher and primary historian of the County Championship, caught up with the last surviving member of that Northamptonshire side of the late 1930s. Cyril Perkins played 56 Championship games without a victory, still a record for county cricket. A photograph in the definitive history of Northamptonshire CCC, by Matthew Engel and Andrew Radd, shows three fine cricketers from the single village of Wollaston, one of them Perkins, a tall, strong, strapping lad who could bowl left-arm spin (except that the second Kiwi in the team, the wicketkeeper Ken James, made him bowl the wrong line). Perkins could bowl alright: he went on to become far and away the leading all-time wicket-taker for Suffolk.

'We did get a bit despondent at times,' Perkins told Chalke in *The Way It Was*. 'We had a first-innings lead in quite a few matches and we didn't win any of them. But in the end you get so used to not winning that you just accept it. The members got used to it, too. They saw some cricket.' And one young spectator at Wantage Road in the late 1930s was inspired to help the club when his turn came.

Having gone four years before winning a Championship match, Northamptonshire went another seven years before their next win: not a successful run, but then six of those 11 summers were lost to war. Nelson too was lost, when a bomb landed on his officers' mess in 1940.

Northamptonshire, like Somerset, have never won the County Championship. At least Nelson broke their habit of winning the wooden spoon.

* * *

Harvard Business School must have students combing economic history to find the most efficient business model. The East India Company must have been superlative at stripping every penny of profit from wherever they plundered. But has anyone done a module on the most inefficient business that ever was?

Or maybe you cannot count English county cricket, for much of its existence, as a business model. Local gentry and a few prosperous merchants – more old money than new – would decide that their county ought to have a cricket team: why, they might even play a spot of cricket themselves for this new club. So a few hundred chaps would subscribe a guinea per year, a few professionals and a groundsman would be engaged and, lo and behold, Loamshire are competing – or at least participating in – the County Championship.

It was all very well after the two world wars when spectators flocked. Where better to forget, or grieve, or enjoy the sun and company of friends and strangers, than at a cricket match? But when the crowds tailed off, in the 1930s and 1950s, what then? The Duke of Devonshire would put his hand in his pocket to keep Derbyshire going, but death duties hammered other patrons. The existence of many counties was hand-to-mouth, the rescue package being the several hundred pounds which MCC would distribute to each county every four years after a tour of Australia.

Major counties which owned Test match grounds – like Lancashire, Surrey and Yorkshire, each with the best part of 10,000 members or more – were safe. But if you are writing an essay for your MBA on county cricket, it would be safe to assert that Derbyshire, Leicestershire and Northamptonshire have survived largely because of one man in each case, in defiance of economics.

At Derby he was William Taylor; at Leicester he was Mike Turner; at Northampton he was Ken Turner (no relation). Each of them served for several decades as 'the secretary', but their counties survived because they were so much more. With the aid of nothing more than a typist, and a part-time accountant, who might be a committee member doing it for free or on the cheap, these three officials tried every avenue to keep their county flags flying.

It is fortunate that one of them, Ken Turner, recorded his memoirs (in a diary, not a published book) to enable posterity to understand what county cricket used to be like. Ring up a county club now and you will be offered the chance to press 1 for membership enquiries, 2 for the banqueting department, 3 for match ticket sales, 4 for the indoor school, etc. These three secretaries organised everything; each was a chief executive with a staff of one.

Ken Turner was one of those small boys at Wantage Road who sat through those four years without a victory: 'I went to the County Ground with the *Manchester Guardian*, as it was then, a well-thumbed record book, sandwiches and high hopes for Northamptonshire which, alas, were rarely fulfilled.' After a busy war he came back to Northampton and heard that the club's incumbent secretary needed an assistant. The secretary was Lt-Col Alleyne St George Caldwell, so we can imagine he did not lick the back of envelopes himself when posting out membership cards.

When Turner succeeded the lieutenant-colonel as secretary, he had one piece of luck: Freddie Brown became the Northamptonshire captain. Here was an amateur not only worth his place but almost everything that an amateur cricketer in those days should have been, full of zest in leading from the front. 'Beautiful cabbages – hearts like Freddie Brown!' This was the cry of barrow-boys in Australia in

1950/51 when Brown finally led England to their first postwar victory against Australia.

Turner made sure this luck continued by hitting on the financial wheeze of organising football pools. Warwickshire had started the scheme, and by 1959 it was judged to be illegal, but for five years tens of thousands of people paid a shilling a week to do the football pools and subsidise Northamptonshire.

'We raised £115,000,' Turner recorded in his diary, 'and miraculously a capital reserve of £80,000 was accumulated in the fifties on the shillings subscribed for the football competition.' At one point 60% of Northamptonshire's income came from football pools. For one of the rare periods in Championship history – arguably the only period – there was a level playing field financially. Grander counties disdained anything so tacky as football pools, preferring to be 'poor but respectable'.

Money meant players and, to Turner, lots of them. Bear in mind he had been in the army and worked in the military government in Germany afterwards. He wanted a squad of first- and second-team players and soon Northamptonshire had 29 players on their staff, more than any other county. In addition to a first XI he wanted recruits to be trained like an extension of national service. Coaches, such as the county's former batsman Brian Reynolds, were in effect regimental sergeant-majors.

'Bowl straight, you prat!' was the sole instruction that one county bowling coach had for his bowlers. 'Play straight!' was the standard instruction for batsmen. This system produced tough cricketers, but uninspired and defensive ones, focused on their averages at the end of the season, hence their contracts and careers. On the plus side, these recruits grew up together and shared the same core values, including loyalty to their club.

By 1965 Northamptonshire had worked their way up from the bottom of the ladder to the top, the very top. They completed their season early: back then Northampton Town required the other side of the Wantage Road ground for football. Worcestershire, meanwhile, the current champions, had two matches left to play and had to win them both to prevent Northamptonshire winning their first title.

Northamptonshire were a team without stars in 1965, although Milburn was about to be recognised as one. Their surnames give us a flavour of unpretentiousness: Watts, Steele, Crump, Norman, Kettle, Sully. The most effective were the brothers Watts, Jim the future captain and Peter the leg-spinner, and the cousins David Steele and Brian Crump, all four all-rounders. Keith Andrew was captain, and possibly the finest of all English wicketkeepers to that point.

Then Colin Ingleby-Mackenzie went and declared. Worcestershire were playing Hampshire at Bournemouth, where it had rained. The home captain declared 146 behind on first innings which 'caused a great deal of controversy', according to *Wisden* which added, 'but this was the pattern of many other matches during the wet season'. After negotiations, Hampshire's target was only 147, but Worcestershire had read the damp pitch and conditions rather better. Worcestershire rolled over Hampshire in 16.3 overs for 31, went on to defeat Sussex in their final game and retained their title by four points ahead of Northamptonshire.

Ken Turner had noticed something else: that about half of most England Test cricketers – i.e. the best cricketers in the country – came from minor counties, like the greatest batsman, Jack Hobbs from Cambridge and the greatest bowler, Syd Barnes from Staffordshire. Is this coincidence, he asked? It has been observed that cricketers, especially batsmen, who are not brought up at first-class counties and their academies have a freedom of self-expression which has not been coached out of them.

Turner therefore became, in addition to secretary, the first talent ID scout in professional cricket. Northamptonshire's second XI joined the Minor Counties Championship in 1950 and were thus able to see young talent for themselves. Traditionally, players were recruited by word of mouth, or after they or their parents had written in to ask for a trial: not very scientific. Turner established a network of eyes and ears, especially in the North-East, where not only Colin Milburn was found but a teacher named Doug Ferguson recommended Peter Willey, Geoff Cook, Neil Mallender and Richard Williams; and in Staffordshire, whence came David Steele and his cousin Brian Crump.

This talent identification system, however, was not quite flawless. When Milburn turned up at Wantage Road for his trial, a couple of old pros took a look at him in the nets and were not impressed. Heads were shaken; nay, lad, not the right approach at all; what's the point of hitting every ball out of the ground for six? They let Milburn go back to Durham and it was only when he scored his century for them against the 1959 Indian tourists that Turner out-bid Warwickshire to sign him.

Turner's revolutionary methods kept Northamptonshire afloat until a benefactor came along in the form of Lynn Wilson. He was born into the property and construction business, played enough at Oakham School to have a few games for Northants seconds, and iced the county's cake. He put a million pounds, about one-third of the cost, into the indoor school which replaced the old football infrastructure of Northampton Town; and he enabled Northamptonshire to sign some of the game's greatest names.

Dennis Lillee, Kapil Dev, Curtly Ambrose, Bishen Bedi and Anil Kumble – never mind Frank Tyson. Surely no county – no country – has fielded a better attack than that quintet, who took more than 2,000 Test wickets, in their prime. True, Lillee was past his best when he went to Wantage Road, and Kapil did not bust a gut, but what about the other three? Ambrose, signed with some prescience after one first-class game, was the last bowler never to be taken apart; Bedi was the maestro of left-arm spin; Kumble was unique, as an over-spinner, but raised eyebrows when he was signed to replace Ambrose in 1995. After three games, and barely a wicket, his captain Allan Lamb asked what was wrong. Kumble replied he was too cold, so Lamb whisked him off to M & S for long johns. Kumble finished the season with 105 first-class wickets, pushing Northamptonshire into third place, another of their near-misses.

***

Like Essex, Northamptonshire are a prime example of a cricket-playing county that has used all its resources to achieve success – not in the 1930s, of course, but in the course of the last decade. Still no County Championship title, but they have won the T20 trophy twice. (Yorkshire have never won the T20, and Surrey only once, in the inaugural year of 2003.)

Northamptonshire cleverly used data. In the T20 competition of 2012 they hit only 19 sixes and finished bottom of their group for the second year in a row. Across the seasons of 2011 and 2012 they won three T20 games and lost 18.

They spent the next winter toughening up and practising white-ball skills half the time, not 20% as before; and they hit 73 sixes in 2013 in the process of winning the title. Alright, it was evident from the first T20 games ever played by counties that the team hitting more sixes would normally win the game, but there was more to Northamptonshire's title than that.

One example given by Tim Wigmore, the leading media analyst of T20, was that when Northamptonshire visited Durham, their players discussed the size of the boundaries at Chester-le-Street. Northamptonshire obviously wanted short boundaries, for the benefit of their six-hitters, but simply looking at the ground they could not agree whether the boundaries were long or short. Being able to think on their feet and move quickly, like only a small unit can, the new coach David Ripley went to some local builders to buy the equipment which measures an area of ground and took it to all their games.

Leicestershire had dominated the T20 in its early years. They saw the wide boundaries to either side at Grace Road – the ground had been owned by the council and used to stage two school games side by side – and employed two spinners to bowl short of a length and have visiting batsmen caught in the deep leg side. Northamptonshire, prompted by their analyst Richard Barker, evolved a stage further. By preparing short boundaries at Wantage Road, they not only played to their side's new strength of six-hitting, they minimised the need for running twos – many of their players being hefty and not swift between wickets.

'Before the quarter-final at Hove in 2015, Northants' measuring wheel found that there was an unusually short boundary up the hill, with the wind howling to the leg side,' Wigmore wrote. 'David Willey promptly smashed 34 off a single over from Mike Yardy during a blistering century. Northants also always have in mind opposing bowlers they can target if they are behind the game.'

Ken Turner's philosophy – that a large squad is essential – no longer seems to apply, not at least in the newest format. 'In T20, a smaller squad can render batsmen less fearful that a loose shot or two will lead to being dropped,' Wigmore noted. He quotes the Northamptonshire all-rounder Stephen Crook, who had played in far larger squads at Lancashire and Middlesex: 'You don't feel like you're looking over your shoulder the whole time. You then play fearless cricket. It becomes a less selfish environment.'

Wigmore concluded: 'The shallowness of Northamptonshire's squad, and the camaraderie between players, cultivates a culture of selflessness and honesty.'

* * *

Do former wicketkeepers make particularly astute coaches? After all, they grow up watching intently every ball that comes their way and giving advice to their captain whenever he asks, or not. David Ripley, in any event, achieved remarkably much with remarkably little after taking over as head coach in 2013, both in red ball and white ball, as he secured promotion to the first division before moving to newer but equally important pastures on behalf of Northamptonshire.

Ripley has an eye for a bargain, especially ones that have been overlooked by Yorkshire, having been one himself (Keith Andrew comes first in the county's list of most wicketkeeping dismissals, Ripley fourth). Ben Sanderson from Sheffield played a handful of matches for Yorkshire, drifted out of the game, then took more than 200 wickets in the next four Championship seasons after Ripley called him back, besides being a vital death-bowler in their last T20 title.

South Africa's under-19 captain is usually a bargain. I watched Ricardo Vasconcelos's debut for Northamptonshire in 2018, aged 20, when he immediately looked the part of a batsman who knows his game and can bat a long time (he keeps wicket too). No county awards a five-year contract lightly, especially to someone with a Portuguese surname and passport. Northamptonshire did, after their players renamed him Dave, for short.

A reward for Sanderson powering Northamptonshire back into the first division at the end of 2019 was a trip to the Cayman Islands. With their president Lord Naseby as intermediary, since he has a property in the islands, Northamptonshire now have a link with the Caymans.

'We took our academy team out there and started with coach education and schools,' says Northamptonshire's chairman, Gavin Warren. 'In March 2020 we took the first team out to Singapore at the invitation of their Chamber of Commerce but we had to cancel our gala dinner there and come home when the virus struck.' Small acorns, but worthwhile for a small county to plant.

Having had debts of more than £4m in 2015, 'we are now in a really good place', says Warren, a property developer who has followed – consciously – in the footsteps of Lynn Wilson. The debt was turned round by issuing shares of £250 to anyone who wanted to buy them, with a limitation of £100,000. 'As always great ideas come about over a cup of tea,' Warren recalls. 'My vice-chairman Ian Peck [a Cambridge double Blue] and I were discussing various ideas – bonds, loans, selling assets, etc. – when Ian said his father-in-law was a shareholder at Leicester racecourse. This had come about because the racecourse had written to fans and sponsors asking them to invest in the course to give it the best chance of surviving through financial challenges.

'We thought that we had asked the same benefactors time and time for help and we needed to offer them something in return, moreover making sure it was accessible to members regardless of wealth,' Warren added. 'Our aim was to raise £1m and we raised just short of £1.2m, 20% over target.'

Ken Turner would have been pleased with that fundraising wheeze, and with Northamptonshire's continued use of networks in the north of England to unearth bargains.

***

Northampton itself urgently needs Northamptonshire CCC to survive. The city of cobblers has become very down at heel. In the centre, even the shops selling stuff for a pound had closed before Covid. When the lights are switched on at Wantage Road for a T20 game on a weekday evening, it is not quite like the home games of Northampton Saints rugby, but a sense of well-being and excitement does descend on the surrounding streets.

The ground on such occasions combines warmth and English eccentricity with the fine facilities of the indoor school and an outfield which has been re-laid. In England we can forget that professional cricket around the world is increasingly played in soulless stadia and concrete bowls. Not county cricket, not Wantage Road with its former score box that could have served as a signal box on a pre-Beeching branch line. When Northamptonshire were promoted in 1905 they were told they needed a press box but baulked at the cost of £72, before realising it was unavoidable, then squeezing in the scorers as well. Media have been moved to behind the arm, and the ground floor of the old box was turned into a second-hand bookstall run by their supporters' club.

To grow, not atrophy, Northamptonshire's latest idea has been to establish an academy in Luton, where they used to play the odd first-class match at Wardown Park. The scheme was the brainchild of Amran Malik, the Lord's Taverners Wicketz coach in Luton but much more besides: a visionary in fact because, after gaining a business management degree and having been interested only in football, he turned to cricket when his sons started to play it and saw the existing pathways for what they were worth: not much.

Malik's project to promote cricket in Luton, partly by bringing in Northamptonshire's skills, is the only cricket project in Britain backed by the United Nations' Department of Economic and Social Affairs. This is where David Ripley now presides, at the Northamptonshire Steelbacks academy in Luton. Until 2017 the only outdoor cricket nets were to be found at the Luton Town and Indians CC at Wardown Park, and no indoor nets at all. But – and this was a first – Northamptonshire followed up Amran's brainwave by setting up an academy outside their own borders. A model for most counties to follow?

Sports traditionally do not work together. Even in cricket, charity organisations do not work together. In Luton they do. Amran has devised a pathway for everyone (male and female) who wants to play cricket up to the age of 24, not only to play cricket but to grow and acquire qualifications along the way. Everyone is accommodated. If you are involved in anti-social behaviour then Combat Cricket may be the course for you as it harnesses young people's energies.

Amran has rolled out the same template in Peterborough, and been recruited to promote the ECB Core Cities project. 'I've seen very similar situations where there is an appetite to play, but just not the parental support or financial prowess. If there is a Steelbacks-style academy in the vicinity I think we might be on to an urban talent identification model which doesn't replace but complements the current [county-based] system and makes it more inclusive.'

What our 18 first-class counties do on the field is important. No less is what they do off the field within their own borders, and beyond.

Nottinghamshire

SUPPOSE ROBIN Hood had been born and brought up in Leicester, and Friar Tuck had moved to Nottinghamshire from a monastery down south, and Maid Marian hailed from Northampton, and Little John from Derbyshire, where he is reputedly buried in the village of Hathersage.

Whereas spice is added to the stories about Robin Hood and his merry men if the Sheriff of Nottingham is an outsider, sent from London to enforce the wicked rule of King John, it detracts if Hood and his merry men have grown up far from Sherwood Forest, and have only moved there to promote their careers.

Every county in this age of social mobility is bound to have plenty of cricketers imported from other first-class counties and minor counties, even Yorkshire who relied on their own home-born until the 1990s. But it surely has to be a matter of degree.

Nottinghamshire have won their share of white-ball titles in recent years: the 20-over (twice), 40-over and 50-over trophies. Yet in the Championship they went through a barren period that was astonishing for any county, let alone one of their resources: from June 2018 until May 2021, they drew 12 and lost 18 of their 30 matches. Their batting line-up consisted entirely of signings from other first-class counties: Ben Slater from Derbyshire, Haseeb Hameed from Lancashire, Ben Duckett from Northamptonshire, Joe Clarke from Worcestershire, Chris Nash from Sussex and Steve Mullaney, the captain, from Lancashire. Would they not have fared better if one or two of their batsmen had been Robin Hood's descendants?

Nottinghamshire, from the very beginning, have been one of the wealthiest of the 18 first-class counties, though some of the reasons are not obvious. There was no more money in lace than steel or cotton, and Nottinghamshire's population is no larger than Derbyshire's as the traditional borders go.

Since 1899, however, Trent Bridge has been staging Test matches on almost an annual basis, or else a couple of plum England white-ball fixtures guaranteed to bring in capacity crowds of 15,000. Nottinghamshire's white-ball team has long been vibrant, with Alex Hales to open, and any T20 game packs in 10,000 of an evening and a full house for a home quarter-final. No wonder club membership has numbered around 8,000.

So there is plenty of cash to splash on players: Nottinghamshire's recent accounts stated that they have over a million pounds in the bank, not tied up in assets but ready to hand. Is it possible that they have had too much money to spend on importing ready-made players? Conceivably. For certain they have had a lot of downs as well as ups: while they won the Championship in 2005 and 2010, they have been relegated from the first division five times in the 20-odd years of two divisions, which is almost as much yo-yoing as far less affluent Worcestershire.

***

Trent Bridge itself is another reason, money aside, why ambitious cricketers head to Nottingham. Outside Lord's at any rate, is there a better Test ground in England? The walk from the city centre and railway station across the River Trent with its bracing breeze; the pavilion which was built for the 1899 Ashes Test and whose dressing rooms still serve, one upstairs, one down; the proximity of useful shops outside the main gate and in the Radcliffe Road, which makes the ground feel as though it is right in the community; the blending of ancient and modern. This cricket ground looks the two neighbouring football clubs in the eye, not as an inferior, as cricket so often is elsewhere.

No county has played so few games away from its headquarters as Nottinghamshire, which in itself speaks volumes for Trent Bridge. Pitches through the ages have been conducive to batting, but usually have a decent carry for new-ball bowlers – which, in itself, is a worthy feat of groundsmanship for, in my observation, pitches located beside a river naturally tend to be slow. (Yes, I know the WACA in Perth lies beside the Swan but the soil is imported clay from south of the city, inland.)

Trent Bridge was the creation of the man I have come to consider the most influential person in the shaping of English cricket – even more so than WG Grace, because Grace might never have devoted himself to cricket but for William Clarke. Cricket-writing about the past and present is largely done in the south of England, whether its exponents have been born in the north or south, because of the gravitational pull of London, its newspapers and publishers. This imbalance has led, I believe, to an under-estimation of Clarke's legacies.

Clarke was a bricklayer, born in 1798, who married the landlady of the Trent Bridge Inn and, using his professional skills, made the surrounding field into the cricket ground we admire today. 'He has displayed great judgement in laying out the Trent Bridge ground and the admirable condition in which it is kept rendered it a delightful place.' This was the *Nottingham Review* of August 1838, quoted by Peter Wynne-

Thomas in his superbly researched book, *Nottinghamshire Cricketers 1821–1914*. (I have to admit that when this book was published in 1972, most teenaged boys were spending their pocket money on flared jeans and leather jackets or pop concerts on the Isle of Wight, but I never regretted this sum of £5.25p.)

Clarke's legacy to this day has been maintained. He would be especially pleased that the new Radcliffe Road stand was built with 500,000 bricks. In fact, he would probably have landed the contract for laying them or threatened to ban all Nottinghamshire CCC staff from the Trent Bridge Inn if he did not win the contract.

There is much more to Clarke though than the creation of Trent Bridge. Secondly, he was a very artful bowler. 'Instead of delivering the ball from the height of the hip, he at the last moment bent back his elbow, bringing the ball almost under his right arm-pit, and delivered the ball thus from as great a height as it was possible to attain and still be under-hand,' wrote one contemporary. Although he lost one eye playing Fives in his twenties Clarke was so artful – so quick to analyse a batsman and bowl to his weak points – that he would regularly take 300 wickets in a season and, once, more than 400 wickets for his All England XI.

Yes, the All England XI. The first England cricket team was another of Clarke's creations.

After getting Nottinghamshire cricket up and running at Trent Bridge, Clarke moved to London and joined the MCC groundstaff when he was approaching 50, being still the craftiest of bowlers (he was acclaimed as the first who bowled to his field for catches rather than to knock stumps down). There he met the most notable cricketers of his day – and realised the sport's enormous commercial potential, completely untapped, but ready to be exploited owing to the new railways.

DISAPPEARING WORLD

Thus Clarke formed the All England XI in 1846 to tour the country, play cricket and cash in. MCC was a gentlemen's club, like many others in London: it did not exist to popularise the game. This is what Clarke did, by writing round for matches, tapping areas outside London, arranging fixtures against XXII of Newcastle or XVIII of Sheffield, and – what is more – by making cricket equipment to sell while on the road, thus starting the Nottingham tradition of bat-making still maintained by Gunn and Moore.

'One never sees such holiday-making and high jinx as we used to see in the All England days,' wrote one of Clarke's players, Richard Daft, in later life. Note the social context: in 1850 a Factory Act granted workers Saturday afternoon off and finally the Industrial Revolution allowed workers some leisure. 'The match was the topic of conversation months before the event took place. Special committees were formed to get up entertainments in the evenings, and when the day arrived the excitement was often intense.'

By 1854 the All England XI are playing a three-day game in Bristol at a ground made by a fellow called Grace, who has several sons keen on the game. One of those sons, aged 14, fields so athletically at long-stop that William Clarke gives young Edward a bat. His six-year-old brother is watching from the family pony-trap – watching these 11 touring cricketers playing cricket both for fun and a living (Clarke paid about five pounds per game – several times the average weekly wage).

Clarke also gives Mrs Grace a little instructional book entitled *Cricket Notes*, to which Clarke himself has contributed the section about bowling, and which he signed as 'Secretary, All England Eleven'. It becomes a family heirloom and source of inspiration.

Four years later, when that six-year-old boy named William Gilbert is ten, his mother writes to Clarke's successor as the captain of the All England XI, George Parr of Nottingham, saying that while Edward is good at batting, WG is even better, because he can play on the back foot as well as front.

WG goes on to play his first matches of note against the All England XI. Some players then revolted in favour of higher pay and formed the breakaway United All England XI. Grace was playing for another breakaway team, the United South XI, when in 1876 he scored 400 not out against XXII of Grimsby. His gigantic run-making that season seized the nation by the ears, making cricket the summer sport – and this had only been possible because Clarke had demonstrated that money could be made out of cricket. Grace was an all-round athlete in his youth: but for the openings created by Clarke he might have stuck with track and field, or boxing and doctoring, and never played cricket after childhood.

***

Nottingham therefore produces the first professional cricketers of substance in William Clarke, George Parr, Richard Daft, Alfred Shaw and Arthur Shrewsbury. Some of them are also landlords of inns, or owners of shops selling sports equipment; pillars of the community, not forelock-tuggers; they know their own worth as the best professional cricketers in England, not only Nottinghamshire, and are ready to strike if they see fit. And they not only spread cricket around Britain, as never before, but abroad.

The first of all touring teams, to the United States and Canada in 1859, was captained by George Parr whom Clarke had coached and mentored. Parr also led the second of the first two touring teams to Australia, in 1863/64: they went unbeaten through their tour and cleared £250 per man. In 1879 Richard Daft led another team of professionals to the

USA, when a crowd totalling 25,000 watched their three-day game against Philadelphia.

The most ambitious of all England cricket tours, in 1881/82, was promoted by Shaw, who was also the captain, by Shrewsbury and by James Lillywhite, the Sussex pro who had captained England in the inaugural Test of 1876/77. Their team sailed to the USA, crossed the country by train while playing games en route, voyaged to Australia and played a Test there before going to New Zealand, then returned to Australia for three more Tests. They were playing for almost six months and even though cricket crowds were slumping in America, it was a profitable venture. Shaw and Shrewsbury promoted three more tours of the Antipodes in the 1880s, with Shrewsbury as the England captain. Shaw, having organised these merry men all winter, with the enormous amount of paperwork that entailed, captained Nottinghamshire to the County Championship title, outright, in four consecutive summers in the 1880s, the county's golden age.

***

It is good that while Nottinghamshire sign their batsmen from other counties, they still produce their own pace bowlers. The collieries have closed, along with their cricket grounds – about 25 colliery grounds disappeared, according to Peter Wynne-Thomas – but strapping local lads are still taking the new ball.

When Nottinghamshire won the Championship in 1929, their five main bowlers all came from collieries, starting with Harold Larwood and Bill Voce, who were good enough to break the hold which Lancashire had on the County Championship (Lancashire won it from 1926–28 and again in 1930). Larwood and Voce would go to the Trent Bridge Inn at lunchtime for a few pints, pulled by Mr and Mrs Clarke's successors, then roll up their sleeves and sweat it out in the afternoon, if opposing batsmen hung around that long.

Trent Bridge offered Larwood and Voce two advantages. 'Trent Bridge wickets are the fastest in England, that quickening marl being used almost to extremes,' wrote Fred Root, who played a few Tests contemporaneously. The names of the best groundsmen are never recorded like those of cricketers – another feature of cricket's historiography – but Walter Marshall was the man who encouraged Larwood and Voce to become Bradman-busters.

Larwood and Voce had a second asset when playing at home: Trent Bridge in their day had no sightscreens. Imagine the quality of light on a cloudy day in an industrial city which had factories and tens of thousands of houses belching smoke – and no sightscreens, at either end. The person who sparked the players' demand for sightscreens was Herbert Sutcliffe, the Yorkshire opening batsman, who lost sight of a ball against the background of the Oval pavilion at a crucial moment in the 1926 Ashes – but it was a slow process. County members did not want their view, from the best seats behind the arm, impeded.

***

Nottingham, strange as it may now seem, has been home to two teams of first-class quality and status: Nottinghamshire CCC and, just down the Loughborough Road in West Bridgford, Sir Julien Cahn's XI. Here was cricket's biggest ego-trip – though who could blame him? – and it poured more money into the county coffers.

Cahn made his millions out of a new scheme, selling furniture on hire purchase. The son of a Jewish emigrant from Germany, he, like the poet Siegfried Sassoon, made himself more English than English by playing cricket and hunting foxes. He used some of his wealth to become a most admirable philanthropist, saving Newstead Abbey by buying Byron's home for the nation, and founding a charity which offered gas and oxygen to women in childbirth. In addition to his West Bridgford ground, he bought Stanford Hall in Lincolnshire and installed another ground; together they staged the last flowerings of country house cricket.

Cahn was also vain, perhaps through underlying insecurity, and took himself very seriously. So one of the unwritten rules was that Sir Julien Cahn's XI could not lose: and he hired so many Test and top-class players, from Australia, New Zealand and South Africa, that 'his team lost only 19 of the 621 matches that they played between 1923 and 1939, and their winter tours – to such places as Canada, Argentina, Jamaica, Ceylon and New Zealand – were spoken of for years afterwards' according to Stephen Chalke in *The Way It Was*. His overseas players could manage one of his 300 stores if they wanted a winter job.

Cahn's hospitality was lavish – and the humour he unconsciously supplied was abundant too. For the second unwritten law was that Cahn could not be dismissed for nought, or be hit for 36 off an over, as he would have been if merit had determined. So he had his own umpire, John Gunn of the famous bat-making family, and his own special pair of pads – an extreme version of the kind that Graham Roope used to wear when batting for Surrey and England in the 1970s. Cahn's chauffeur, accustomed to blowing up tyres, would inflate these pneumatic pads – until the day they burst when Cahn was batting, and he lost face, and the chauffeur was instantly sacked.

As Fred Root, no relation to Joe, enjoyed country house cricket in his old age, he said most diplomatically in his book, *A Cricket Pro's Lot*: 'Sir Julien plays himself, gets runs and wickets.' Well, this is what the scorebook was made to record. But the ball would hit his pads (perhaps plumb in front), then whizz away for leg-byes, only the umpire would signal them as runs off Sir Julien's bat. We have EW Swanton's word: 'The pads were very large, and the ball bounced readily off them for leg-byes, which the umpires conveniently forgot to signal.'

MCC, of course, had no truck with new money but Nottinghamshire CCC made Cahn their president, and they inherited his unrivalled collection of bats, which are now exhibited in the pavilion at Trent Bridge. If you walk down the steps from those dressing rooms which were built for the 1899 Ashes and look to your right you can see some of the bats used by players in the ground's inaugural Test.

What happier way to have escaped the advancing horrors of Nazi Germany in 1939 than playing for Sir Julien Cahn's XI? A couple of Aussie spinners to do the bowling when you played serious teams, like the touring West Indians; games against Bedfordshire and, into the August of that year, against Scotland and Ireland. A grand week of hospitality and privilege, and some excellent cricket: yes, what better way to go?

* * *

Five thousand pounds for the 1968 season is the equivalent of six figures today: that was the highest bid, made by Nottinghamshire, for the services of the greatest all-round cricketer, Garfield Sobers, when instant registration was introduced in 1968. It may not sound much, but this was pre-Packer, and by comparison some England players were earning less than £1,000 per year.

Nottinghamshire after the Second World War had been content with being well-off and unsuccessful. In 1951 they finished bottom of the table for the first time; passed the wooden spoon on to Somerset, who finished bottom for the next four seasons; then re-claimed it in 1958, 1959, 1961, 1965 and 1966. The Trent Bridge pitches became flat, indeed the whole set-up was flat, yet the Stags were content to lean on past glories.

It was in 1965 that I first visited Trent Bridge. It was all very tranquil as the ground slumbered in August heat, far from the noise and drama of Bramall Lane. I sat in the West Bridgford stand, which then consisted of two tiers of wooden benches. Parr's Tree still stood near the Trent Bridge Inn: named after Parr because he used to slog-sweep the ball into its branches. The Championship match between Nottinghamshire and Leicestershire proceeded sedately. But on the last of the three days, which I did not attend, a world hitting record was set: Clive Inman, the Sinhalese left-hander, reached 50 in only eight minutes. Norman Hill, the home opener, bowled two overs of lollipops for Inman to smash leg-side, for 18 off one over, 32 off his second. The declaration set Nottinghamshire 258 to win in two and a half hours: far too steep. Still, the ploy of declaration bowling and setting a target was an indication of how the county game was speeding up. These counties had been two of the four that had participated in the Midlands Knock-out competition of 1962 and, thereafter, the Gillette Cup.

Sobers, in his first season, raised Nottinghamshire from 15th to fourth. It will always be one of the game's indelible images, when Sobers hit Malcolm Nash for six sixes in an over at Swansea in 1968. Remember those were the days of bats weighing little more than two pounds. The key was the arc in which Sobers swung his bat, well over 360 degrees. It was not only that he raised his bat to point vertically upwards in his backlift; players that dared to field anywhere close to Sobers would recount how they could hear the bat slap against the back of his shirt as he completed his follow-through. In 1969, however, he was away for half the season captaining West Indies on their tour of England, and in 1970 he was captaining the Rest of the World in their five

Tests. It was back to the bottom half of the table, until an historic moment.

'In late 1977 Nottinghamshire became the first county to have not a secretary but a chief executive who would make all the day-to-day decisions without referring to the committee,' Stephen Chalke wrote in *Summer's Crown*. 'Philip Carling, who had developed the money-spinning Trent Bridge Squash Club, was appointed but he did not want the hiring and firing of players to fall within his remit.' So Ken Taylor became the manager, a former Warwickshire batsman, aged 61. 'He [Taylor] took us by the scruff of the neck,' said Clive Rice, who in 1981 captained Nottinghamshire to their first Championship since 1929.

I doubt whether batting in county cricket has been more consistently demanding since Rice and Richard Hadlee were backed by Kevin Cooper, and by the groundsman Ron Allsop, who dovetailed his pitches to match Nottinghamshire's colours, with Eddie Hemmings to flush out any lingerers. This was value for money alright. Hadlee, the son of an accountant, brought that mindset to achieving the double of 1,000 runs and 100 wickets in the first-class season of 1984. Another Nottinghamshire all-rounder, Franklyn Stephenson, is the only one to have done it since, in 1988.

***

In 2003 Nottinghamshire were one of the first counties to set up an academy under ECB guidelines. A primary question was whether academy players would play for their own clubs or for an Academy XI in the local premier league. The committee decided the Academy XI would participate in the Nottinghamshire Premier League.

One consequence was that, to put an XI into the league every Saturday after first-team call-ups, injuries and so on, almost 20 young players were needed. This in turn meant these players did not receive much individual attention. Now, however, the academy players play for their clubs, which strengthens the whole league structure and allows for more concentrated development. Almost every league in England seems to have declined in overall standard, but the Nottinghamshire Premier still has some strong clubs, with a few patrons funding some well-paid players.

Another committee decision was that Nottinghamshire second XI would not play at Trent Bridge but at the Lady Bay ground down the road. When one of the lads made his first XI debut, it was like being at an away ground, everything new. The pitches at Trent Bridge have more bounce than Lady Bay, and the field different dimensions. It seems bizarre that Nottinghamshire would not give their young players the normal benefits of home advantage.

In casting round for an opening pair after Darren Bicknell and Jason Gallian, Nottinghamshire did not follow the axiom that batsmen brought up in southern counties, which normally have drier and easier pitches, struggle to adjust to northern counties, if they ever do. They signed Will Jefferson from Essex and Neil Edwards and Matt Wood from Somerset, none of them prospering in red or white ball at Trent Bridge, while academy lads were not given a prolonged opportunity to claim a place.

Paul Johnson was the captain then batting coach, at the club for 33 years in all, before joining Leicestershire two years ago – and has since become a Nottinghamshire vice-president. 'I felt our academy players reached a glass ceiling,' he says. No guarantee, of course, that any youngster will succeed when introduced to first-team cricket, but Johnson singles out Sam Kelsall and Sam Wood, who was in the England under-19 side for two years, as two batsmen who deserved more of a chance. Akil Patel, Jake Libby, Matt

Milnes and Luke Wood were other players whose potential was not fulfilled at Trent Bridge.

'A player wasn't a player unless he came from somewhere else, or it seemed that way,' Johnson reflects. 'At times I sat down and thought – why do we bother running an academy and second XI?'

The long-accepted formula used to be that a county, to succeed, needs a core of local lads; on to this core some shrewd signings from other counties or countries are grafted. Nottinghamshire did buck this trend when they won the County Championship in 2005, without any regular player who had been born in the county, and again in 2010, when Paul Franks was the only one. But in 2005 they had Stephen Fleming as captain, the New Zealander who could weld any team together, and in both seasons the rugged Australian David Hussey weighed in with innings of 250.

By the time Nottinghamshire won Division Two of the County Championship in 2022 Lyndon James had replaced Chris Nash in their line-up, so that was one batsman born in the county. So promising was James indeed that another fine local prospect, Joey Evison, had to leave to find first-team opportunities.

Maybe this formula has to be revised and updated. The 11 players in a side still have to be fairly familiar with each other, and know their characteristics, in order to function at their best. But now it may no longer be essential for them to grow up together in one location. This familiarity can be achieved if they play alongside each other for T20 franchises around the world. And this is not so much of an innovation so far as Nottinghamshire, of all counties, are concerned. To travel all round England and across the world, in order to make a living by playing cricket, is what their players were the first to do.

Somerset

ONCE UPON a time there was a Holy Grail. It may or may not have originally come from the Holy Land. King Arthur and his Knights of the Round Table dedicated themselves to finding it. They lived in Avalon, perhaps on Glastonbury Tor, where they could look out over the flooded waters of ancient Wessex, if not on the current site of the Avalon Trading Estate.

The Holy Grail, for Somerset's cricketers, is their first Championship title. Three counties are said to have never won it, but it is manifest that WG Grace and his brothers made neighbouring Gloucestershire the power in the land in the 1870s and won the unofficial title several times. Which leaves Northamptonshire and Somerset.

Their modern knights have come close, so close: six times in this millennium they have finished runners-up. In 2016 they were topping the table with two sessions of the season left: only Middlesex and Yorkshire contrived a target of 240 off 40 overs, which was legal, but why did Yorkshire have to throw all their wickets away even when they had no chance of reaching that target, instead of fighting for a draw?

In 2018 Somerset had only to beat Hampshire at Southampton, only their Kolpak Kyle Abbott zipped in with no less than 17 wickets.

In the absence of a full-scale Championship in 2020, Somerset reached the final of the Bob Willis Trophy at Lord's. To win that would have been a psychological stepping-stone towards the Holy Grail, a dress rehearsal for that first title. They had swept through the five qualifying rounds of their Central group and five of their batsmen scored centuries in the five games. Their pace bowling was so overwhelming that no opponent passed 200, their fielding fresh and hungry as their captain Tom Abell, at wide mid-off, walked in and stalked.

I don't think I've seen better fielding in county cricket than Somerset's in that truncated summer: never in peacetime can appetites for the red-ball game – any live game of cricket – have been so avid. No need for another fielder in front of the wicket on the off side, because Abell covered so much ground, almost the whole arc from the bowler in his follow-through to cover: they could pack the slips and post one man at point, behind square. Craig Overton, pounding in off a new and smoother run-up, could bowl any length he liked on or outside off stump, confident that no batsman could score in front of the wicket on the off side. Abell would swoop like the top hockey player he was, dive and stop; as a leader, a fine successor to King Arthur.

Somerset, though missing their only experienced batsman James Hildreth through injury in the BWT final, cobbled together 301 on a slow, new-ball Lord's pitch. With a biting wind from the north, bad light and showers, it was likely that first-innings lead would decide the outcome. Only two Essex batsmen reached 30 first time round, one of them their captain Tom Westley who was out for 51. Somerset would surely have made the breakthrough and won this dress rehearsal for the County Championship, but for one man.

He was, too, a knight in shining armour who thwarted them. One version of the Arthurian legend has Sir Galahad finding the Holy Grail, but the victor on this occasion was Sir Alastair. Wielding a bat as mighty as Excalibur, Cook scored 172 to win this one-off competition for the team from Essex, not Wessex, and who could take offence at a victor so un-triumphalist? Somerset, yet again, came second.

It is some consolation, if not much, that Somerset are known as everyone's second-favourite county. I think the romance of the Arthurian legend plays its part in this partiality. Some pranksters in Victorian times buried a dish near Glastonbury and 'discovered' the grail, before their hoax was realised, which served to keep the legend alive. As do films and novels like *The Once and Future King*, stretching right back to Sir Thomas Malory's *Morte d'Arthur*, which was Caxton's best-selling bodice-ripper, featuring Lady Guinevere.

I too have felt the lure of Glastonbury, and climbed the Tor, and looked down on the Morlands ground. Somerset used to play a game or two there in a pre-Pilton Glastonbury festival, and Jos Buttler played his first league cricket for the club in his early teens. But the reality does not quite live up to this romantic image. Somerset is mainly agriculture, and agricultural services. As you drive into Taunton from the motorway, the local priorities are spelled out by the sign pointing towards the centre and proclaiming in order:

Market
Cricket
Theatre

We dream of sun-kissed villages in the Quantocks with two-word names, like Nether This or Middle That, but we are less enchanted if we drive to them down a narrow lane and get stuck behind a muck-spreader. A few years ago my wife had to go abroad for a fortnight and I put my name down for eight games, starting with a Forty Club game at

Morlands. I had only been able to play on Sundays and in the odd midweek game for my club Hinton Charterhouse (no seniors county competition in those days, the over-50s and 60s and so on). Where better to start this indulgence than Glastonbury?

After I had changed and looked at the ground, I saw shades of Jack White and Arthur Wellard, as well as the blossoming Buttler trying his first ramps and reverses. The Morlands company that owned the ground ran a tannery, producing sheepskins and related products, and everything was neat and functional, as you would expect from a Quaker company, yet no rural idyll. Then, after less than an hour of fielding first, before I could bowl or bat, I turned at gully to pursue a ball to third man and pulled a fetlock. Couldn't run, could barely hobble. Out for at least a fortnight.

In addition to Somerset's romantic image, their cricket team have had a reputation for unpredictability and inconsistency, which may be another reason why they have become 'second-favourite county'. Trevor Bailey – doyen of Essex, England and *Test Match Special* – wrote of Somerset in *Championship Cricket*, 'They have always been gloriously, and at times infuriatingly unpredictable. Thus a Somerset supporter is tolerant and must possess a sense of humour. Life would be impossible without it! He has, however, the satisfaction of knowing that his team may at any moment pull off a totally unexpected victory over the champions after having just lost convincingly three matches on the trot.'

Since 1961 however, when Bailey wrote, Somerset have become consistent – all too consistent, it could be said, as when they finished runners-up in the Championship three times between 2016 and 2019. And since the invention of limited-overs county cricket they have done consistently well and won their first trophies. Five of them were won *circa* 1980, when the Knights of the Round Table featured Sir

Vivian and his companions-at-arms, Sir Ian and Sir Joel. That last step over the line, however, is always the hardest, and never more so than in the case of Somerset's first elusive Championship. More than 130 years, and still waiting.

* * *

The historic cause of Somerset's systemic inconsistency was that, having a small county ground to generate revenue, they could afford few professionals. Until after the Second World War the majority of their team consisted of amateurs. When the best of them were available, the team could be very, very good; when they were away working, or on holiday, Somerset were liable to be dreadful.

No new county can quite have seized the imagination of cricket followers so quickly as Somerset did soon after they were admitted to the Championship in 1890. The following season they beat the county champions Surrey in an epic finish at Taunton, when their Australian Oxford Blue Sammy Woods bowled Surrey's last man in the last possible over.

'Though Somerset have only for two years been reckoned among the first-class counties, they have done many things to render themselves famous in the cricket world,' *Wisden* announced the following year. 'Among all their achievements, however, nothing has been more extraordinary or has caused such a vast amount of excitement as what was done in this match against Yorkshire.'

In their first decade it became standard for Somerset to field nine amateurs, and two professionals to do most of the bowling: a pace bowler and Edwin Tyler, a tall, rather gaunt-looking left-arm spinner, who suddenly disappeared when county captains were prompted by MCC in 1900 to clamp down on throwing. Until then Tyler would open the bowling for Somerset and continue to deliver the ball

– one way or another – for most of the innings. In 1892, in this 'extraordinary' match against Yorkshire, he took seven of their wickets in his 50 overs to dismiss them for 299, whereupon the highest opening stand in first-class cricket, to that point, unfolded. It remains Somerset's highest ever for the first wicket.

Wisden was all a-twitter, if not on Twitter. 'A performance of altogether exceptional merit,' it reported of the opening stand of 346 by Lionel Palairet and Herbert Hewett in only three and a half hours. Palairet was one of the minor stars of what Neville Cardus called cricket's Golden Age. Oxford's current captain, a forerunner of CB Fry at Repton, a superlative driver of the ball, a Corinthian at soccer, he opened the batting straight after filling in as wicketkeeper, scoring 146 in 'a style that was absolutely a model to young cricketers'. The left-handed Hewett was another Oxford Blue, and the Somerset captain until he fell out with the committee in 1893, something of a portent. At lunch, when the score was 301/0 – 'this being the first time that 300 had been put on the board without a wicket down' – a 'special photograph' was taken of the figures. When Hewett was dismissed for 201, this opening partnership had 'created tremendous sensation throughout the cricket world'.

As for Somerset's victory at Headingley in 1901, it was 'the sensational match of the whole season' according to *Wisden*. Somerset were dismissed for 87, Yorkshire scored 325, whereupon Somerset responded with 630 against an attack that took about 10,000 first-class wickets – yes, ten thousand – and went on to win easily. When their train returned them to Taunton around midnight, the townsfolk – alerted by telegram – came out to meet, greet and fete them. Lionel Palairet had inspired the revival with 173. The number of professionals had increased to five, including the all-rounder signed from Surrey, Len Braund. He also made a hundred and was soon England's leg-spinning all-rounder and their first world-class slip.

When their lack of depth was exposed, Somerset were horrid. In 1895 Essex scored 695 and won by an innings and heaps. After 60.3 overs, and a single day off, Tyler bowled another 59 overs against Lancashire as they scored 801, Archie MacLaren's 424 a new world record innings. Was it then that Tyler's action became a little ragged? Even Palairet could not save them from defeat by an innings and 452 runs. Until Somerset had a hard core of pros they would always be inconsistent, and they could not afford one – so the committee argued – until the mid-1950s.

**

Another reason for Somerset being everyone's second-favourite, or favourite, county is that no other has generated such fine writing. Raymond Robertson-Glasgow, David Foot, Peter Roebuck: no county, or even country, has produced a finer trio. The cricket lover who goes on *Desert Island Discs* need look no further than this triumvirate for the book he is allowed to take.

Robertson-Glasgow was the master of profiling a cricketer in 600 words, Foot in 60 pages. Robertson-Glasgow sketched, from experience, after playing on the field with the man he profiled; Foot painted from observation and empathy.

Roebuck was as witty as they came in the early to mid-1980s, which was the golden age of humour in cricket writing in British newspapers: Alan Gibson, Matthew Engel, Martin Johnson as well as Roebuck. This was before Roebuck's world turned darker in the build-up to Somerset's revolution in the winter of 1986/87. Nevertheless he continued to have profound insights into the players and issues of the day, until his tragic end in Cape Town.

Such is the quality of this trio, Harold Pinter can hardly find a place alongside. Vic Marks and I once had the privilege of an evening drinking Meursault at Pinter's London home – Lady Antonia was not in – as he talked about his hero Arthur Wellard. Wellard set the record for most sixes in a first-class season and kept raising the bar in the 1930s, and was only overtaken by another Somerset all-rounder, now Lord Botham. Perhaps Pinter could have forced his way in and made it a quartet if he had spent more time writing about the Somerset team as a whole, but he was content with immortalising Wellard, and some plays.

***

Somerset can claim to top the county table in other ways, if not Championship titles. No county has more wicketkeepers commemorated in stained-glass windows in rural churches, if only one. The Reverend Archibald Wickham was devoted to wicketkeeping and butterflies, as well as his flock in Brent Knoll, of course. After his death the church installed a colourful window displaying a pair of wicketkeeping gloves, which were opened like a Bible, about to receive; and a butterfly net.

According to Foot, Somerset head another table: more suicides than any other first-class county. The most famous was Harold Gimblett, the holder of most of the individual batting records for Somerset until Viv Richards or Marcus Trescothick surpassed him. Gimblett either set or exemplified a trend, being a cricketer keener to represent Somerset than travel to a big city to represent his country (Roebuck admitted to the same reticence, or at least ambivalence). The stresses of fame became too much at times during Gimblett's career and his retirement, until he dictated his thoughts on to tape, which he left to Foot to write up; then turned out the light.

A less famous, yet far more understandable, suicide was Fred Hardy, a journeyman pro if ever there was. Hardy played 100 first-class matches in the dozen years leading up to the First World War but was never a regular, always up and down the order, varying from opener to No.11, always one to be omitted when the amateurs were free in the holidays and fancied a game.

In March 1916, when he had to return to the Western Front, Hardy caught the train to London. On his final journey, as a native of Dorset bound for Flanders and its mud, he might have remembered some of the 91 wickets he had taken with medium pace, or catching Victor Trumper at slip when Somerset played the Australians in 1902, or his innings of 91 against Kent. The inquest found that Hardy had been fortifying his nerves, like the shot of brandy doled out before you went over the top. Perhaps in his mind's eye, looking out of the train window, Hardy replayed a couple of his favourite cover drives or, to complete his hundred against Kent in August 1910, he hit a couple of fours to the Taunton boundary to reach 99 then took a quick single, before he walked down into the lavatories at King's Cross station and cut his throat.

**

Somerset have been joined with Northamptonshire for a simple reason: these two counties, along with Worcestershire, had the smallest populations until county boundaries were redefined in 1961. At least Somerset's population is spread over a wide area, with space to breathe and play, outside south Bristol at least. Before Covid the county had 250 cricket grounds; and part of the population has always been farming stock, bringing their physical and other attributes to the table.

For example, the most effective spinner England have had in an Ashes series in Australia in the last hundred years has not been Hedley Verity, nor Jim Laker, nor Graeme Swann – and you cannot count 1978/79, during World Series, when Australia's naifs gave themselves up artlessly to off spin. It is Jack White, or 'Farmer' as he was known. Tough, real tough. The stamina born of farm work from an early age, not sitting in front of a screen, enabled him to average 80 overs per Test in the heat of 1928/29 and gave his captain control over Australia (less than two runs an over). White took 25 wickets as England won 4-1.

Robertson-Glasgow tells us perfectly what Farmer was like and how he bowled: 'Jack White is the yeoman, four-square. His work on the field, either cricket or farm, is conducted with an unhurried certainty and an unsurprised understanding of natural obstacles. Whether it was cows or batsmen, he had the treatment for the trouble.'

'The secret of his bowling could be seen, if never quite understood, only from very close. For, besides the length and direction and the variety of flight, he made the ball "do a little" each way on the truest pitch without any advertisement from his fingers, and he made the ball bounce high.'

I did a bit of research on how Australia's batsmen tackled White and was surprised to learn that they focused on playing him to the off side, when one always thinks of Aussie batsmen favouring the leg side. White could thus pack his field on one side of the wicket. The exception was a young fellow who made his debut, then was dropped mid-series before returning to make his first Test hundred, called Don Bradman.

**

England, 20 years ago, went through a similar cycle. Under the captaincy of Nasser Hussain they stopped losing, then started winning under Michael Vaughan. Somerset stopped losing under Brian Close, then started winning trophies under Brian Rose – and boy, had they done some losing. They were bottom of the Championship every year from 1952 to 1955.

Desperate to avoid the stigma of appointing a professional as captain, the Somerset committee cast around for any amateurs: a solicitor in Bath who had gained his second XI colours at school but had not played since? Just the ticket. Gimblett, another of farming stock, scored the fastest hundred of the season when he made his first-class debut in 1935; and he had attended a fee-paying school, the same West Buckland boarding school that nurtured the Overton twins, Craig and Jamie, but he played for Somerset as a professional. Impossible! 'This lack of continuity (i.e., so many amateur captains) has naturally discouraged teamwork,' Bailey observed wryly.

It was only when the grandfather of the England fast bowler Chris Tremlett was appointed in 1956 that Somerset deigned to become competitive. Maurice Tremlett did such a good job that by 1958 the county came third, their highest yet. Somerset's connection with Australia had begun with Sammy Woods, and has continued with Colin McCool, Bill Alley, Greg Chappell, Kerry O'Keefe, Jamie Cox, Justin Langer and Matt Renshaw among others.

But it was an Antiguan, more than any Australian, who infused in Somerset the self-belief to become winners under Rose. Wherever Viv Richards went, he transformed his team into winners: no cricketer has had such a wide and beneficial impact. In a pub in Bath the Somerset committeeman Len Creed dined out for the rest of his life on how he had heard about this teenager in Antigua, brought him to the Lansdown club and unearthed cricket's Koh-i-Noor. In an entertaining new history of Lansdown, more stories are told about Richards: like how he used to visit a friend every day in the hospital next to the ground, and why.

Hence the five trophies around 1980. The bigger the occasion, like a Lord's final, the bigger the innings by Viv Richards. Failure was no option. Somerset's off-field organisation had vastly improved as well. The committee was kept in place by Roy Kerslake, the CEO – or secretary in those days – who had been a player himself.

Let us not omit the element of diversity either. That Somerset side had the broadest range of character that the county has ever known and, arguably, any cricket team had ever known to that stage. Brian Rose the trained teacher and captain who saw all and said little; 'Dasher' Denning and his scruffy blond hair, as West Country Wurzle as could be; the Oxbridge graduates, Peter Roebuck and Vic Marks; Colin Dredge, 'the Demon of Frome' as Alan Gibson dubbed him in *The Times* and 'the best third seamer in England' said Rose, loyally; Joel Garner from Barbados, the tallest and fastest bowler of yorkers; Hallam Moseley, another Barbadian via London, with his gleaming specs and sixes; not to forget Ian Botham.

I used to push the boat out during the Bath festival, by hiring a narrowboat on the Avon after close of play and can vouch that these characters lived life to the full. It made for delightful days, the cricket festival at the Recreation Ground, the only fly in the ointment being the pitches and a pavilion equipped with little more than wooden benches and splinters. In 1965 Somerset played three consecutive Championship games in Bath, and *Wisden* went so far as to say that the first match was staged 'on a travesty of a pitch': forthright words.

Batting did not get any easier either. Somerset won the first game in two days by an innings after scoring 190 and dismissing Worcestershire for 143 and 43; they won the second game in two days by seven wickets after dismissing Hampshire for 64 and 77; and they lost the third game by

200 runs after being bowled out for 133 and 62. No batsman in the course of those three matches scored more than 60. My judgement of the Rec is a little biased by the fond memory of playing one of my finest cover-drives there – alright, my only fine cover-drive – and I thought the square, though it looked rough, was acceptable for club games. But professional fast bowling which exploited the unevenness would have been too dangerous, and the Rec had to close to county cricket. Thus Somerset withdrew from the north of the county.

The golden years of the 1980s ended in tears. At issue was the question of Somerset's overseas player. As the rules were changing, Somerset could either keep both Richards and Garner as they aged or re-engage the young Martin Crowe; and the culture which they brought was relevant too. Crowe became a Knight of the Round Table during his season with Somerset in 1984, a latter-day Sir Lancelot, the personification of orthodox strokeplay, clean and wholesome, in pursuit of perfection and rapidly attaining it. He then injured his back while playing for New Zealand and had to give up pace bowling. By the winter of 1986/87 Crowe was offering magnificent runs in all formats but not the 50 first-class wickets he managed in 1984. Then he had covered for Richards and Garner, as one for the price of two; but not when his back went. It would have been wiser to have kept the West Indians, won the odd one-day trophy, and let them move on. Evolution not revolution.

Somerset subsequently looked to South Africa for their overseas players and even coaches. This was a cul de sac, except when Graeme Smith, briefly, seized them by the scruff and led them to their only T20 trophy in 2005. The work ethic has been as strong as any county's, the membership loyal, and Somerset have reached second place in the Championship, all too often. Something has been missing: that element, that piece of chemistry, to get them over the line.

It is not a question of captaincy. Abell, like Graeme Smith at the outset of his career with South Africa, has been installed as captain in effect for life, and rightly, with all the stability and continuity and long-term planning entailed. Abell went through a baptism in which he nearly drowned: when he scored one run in his first four Championship innings as captain, everyone was ready to say that he was not up to the mark. But he has emerged, scathed, tougher, and when the knights charge down Glastonbury Tor to fight for Avalon, Abell will be leading with his Excalibur.

But something else is missing. Could it be diversity? Before most cricketers travelled by car, a group of Somerset players would daily meet at Bristol Temple Meads and take the train to Taunton, such as Horace Hazell, who succeeded Jack White and preceded Jack Leach. Somerset seem to have given up on south Bristol. They used to play the odd Sunday game at both Brislington and Imperial, where Shane Warne played for an Epicurean summer, but all their games are at Taunton now that the Weston-super-Mare and Bath festivals have also gone. The epicentre has shifted south, and a Memorandum of Understanding has been signed with Devon, who are now supplying Somerset with plenty of fine young cricketers, including Tom Lammonby, who made a century almost as fine as Cook's in the Bob Willis Trophy final.

Like the England Test side, Somerset's batsmen all came from public schools once Marcus Trescothick had retired. It is fine if some players come from public schools – after all, some of those glorious days of the past were inspired by Palairet from Repton and Hewett from Harrow – but not if they all do, because then they tend to react to a crisis in the same way. Too much homogeneity is unhealthy, in cricket as in nature. We never want all our bowlers to bowl the same way, so why do we want batsmen who play the same way?

The Knights of the Round Table, according to some versions, never did find the Holy Grail. However, Exeter Chiefs, as another Wessex parallel, have become national winners in club rugby. In any event, it will be a constant source of interest to see whether Somerset ever do make it over the line, without the aid of Merlin to conjure up some magic.

Surrey

WHEN ROME won the Punic Wars, finally, a wise senator warned the people. Having Carthage as a rival had kept Rome honest. Henceforth a more insidious danger lay in holding the monopoly as the West's only super power.

Surrey have the Oval. Surrey therefore are the first-class county with the richest resources (MCC, not Middlesex, own Lord's). From the moment the Oval became the first modern venue for commercialised sport – by staging the first of all Tests in England in 1880, and the second in 1882, as well as FA Cup football – Surrey may not have maximised the Oval at certain times, but overall they have had the most cash to splash. A unique position, and a difficult one as the senator warned, if decadence is to be avoided and envy to be averted.

Blessed with the Oval's financial muscle and the revenue it generated, Surrey were effectively the first county to make major signings from other first-class counties. They were also the first to make signings from minor counties: of the first three batsmen to score one hundred first-class centuries, one was WG Grace and the other two were batsmen whom Surrey signed from Cambridgeshire, Tom Hayward and Sir Jack Hobbs.

When they brought in Kumar Sangakkara while still the world's best batsman, to show lads like Rory Burns and

Ollie Pope how to go about it, Surrey were following their own well-worn path.

Their director of cricket Alec Stewart appears to have eyes and ears around the cricket world. As soon as a top-class South African cricketer has retired, or before, he is on his way to the Oval. The rand is weak against the Kennington pound. Yet combing the world as well as Britain is nothing new for Surrey. Before the First World War, Surrey were signing an Australian who was tipped to be the next sensation, and briefly was, before he got into trouble with the police, harbinger of the Tom Maynard tragedy almost exactly a century later.

When the potential has been used wisely, Surrey have been the overwhelming power in the land, in roughly three separate periods. First was the 1890s, when they won the County Championship six times. Second was the 1950s, when they set the record for seven Championships in a row. Third was the period from 1999 to 2003, when they won three white-ball trophies in addition to three Championships. Twenty outright titles in all and one shared, second only to Yorkshire.

The Oval used to be the home of Cockney cricket. Surrey made their highest ever score of 811 in 1899, against Somerset at the Oval, when Bobby Abel made their highest ever individual innings of 357 (Kevin Pietersen fell two runs short). Abel was known as The Guv'nor. For the last 60 years the dominant figures have been the Stewarts, father and son. Micky was a member of their 1950s side and, as a short-leg fielder to Jim Laker and Tony Lock, set a world record – yet to be surpassed by an outfielder – for seven catches in one innings, before becoming the club's first professional captain and leading them to the Championship in 1971. Then he became the first paid manager of a county club (Cyril Washbrook had not been paid as Lancashire's manager in the 1960s), before becoming England's first permanent coach.

Now it is Alec Stewart who directs the county's cricket. Surrey have gone from The Guv'nor to The Gaffer, yet the cash remains. Those many evenings of sell-out T20 games – and all the hospitality profits – enabled Surrey to endure the Covid lockdown without putting their players on furlough, like Lancashire alone of other shires. The Cockney element though has disappeared, to be replaced by something more cosmopolitan. The majority of their pace bowlers in recent years have originated from either southern or South Africa.

Along the way, some of the game's greatest names have had Kennington's gasometers for their backdrop. Throw in Mark Ramprakash, who averaged 66 for Surrey, alongside Sir Jack Hobbs, Tom Hayward, Andy Sandham and John Edrich, and no county has produced so many batsmen who have made 100 first-class centuries. Jim Laker and Tony Lock at their peak were almost indisputably the most effective pair of spinners ever on English pitches. The first three pace bowlers in England widely labelled great were George Lohmann, Tom Richardson and Bill Lockwood, all of Surrey. With Douglas Jardine to captain them, or Peter May if a less confrontational leader is required, or a more imaginative one in Adam Hollioake, the Brown Caps All-time XI could take on any team in the universe – although it would help if the match was officiated by neutral umpires from Mars who could not understand the sledging for which Surrey have in the past been renowned.

***

What is the easiest way to win the FA Cup? Start the competition, make yourself captain of your team, and stage the final on your own ground.

Surrey have not only produced, or sometimes signed, some of England's best cricketers, they have had the best administrator too. Charles Alcock should be recognised as the most influential sports administrator of all time because he turned both cricket and football into mass entertainments, at the Oval.

After becoming Surrey's secretary, Alcock – like his successor Geoffrey Howard in the 1950s – arranged all the fixtures for all the counties and for teams touring England. Having drawn up the fixtures for the Australians' tour of England in 1880, Alcock had the bright idea of replacing their late-season game against Sussex at Hove with a match at the Oval between England and Australia, or a 'Test' match. WG Grace, modern sport's first star, did not have a ground worthy of his talents in his native Bristol, but the Oval could accommodate 10,000 spectators even at its most rudimentary; and when WG scored 152 in that inaugural Test in England (there had been three in Australia), and England won in spite of a dramatic collapse, the sport took off. Such was the public demand that the Australians kept coming back to England every couple of years, to the verge of overkill.

Alcock also played in the first FA Cup in 1871/72 in addition to organising the competition, which comprised 15 teams, including Queen's Park from Glasgow. He captained Wanderers, who defeated Royal Engineers in the final at the Oval. By 1889 the number of teams in the FA Cup had increased to three figures and the final between Preston North End and West Bromwich Albion was watched by 27,000 at the Oval, a capacity crowd, as there was for a day of Surrey's Championship match against Nottinghamshire.

Staging pop concerts or baseball at cricket grounds is nothing new. At the Oval Alcock staged cricket, football, rugby, athletics, cycling and lacrosse – anything to raise the money to improve the infrastructure and Surrey's cricket team. He knew his own worth, too. *Wisden* in 1873 records that '£250 [was] paid for the first time as Secretary's salary' i.e., Alcock's. The construction of a new committee room, by comparison, cost £100.

According to Stephen Chalke in *Summer's Crown*, Alcock agreed with the Duchy of Cornwall a new lease for the Oval in the 1890s and built the brick, two-turreted pavilion which survives as the ground's architectural focus. According to the same *Wisden* of 1873, when the Surrey president Lieutenant-Colonel F Marshall gave his speech at the annual dinner, he observed that on the basis of his military experience 'men who excelled in sports – especially cricketers – always proved to be the best soldiers'. Jack Hobbs, however, was later considered to be such a national treasure that he was sent, not to the trenches, but to a munitions factory in Bradford, to keep his hand in by playing in their wartime league.

As if Alcock did not do enough as the primary administrator of cricket and football, he launched and edited the *Football Annual* and *Cricket*, a fine magazine which he edited until he died in 1907. He had been Surrey's secretary for 35 years, and through his fund-raising had enabled the county to assemble a hard core of professionals that was matched by no county except Yorkshire, who only recruited players born within their own borders. Two of the pace bowlers Alcock signed from Nottinghamshire, John Sharpe and Bill Lockwood, went on to represent England as well as Surrey. Yes, it is an age-old path from the north of England to Kennington.

***

Only one drawback to being a pace bowler at the Oval: Surrey may give you a longer and more lucrative contract than any other county, but you have to bowl on what have usually been the best batting pitches in the country. All those batsmen who have scored 100 first-class hundreds! Surrey's money also bought the heaviest rollers from the 1890s onwards, and the carthorses to pull them. Len Hutton scored 364 on one of 'Bosser' Martin's creations. Manifestly, when Tony Lock and Jim Laker wanted result pitches, the Oval's strips were prepared, or unprepared, accordingly, and Surrey went through a whole season without a single draw during their seven-title sequence; but generally they have been the flattest.

Necessity being the mother of invention, the Oval can also be regarded as the English home of the slower ball. Jade Dernbach did so much to popularise his particular form of that delivery, releasing it out of the back of the hand, his wrist twisted 180 degrees so that the seam still went vertically down the pitch; and the Currans, Tom and Sam, became leading exponents too. When Liam Plunkett joined Surrey, he had a sympathetic environment in which to prepare for England's World Cup victory in 2019.

Not only the modern home, however. Ranjitsinhji, no less, thought Lockwood the most difficult bowler he ever faced because of his slower ball. 'It took the cricket world by storm when it made its first appearance,' wrote WA Bettesworth in 1898. 'The bowler has mastered an extremely difficult art of changing from very fast to slow without apparently altering his action in the slightest degree.'

CB Fry proclaimed: 'Lockwood was medium size (5ft 10in in fact), well-built, loose-shouldered, and he had a long bounding run and a lovely action, and both he and his partner Tom Richardson 'on the truest wicket could break the ball back from outside the off-stump to hit the leg.' I would love to be added to a Zoom call between Lockwood, Lohmann and the Currans. The ancients would surely have much to learn from the moderns, who have so much more time to practise and experiment (no indoor school that I know of existed before the First World War). But maybe there is a grip or a different kind of delivery which has become extinct?

The sheer numbers of Lohmann and Richardson are staggering. Lohmann still tops the all-time Test bowling averages with his 112 wickets at only 10.75 each, bowling all sorts of medium pace. From 1886 to 1892 inclusive he took more than 150 first-class wickets per season, and twice in that time he also toured Australia and bowled most of the winter too. Surrey, and Alcock, used their resources to send Lohmann to South Africa to rehabilitate when he got TB, but he was burned out and died aged 36.

Bowling pace, flat out, did not do much for Richardson's longevity either. In three consecutive seasons in the mid-1890s he delivered more than 1,300 overs and took, respectively, 290, 246 and 273 first-class wickets – with a tour of Australia on either side in which he did most of the bowling in the five Tests. It was easy to mop up tailenders in times past as they did not hang around or practise their batting. But who bowls more than 8,000 balls in a competitive summer nowadays? Richardson was dead at 41.

***

Some people dislike Surrey for their strutting or foul language in the past or their signings in the present. I admit to a soft spot for every county. I used to go to the Oval quite regularly around 1970. My stepmother was not wicked but she was unable to cope with marriage, at any rate to my father, and her flat in London was not my idea of home. She would stub her cigarettes out in a plate of food and hit the sherry bottle. While contemporaries headed to the Isle of Wight Festival or the south of France to indulge teenaged desires, I took the Northern line and sat on the empty terracing.

Robin Jackman, the Cockney Sparrow as Alan Gibson dubbed him, used to run in a long way, scattering the pecking pigeons; and the wily Intikhab Alam – he was always 'wily' or else 'burly' – would wheel away. The Oval was the ideal place after visiting the dentist. The cricket was as far as could be from village greens, flower baskets and cream teas. It was either the Oval or back to that flat and listen to Leonard Cohen.

The liveliest of all places to watch county cricket day-in day-out must have been the Oval before the First World War. The quality of air would not have been ideal amid the belching chimneys and fuming buses of Vauxhall, although the stage was never reached when play was suspended for air pollution, as it has been of late in Delhi. But there was not only great bowling to be seen; and Hobbs at his peak (he scored more centuries after the First World War, but only because the standard of bowling had plummeted); and Abel the Guv'nor; and Hayward (who never made a pair until his final game when he was run out and cried in the dressing room). The crowd itself was to be observed.

The biggest attendance for a county match – no precise number because members did not have to go through turnstiles – has probably been that for the Surrey v Yorkshire match in 1906: more than 80,000 attended the Oval over the three days, including 66,923 who paid for admission, plus members. Never has the County Championship bulked so big in the British consciousness as it did at the turn of the last century but one. 'Cricket has never been more popular than it is now, and for much of this popularity the skilled county teams in their keen competition for the championship are responsible,' declared *The Times* in 1896.

So large were the Oval's crowds that a poet made a living out of them. In the West Indies a generation ago a record would be quickly made to commemorate an event on the cricket field, but Albert Craig would compose a poem the same day and print it on a hand-press he carried with him, selling the sheet to spectators for two pence. To give Craig credit, he never called himself 'the Surrey poet' or even a poet at all, only 'a rhymester'. The following, to mark Hobbs's 162 against Worcestershire at the Oval in 1906, gives the flavour:

> *Joy reigns supreme amongst the Surrey throng,*
> *Patrons break out in one triumphant song;*
> *Young Hobbs we loved as hero of today,*
> *Gaily he steers along his conquering way.*

Instant verse, however clunky, must add to a sporting occasion, as much as a few tweets. I like the fact that Craig used to admit that anyone could write verse like his but that it took talent to make people cough up tuppence to buy it. The Prince of Wales sent a letter to Craig when he was gravely ill. Bobby Abel organised his funeral. It has always been rare for players to care much about their supporters – until they started ringing around county members at the start of Covid. So Craig must have struck a chord.

It was a man in the Oval crowd who was captured for posterity by Dudley Carew, who was rich enough to go round the country watching cricket in 1926 when the General Strike was on. He went to the Oval for a game and, so he wrote in his diary of that season *England Over*, met 'an elderly man who will talk to you for as long as you care to listen of Abel and Richardson, Lohmann and Lockwood. One notices the square-toed, unpolished boots, the rucked waistcoat with the spot or two of grease on it, the clean, ill-fitting collar, and one wonders, if one has an inquisitive mind, what manner of life this man has led... Who is his

God, and what in life or in death does he most fear? One wants desperately to pierce the reality behind the clothes and talk, and it is only after one has been listening to him for some time that one begins to realise that the reality may lie precisely in those words – "Abel," "boundary," "slow-bowler" – he is perpetually muttering … Looking at the particular old man to whom I spoke, the conviction grew on me that *this* was reality for him, this ground, this score-board and these slim, yellow stumps, and that he would carry out with him into the darkness, not the recollection of a woman's lips against his own or of the laboured, weakening breath of a child, but rather of Richardson walking back to begin his run or of Hobbs lifting his cap after completing his century.'

* * *

Surrey's playing staff was not all present and correct at the start of the 2020 season when Covid eventually allowed it to begin:

Hashim Amla – Stuck in South Africa, could not get visa or flights

Gus Atkinson – Still rehabbing (back)

Gareth Batty – Unavailable for red-ball games

Scott Borthwick – Available

Rory Burns – England bubble

Rikki Clarke – Available

Jordan Clark – Available (but suffered a side strain in the first BWT game and subsequent ankle injury, out until T20 finals day)

Sam Curran – England bubble

Tom Curran – England bubble

Jade Dernbach – Injured (groin, out for the season)

Matt Dunn – Available
Laurie Evans – Still with Sussex
Ben Foakes – England bubble
Will Jacks – Available
Nick Kimber – Injured (back and knee patella tendonitis, out for the season)
Conor McKerr – Injured (knee, required an operation, out for the season)
Daniel Moriarty – Available
Morne Morkel – Stuck in Sydney, couldn't get visa or flights. Once he arrived, required ankle operation after standing on a ball having played one game
Jamie Overton – Still with Somerset before moving to the Oval
Ryan Patel – Available (subsequently suffered knee injury which required an operation and put him out for the season)
Liam Plunkett – Injured (hamstring)
Ollie Pope – England bubble
Nico Reifer – Stuck in Barbados
Jason Roy – England bubble
Jamie Smith – Available
Mark Stoneman – Available
James Taylor – Available
Reece Topley – England bubble
Amar Virdi – Available

Surrey had seven players in one England bubble or the other while no other county laboured under such a handicap. It is therefore to some extent understandable, and justifiable, that Surrey should use their unique resources to sign more players from other counties and countries than anybody else.

But the other viewpoint should be considered. When Surrey visited Durham in 2016 and Alec Stewart took

Scott Borthwick and Mark Stoneman out to dinner and made them an offer they did not refuse, Durham supporters said goodbye in effect to the first division of the County Championship. They finished fourth in 2016, their 11th consecutive season in the first division. In 2017 they were demoted, as might have been predicted, having lost two proven batsmen at the top of their order, and being in no financial position to replace them. Some Durham supporters will not live to see their side return to the first division.

In the whole history of the County Championship nobody has had any reasonable objection when one county has come along and signed a player of another county who has not been able to find a regular place in his first team. When Surrey signed Jamie Overton, there was an argument that he wanted to take the new ball, and that would be the best thing for him and perhaps eventually England. But in the Bob Willis Trophy final the pitch at Lord's was less responsive to seam than the county pitches which Somerset had played their qualifying games on. Had Jamie Overton still been available, they might have looked at the immense obstacle that is Sir Alastair Cook and decided the extra pace of the two Overtons with the new ball was the likeliest way of dismissing him early, instead of Josh Davey's seam-up accuracy. Somerset supporters could feel aggrieved at Surrey for depriving them, not of their first Championship title but of the stepping-stone to it, the Bob Willis Trophy.

It was different when Surrey signed two of the first three batsmen to score 100 first-class hundreds. Cambridgeshire was one of cricket's earliest nurseries: the university and its colleges needed skilled cricketers to maintain grounds and coach and bowl at students. Tom Hayward's father Daniel was in charge of Parker's Piece, 'a huge responsibility given that more than forty cricket clubs played there during the summer' according to Leo McKinstry in his biography of

Hobbs, *England's Greatest Cricketer*. But Cambridgeshire did not have the ground and crowds to support a professional team, so Tom Hayward went to the Oval; and he arranged for Hobbs, the son of a college servant, to follow him (after Essex had rejected an approach by Hobbs, without giving him a trial).

Alan Marshal had all the physical advantages, as a pace-bowling all-rounder of 6ft 3in, to be a star in the Indian Premier League. Born in Queensland before they joined the Sheffield Shield, he qualified for Surrey by two years' residence. In his second season he was a *Wisden* Cricketer of the Year alongside Hobbs. The *Wisden* editor Sydney Pardon wrote: 'Some of Marshal's hits at the Oval were beyond the capacity of any other batsman now playing first-class cricket. He lacks Jessop's ability to score in all directions but with his immense advantages of height and reach he certainly can send the ball further. In every way he is a thorough cricketer.'

Instead of culminating on a podium in the IPL, Marshal's career nosedived in the streets of Chesterfield. Some horseplay during a Surrey away game got out of hand, and he gave a false name to the police. Surrey sent him back to Australia in 1910 for 'insubordination'. A portent of the tragedy a century later.

***

The Oval used to be almost as synonymous with sledging as with high scoring. An impartial testimony comes from 'Tiger' Smith, who was an umpire after keeping wicket for Warwickshire and England. His testimony does not tally with the notion that sledging is a modern phenomenon: 'Surrey weren't a pleasant side to umpire in those days [around 1930]. Fender [the captain Percy Fender] liked his own way, and the air was blue from the amateurs when things weren't going right ... they'd take the mickey out of the batsmen to upset them and I know Jack Hobbs was happy to be out of it eventually. It was a complete contrast to other games,' Smith recorded.

When Surrey were county champions for seven consecutive seasons in the 1950s, they were not renowned for taciturnity. While Jim Laker was quiet and old-fashioned as he went about his off spin, and Alec Bedser enjoyed the odd moan off the field, Tony Lock was heard to mutter at short leg – and he also had the habit of walking in a couple of paces, at short leg, as the ball was being bowled. Throw in the fact that Lock threw and playing against Surrey must have been quite annoying. According to Ted Dexter, it was on England's 1958/59 tour of New Zealand that Lock was shown some film footage of his action, which had been taken by the New Zealand player Geoff Rabone; and Lock was so appalled, and contrite, that he went back to the drawing board and *bowled* for the rest of his career. Into the 1960s the sledging was directed as much at junior Surrey players as at opponents.

***

That senator who warned about the dangers of holding a monopoly of power was proved correct both in Rome and at the Oval. Too much money spent in the wrong way led to a decadent culture. Tom Maynard's death on the railway tracks when escaping from police in 2012 at the age of 23 was as sad as any event in cricket's peacetime history, along with the death of Ben Hollioake in a car crash in Perth aged 24.

Maynard's death fired a shot across Surrey's bows. A new code of standards was put in place; youngsters were told what was expected of them, often in one-on-one conversations with older players; the club's history was introduced; and the behaviour of the current generation on and off the field appears exemplary. Initiatives like their ACE project to assist the Afro-Caribbean community are admirable too. An Oval Test used to be the home of the Afro-Caribbean community until the 1990s, when Surrey banned musical instruments. The ACE project is led by the remarkable Ebony Rainford-Brent, an all-rounder in more than one sense, and the first Afro-Caribbean to represent England Women.

Winning the County Championship of 2022 was proof of the new pudding: it was a classic example of teamwork. Of modern teamwork, that is, because spin had no more than a walk-on part, as at most counties, but still: it was anything but the work of a few individuals.

It is not quite a virtuous circle. But, particularly if Surrey can resist the temptation to pluck the ripest fruit from other counties, it is a pretty virtuous Oval.

Sussex

IF ANY single county lies at the heart of English cricket, and forms its spiritual centre, it is Sussex.

Sussex may or may not have been cricket's cradle: the Dukes of Richmond were pioneers at Goodwood by employing the first semi-professional cricketers, and we know that the Sussex village of Slindon had the strongest team in England in the early 1740s; but Kent, and East London, were cradles too. What makes Sussex unique is that, if we close our eyes and think of a cricket match, especially a village cricket match, the setting is likely to be the South Downs or Weald.

Fine writers and poets established this image by having their hearts and homes in Sussex. During and after the Great War they nourished the longing for quintessentially English life back home. Those were the days when soldiers – officers and men – kept a small volume of poetry in their pocket for solace.

The Cricket Match by Hugh de Selincourt begins on Saturday, 4 August 1921 in Sussex: 'The Recreation Ground at Tiddingfold stood on the road to Raveley. From the Pavilion you could look up the slope to the centre of the village on to the background of Downs which spread away to the right in a beautiful, sloping line.' In 1978 John Parker published an updated version, *The Village Cricket Match*: he lived in Sussex, and his son Paul represented that county and England once.

But if five lines can sum up the place of cricket in English life, they are those composed by Edmund Blunden, who won the Military Cross in the First World War and had his lungs damaged by gas while serving in the Royal Sussex Regiment. In the late 1920s Blunden became the professor of English at Tokyo university, where he had 'home thoughts from abroad'. A Japanese colleague told Blunden there was one thing in England he could not understand: cricket, of course. So in the five lines of this sonnet Blunden sums up the game and its place in English life:

> *Far out in the valley the sun was gilding green*
> *Those meadows which in England most are seen,*
> *Where churchyard, church, inn, forge and loft stand round*
> *With cottages, and through the ages bound*
> *The duckpond, and the stocks, and cricket-ground.*

Blunden is not being over-sentimental here in recalling the England of his youth, because he refers to the stocks, which would not have long been out of use when he was born in 1896. Before the Great War he had lived in Sussex and attended Christ's Hospital school near Horsham, as the Sussex and England fast bowler John Snow was to do.

Down at a slightly lower literary level we find Jennings and Darbishire. 'Oh, spiffing wheeze, sir!' they would exclaim when their benign housemaster, Mr Carter, suggests going to watch Sussex. Their prep school Linbury Court is all about Matron being jolly kind, and the teas being jolly spiffing, and lots of cricket house matches in the summer term. Nothing to spoil this idyll except Old Wilko losing his temper, but only temporarily, because underneath he has a heart of gold.

'At the far end of the school grounds, where the playing fields (yes, plural!) give place to farmland, a narrow pathway leads across the meadow and winds its way up the landward slope of the South Downs. The track skirts the village of Linbury, and comes out on the Dunhambury road not far from the old Roman camp site,' so Anthony Buckeridge wrote in *Jennings' Diary*. In another novel, Jennings and Darbishire escape to watch Sussex play (a Championship match of course) at Dunhambury and are given a lift to the ground by the county's famous amateur batsman RJ Findlater, who finds a couple of seats for them in the pavilion! In return, the boys spot a thief in the dressing room … All wildly implausible now: Findlater would have driven to the ground much earlier to do his warm-ups and nets hours before the start, but less so then. And they all lived happily ever after.

Spanning verse and prose came Alan Ross. Born in India, he went to two schools in Sussex while his parents continued to live in Calcutta, and cricket was obviously his emotional surrogate: 'I was lucky that my arrival at St Andrews, East Grinstead, coincided with a revival of fortune for Sussex cricket,' Ross wrote in his autobiography *Blindfold Games*. 'After the pre-Great War golden age of Ranjitsinhji and Fry, 'old' George Cox and Fred Tate, the Relfs and Joe Vine, Sussex went into comparative decline during the twenties. I came to St Andrews in the summer of 1932 and that year, under Duleepsinhji, Sussex were runners-up in the Championship, as they were to be again in the next two years.'

'Under Duleepsinhji': a pithy phrase, and noteworthy in this context. Ross identifies with Duleep, and not only because they were both born in India. 'Duleep's physical frailty – even before tuberculosis destroyed him he had suffered continuously with chest trouble, as had Ranji too – especially endeared him to me, since I was extremely small for my age and thin.' The fact that Duleepsinhji was the first non-white to captain a county cricket team passes unremarked. Being the nephew of Ranjitsinhji gave Duleepsinhji enormous kudos, yet it had not been enough for him to be appointed the captain of school teams in England.

'When the term ended it looked as if Sussex might even win the Championship for the first time in their history. I spent every moment I could during the holidays watching them play at Hove or Eastbourne, but sadly Duleep's health broke down at a crucial moment in August and without their best batsman Sussex could not quite manage it. Duleep, all charm and elegance at the wicket, never played first-class cricket again.' But he still averages 58 from his 12 Tests for England.

Ross set some of his many poems in Brighton and the county ground at Hove: 'Regency Squares, the Pavilion, oysters and mussels and gin' is a neat summary in 'Cricket at Brighton'. My favourite is the one he wrote about Sussex's Jim Parks batting in an away match against Kent at Tunbridge Wells. The Parks family has given birth to so many cricketers it should be explained this is Jim Parks junior: the one who set the modern trend for wicketkeeper-batsmen by converting to wicketkeeping after his schooldays and averaging 32 in his 46 Tests for England. This poem begins:

> *Parks takes ten off two successive balls from Wright,*
> *A cut to the rhododendrons and a hook for six.*
> *And memory begins suddenly to play its tricks:*
> *I see his father batting, as, if here, he might.*

For Jim Parks senior, his father, had also played for Sussex and, once, for England; and he will always remain the only cricketer to score 3,000 runs and take 100 wickets in a first-class season.

My favourite cricket poem though – if we can allow that Francis Thompson was writing primarily about his own declining life in 'At Lord's', though the refrain is 'O my Hornby and my Barlow long ago' – has to be that Blunden sonnet in which he explains to his Japanese colleague the attraction of cricket. It ends:

> *And I fell silent, while kind memories played*
> *Bat and ball in the sunny past, not much dismayed*
> *Why these things were, and why I liked them so.*
> *O my Relf and Jessop and Hutchings long ago.*

***

Sussex, more than any other, is the county of families: of fathers and sons, of brothers, of uncles and nephews like Kumar Shri Ranjitisinhji and Duleepsinhji.

Why should this be? Does the answer lie in Sussex's soil, or water? I confess I have not been through the records of every first-class county to see which has the highest proportion of close blood relations. So may it suffice that Sussex are renowned as the county with the most family connections? Gloucestershire began with the Grace brothers, and have recently had four pairs of brothers on their staff, but not so many as Sussex in between times.

Alan Ross sketched some of them, like the Langridge brothers, John – who holds most of Sussex's batting records – and James. 'John Langridge, tall and loose-limbed, was never the prettiest of players, very square-on to the bowler and often boring. But just when he had sent even the most loyal Sussex supporter to sleep he would start to cut and pull and generally make hay ... He went through an obsessive ritual at the wicket, touching almost every part of his anatomy from his cap to his box while awaiting the ball.' A successor to Phil Mead, a forerunner of Steve Smith and Rory Burns.

'James Langridge, elder brother to John, was a left-handed all-rounder of almost sleepy gracefulness. Nothing he ever did appeared hurried. He was a batsman and spin bowler of classic correctness, possessed of an effortless cover-drive and, as a bowler, of spin and flight.' His son Richard – John's nephew – in turn became a left-handed batsman for Sussex.

Other brothers include the Gilligans, the Greigs, the Newells, the Parkses, the Oakeses, the Relfs (it was presumably Albert referenced in Blunden's last line), and the Wells brothers ... but the Cornfords, Jim and 'Tich', though contemporaries, were not related. Jim Parks senior, brother of Harry, and the man who scored 3,000 runs and took 100 wickets, was according to Ross, 'a neat, bird-like man, his head sunk into his shoulders so that he appeared to have no neck ... and he had the red face and voice of the typical countryman. Batting, he stood still as a scarecrow until the last second, whereupon he would hook or cut abruptly, as if a secret mechanism had been set off ... Bowling, he was a slow-medium off-drifter, who cut the ball both ways and was hard to get away.'

Father-and-son combinations include the Beans, Busses, Coxes, Griffiths, Lenhams, Parkses again, Tates, and Wellses again (Luke the son of Alan). It sounds like a list of British cooking or eating apples; and many professionals among them would have been apple-cheeked and burnished by wind off the sea.

But Ross does not explain why so many blood relations have played for Sussex: nor does any other authority I have consulted. Worldwide there is a pattern: New Zealand and Zimbabwe are the two countries that have had the highest proportion of brothers and fathers and sons in their Test teams: countries with relatively small cricket-playing populations, and largely rural. Growing up with a relative to play with or against, in a family which has the equipment and plenty of space in which to practise, becomes a huge advantage.

Fred Tate, after being the last man out when England needed four runs to win the Old Trafford Test of 1902, is supposed to have brought up his son Maurice with a view to salvaging his family's reputation. Which Tate junior did, as the finest medium-pacer of his day: his record of 38 wickets in the 1924/25 series in Australia, for a losing side too, has never been bettered by an England bowler there.

In a book which celebrates Sussex's first Championship in 2003 – *The Longest Journey*, which it was, given that the club was officially founded in 1839 – the authors Bruce Talbot and Paul Weaver interviewed Charlie Oakes, aged 92, in his nursing home. Blind, forgetful, he nevertheless remembered being brought up in a cottage next to the ground in Horsham. His father was the groundsman and a hard taskmaster if his sons, Charlie and Jack, failed at cricket. 'We had a pretty tough upbringing. My father wasn't very pleased if I didn't do well.' This accounts for at least one pair of Sussex brothers.

There was little more than the average national wage to be earned by playing as a professional for Sussex. Neighbours like Surrey and Kent had larger grounds than Hove, with its capacity nowhere near 10,000, to generate revenue. Some of the causes of the high proportion of relatives in the New Zealand and Zimbabwe teams might apply to Sussex too.

* * *

Another reason why Sussex tugs at the heartstrings of the romantic imagination: out-grounds. Apart from Hove (and Dunhambury), Sussex have played Championship matches at Arundel, Chichester, Eastbourne, Hastings, Horsham and Worthing, in addition to a couple more grounds where first-class cricket (e.g., against Oxford or Cambridge University) has been staged.

When Dudley Carew, during the Second World War, wrote his book about county cricket *To The Wicket*, his opening chapter was on Sussex 'because the downs are in Sussex, because Sussex is the friendliest of all counties' and because Horsham is 'one of the loveliest cricket grounds of all'. Carew was writing in the age of steam. The Horsham ground 'is approached through a churchyard and over a bridge spanning a brook. Round one side of it runs a railway and every now and again a train, which is doubtless prosaic and much like any other train, but somehow contrives to seem oddly primitive and unreal, puffs round and causes the bowler to pause in his run.'

The last time I went to Horsham, rain stopped most of the day's play, and not much romance was to be detected in a diesel rattling past on its way to Clapham Junction, but the setting was still lovely.

The Saffrons at Eastbourne too had its merits: its marquees, and other sports adjoining the cricket arena, and civic dignitaries indulging in cream teas. Chris Arnot's book *Britain's Lost Cricket Festivals* has an amusing photograph of tables set for tea behind several rows of deckchairs. Spectators have their backs to the cricket, not surprisingly, and are looking straight ahead at the white tablecloths and silver cake-stands, still gleaming the best part of a century later. Only a few cakes and buns remain undevoured.

A frequent drawback to the Saffrons was that the pitches were too good – not that Sussex's batsmen would believe it after they recently returned for the odd one-day game – whereas those at Worthing were too bad. Declaration targets are seldom knocked off by ten wickets but it happened at Eastbourne in 1947, when Sussex set Lancashire a declaration target of 233. Mind you, Lancashire were extra-motivated at

Eastbourne: the town mayor had slagged them off in 1931, announcing that it was 'unfortunate' that Lancashire were always the visitors for the festival: 'We are rather tired of them.'

Hastings, on the other hand, came nicely in between Eastbourne's belters and Worthing's minefields, or so Derek Underwood would say. Hastings being so close to Kent, they were the usual visitors for the festival, and Underwood not only took 9-28 there with his left arm but also scored his one first-class century, aged 39.

Hastings was the setting of a terrible accident when the groundsman Len Creese, who had played for Hampshire, saw his young grandson crushed under the heavy roller. Otherwise, memories of the Central Ground have been fond, not least because it was so central, in the heart of town. I never went there before it closed to first-class cricket in 1989, but the county ground at Hove has a similar flavour of tall Victorian terraced houses, their balconies overlooking the field of play ('No vacancy').

Where better to end a county season, after two three-day matches a week for four months, than at the Hastings Festival, when the intensity of the bowling can be guaranteed to dwindle? Gilbert Jessop hit 191 there for the Gentlemen of the South against the Players of the South in 90 minutes, and in those days before 1910 the ball had to be hit out of the ground to count as six. So he did.

For any cricket correspondent, could work have ever been less like work than at a Hastings Festival, when savouring autumn sunshine in a deckchair below the ruined castle? Well, it must have been pretty hectic in 1947 when Denis Compton, representing South of England against the South Africans, broke Jack Hobbs's record of 16 first-class centuries in a season. *Wisden* still captures the occasion: 'When he [Compton] reached three figures the game was held up for five minutes while crowd and players showed their appreciation. His county colleagues Robins and Edrich went on to the field to join in congratulations. Compton dashed down the pitch to the first ball after the resumption and was stumped.' Edrich, conceivably, had slipped his old mate a swig from a hip flask.

Hastings Priory CC chose to accept the offer of a new ground on top of the hill, with some financial inducement, so during the 1990s the Central Ground was turned into a shopping mall. The last words should go to Gerald Brodribb, another in the tradition of writers who attended or taught at Sussex schools: 'The sea is near: the Channel winds blow up from the west and bring the screaming gulls: they swoop on the outfield until the ball hurries them away. There is shelter in this enclosed arena with its terraced walls of houses, and the slanting sunlight shines on distant windows. High above, the ruined castle looks down on this intimate oasis of peace amid the busy town.'

***

Arundel, however, in one of cricket's viler phrases, has 'come to the party' to replace the Worthings and Hastings and Chichesters. The Castle ground at Arundel has become as delightful as any out-ground in county cricket. Idle to compare it with Cheltenham and Scarborough, far more bustling venues in substantial towns. Arundel is as rural as any county cricket ground or out-ground could be.

Before 1990 Arundel had been used for nothing more than one-day warm-ups between the Duke of Norfolk's XI and a touring team: motor down from London for the day and a relaxed tour opener, before moving on to more serious stuff like MCC at Lord's. In 1990 Sussex played a Championship match there for the first time: 'a financial success for Sussex, with more than 3,500 spectators present on the first day' according to *Wisden*.

The Castle ground has two natural advantages, although pedestrians hastening from the station for start of play might not see one of them in that light. It is set on top of a hill, just above the castle. Go through the trees of what is effectively parkland to look down on the river Arun, and one of England's oldest towns, and fertile countryside beyond.

The second natural advantage is the amphitheatre. The Castle end of the ground is flat and open but as you walk to the other end you climb up a grass bank where spectators unfold their deckchairs – up to 3,000 can be accommodated – and look down on the cricketers. What is more, they can hear the players distinctly, such are the acoustics. The sound of bat on ball is different here: a deeper sound, more of a thud. Certain psychologists might say that all cricket grounds, and their pavilions in particular, or their press boxes, hold some primitive appeal to the male psyche, as surrogate wombs: if so, Arundel and its amphitheatre more than most.

Its capacity has been extended to 8,500 but that can stretch the logistics. Over 7,000 were watching Sussex's T20 match against Surrey in 2015 when Rory Burns and Moises Henriques collided horrifically in the field. Ambulances had to treat broken bones on the field before the match was abandoned. A four-day Championship game is a more natural fit, or a 50-over county match.

Sussex give Arundel a staging fee then take what profit they can. There is space for 10,000 cars – £5 for Friends of Arundel Castle CC, £10 for members – so that is a decent earner for a start, then comes the hire of deckchairs. But the costs are considerable, like £1,000 for one marquee for a week. Plenty of permanent toilets around the ground but they have to be maintained. Two full-time groundsmen work at Arundel but Sussex have to send two more from Hove to prepare the pitches. It is not surprising that half the first-class counties think a match on an out-ground is too much hassle.

The presence of so many volunteers, and no doubt the beauty of the setting, have led to annual visits by Sussex ever since 1990. Except in the Covid summer of 2020. Yet the game still went on, because Hampshire made Arundel their base, while England took over their Ageas Bowl at Southampton, and Sussex adhered to Hove.

'Giles White [Hampshire's director of cricket] contacted me in May and said there are murmurings the county programme will start up in late July or August but the Ageas will be needed by England,' remembered James Rufey, the chief operating officer of Arundel Castle CC. 'Of course we said yes and Hampshire started practising here three days a week, using our indoor school which has two wide lanes.

'But a lot of work had to be done, like Covid risk assessments. We had to install six sanitisation points around the ground, and employ an on-site cleaner from 8am to 6pm to go round the ground cleaning handles, etc., and the original marquee could only fit in 14 people for social distancing reasons so that had to be extended. We had to install a one-way system and two live-streaming cameras above each sightscreen.' Hampshire's Bob Willis Trophy games against Surrey and Essex went ahead smoothly, in spite of the hosts not being Sussex, although rain soaking the lower end of the ground made the Essex game a draw.

'I suppose the ethos is to cover all forms of the game in the best possible way.' Thus Rufey summarises the purpose of Arundel. You might expect the Castle ground to stage *The Cricketer* Cup final, and Lords v Commons; but the England Disability XI and Afghan Refugee Cricket Project XI play there too.

***

After rain had washed out the last day of Hampshire v Essex, with Sir Alastair Cook left on 129 not out, I drove the ten miles from Arundel to Slindon. Just as Cook was the finest left-handed batsman in England, so had Richard Newland been: in fact he was the first to be accorded that title. Newland lived in Slindon, and played most of his cricket at Goodwood, remunerated for doing so by the Duke of Richmond.

In the second-oldest surviving scorecard, dating from 1744, when totals were very low, Richard Newland was the only batsman in the Rest of England team to reach double figures in both innings against Kent, as did one of Kent's batsmen. Newland was captain too and known as 'The Champion'. In later life he became a surgeon in Chichester. Batting must have equipped him with manual dexterity.

Newland's reputation is alive in Slindon. I only had to mention his name in the cafe to be given directions to the church where there is a tablet to his memory, only the church was closed. Cricket found a way to keep going during Covid, but just when churches would have been most needed – so one would have thought – they were closed. Find a way: this is what great batsmen do.

**

One last reason why Sussex attracts: they have had so many dashing cricketers worthy of hero-worship.

Their all-time XI might not beat the hard men of Surrey or Yorkshire more than three or four times out of ten, but they would be worth watching on and off the field, especially in Brighton at the height of the season.

1. Charles Burgess Fry. Oxford rugby Blue who represented England at football and cricket. Holder of the world long jump record. A bit of an oddball but he averaged 56 for Sussex.

2. David Sheppard. Became captain of England and Bishop of Liverpool in that order. Led Sussex to second place in 1952 without a fast bowler.
3. Ted Dexter. Would fly to some games in his private plane, then bat like Wally Hammond, or bowl fast, whatever his mood suggested.
4. KS Ranjitsinhji. Revolutionised batting in England by opening up the leg side and playing square of the wicket both sides instead of just driving. First to score a Test century in a session. Averaged 63 for Sussex.
5. KS Duleepsinhji. Similar silky skills to his uncle's. His 333 was the highest individual innings for Sussex until overtaken by Murray Goodwin.
6. Tony Greig. The South African all-rounder who became a zestful big-game player for England.
7. Jim Parks. Batted and bowled leg breaks until he took up wicketkeeping and played for England. Over 36,000 first-class runs: not bad for a keeper and No.7.
8. Imran Khan. Moved from Worcestershire to Sussex for the social life and did not let anyone down. Supreme all-rounder when he wanted to be. Led Pakistan on and off the field.
9. Maurice Tate. Not only a medium-pacer of immense stamina who pitched the ball up, but a strokemaker who came close to a run a ball for England, and averaged more with the bat than ball in Tests.
10. Mushtaq Ahmed. Far and away Sussex's most effective spinner, who won the Championship for them in 2003, 2006 and 2007 – the only occasions they have won it.
11. John Snow. Garth le Roux could be fearsome, but it has to be John Snow, at least until Jofra Archer bowls for Sussex as he did against Australia in 2019.

Who would captain this XI? Fry and Dexter would think they should, Imran would assume he would, but the best candidate might be Sheppard. As a nice touch, he sent a letter to each of his players at the end of the season he captained Sussex; and, as a champion of inter-faith dialogue, his knowledge would not go amiss in this dressing room.

***

Sussex's image has been tarnished a little of late, jeopardising their reputation for healthy and vigorous cricket beside the sea. A crisis was unavoidable: £300,000 had to be cut during the Covid lockdown from their annual budget. But the response, under the aegis of CEO Rob Andrew, cannot have been right.

In addition to the bathwater, the baby, in the form of all their senior players, was thrown out. In August 2021 Sussex fielded the youngest ever side in the history of the Championship: six teenagers, no capped player, and an average age of 19. The county had recently been successful in white-ball formats; soon it was no longer in any.

Some of the teenagers looked to be precociously talented, but they were often left to learn on the job in four-day cricket, when all precedence proves that young batsmen need one old hand to bat around and learn from; and the same with Sussex's bowlers. No point in giving a car to lads without a licence. Experience in general is worth having, but not the experience of losing.

Warwickshire

TOO MANY county cricket grounds lock down for the winter. A groundsman will tend the hallowed square and keep the outfield's stripes neat; a few players, unrequired overseas, will have an indoor net. Overall, the ground sleeps for half the year like a hibernating bear.

Not Edgbaston though. It is growing into a cricket ground like no other in Britain. The Birmingham bear no longer hibernates. Edgbaston will soon be a model for all Test grounds around the world, inhabited and alive 24/7, not deserted, and waiting for its dining room to be booked for a conference or wedding reception.

How much we waste our cricket grounds has struck me ever since I first visited the Bangabandhu. Now this is not one of Signor Berlusconi's nightclubs in downtown Milan. It was Bangladesh's first Test venue, in the centre of Dhaka, where England played their inaugural Test against Bangladesh in 2003/04. Such was Bangladesh's standard in those days – they had been granted Test status with suspicious haste – that what happened underneath the stadium was more interesting than events inside.

Being in Dhaka, where dry land is not cheap, every inch of the Bangabandu stadium was put to use. Under the stand of a cricket ground elsewhere in the world you might find lavatories, or somewhere for the groundsmen to keep mowers, or bars and stalls for vendors on a matchday, or, most often, vacant space. Not in Bangladesh. Every spare space at ground level under the Bangabandu stands was occupied by shops doing business, like selling sports equipment, or white goods, or suitcases and luggage – things that can be stored in spaces where the stand slopes down to ground level.

Cricket grounds, especially in urban areas, should attract people to keep entering them, whatever the season. If for no other reason, the rents from these businesses underneath the stadium could and should bring down the cost of tickets inside. Every Test venue in England charges prices which keep cricket the preserve of the affluent.

Visiting Edgbaston is already becoming a unique experience. Warwickshire CCC, back in 1884, leased 21 acres on which to base their club. It was 'a meadow of rough grazing land' beside the River Rea ('at a fair and reasonable rental, without harrowing conditions'). During the Covid lockdown, when no cricket was being played anywhere in Britain, Edgbaston's car park was turned into an NHS testing centre. The meadow had gone, but this salubrious suburb of Birmingham was as leafy as ever, and the only harrowing thing was the reason for a visit.

***

Edgbaston's development into a year-round stadium is being done in four phases. First was construction of the new pavilion. The old one offered a lovely view behind the arm, but the facilities for television cameras were little better than for Edgbaston's inaugural Test in 1902. After the 2009 Ashes Test, the old pavilion was knocked down and replaced by the huge new stand at a cost of £32m.

The second, current, phase consists of building 375 new apartments on that area of the car park which the NHS used – on the left if you drive in the main entrance. Not only apartments but a veritable plaza of shops, bars, cafes and restaurants on the ground floor so that people will go to Edgbaston cricket ground all year round – and some will live there. Warwickshire sold this land to help pay for the new pavilion, but they retain the option of sharing in the running of these shops and therefore in future profits.

Phase three will consist of a hotel where the Raglan stand is – if you are batting at the pavilion end, this is the area where you slog-sweep the spinners. Old Trafford and Southampton's Ageas Bowl were the two Test venues to have a hotel as part of their ground, and consequently staged every England fixture in 2020, but having a hotel also fits into a 'post-Covid' world, whether it is cricketers or members of the public who are checking in. Again, a hotel keeps a ground alive all year round, especially if it is less basic than Old Trafford's, a little warmer than Southampton's.

Originally this Edgbaston hotel was earmarked to open for the Ashes Test of 2023, but the pandemic prevented this timescale. Before then came the Commonwealth Games which Birmingham staged in 2022 with a women's competition, staged at Edgbaston, part of the Games for the first time.

The fourth and final phase will be rebuilding the Wyatt stand at the City end. Already the Professional Cricketers' Association have an office there, and presumably will do so in future. Should the offices of the England and Wales Cricket Board be based there too?

The ECB, if relocated to Edgbaston, would inevitably have a different perspective. Being in the geographical centre of England, it would have a more objective relationship with MCC who built their offices at Lord's. The relationship between the two has oscillated over the years. At first the two organisations used to overlap too much in personnel. Then MCC prided itself on being Land and Old Money, looking down on the ECB as new money and trade. Subsequently, again, the relationship may have become too cosy and close.

In any event, when there is a major issue like whether Lord's should be allocated two Tests per year, as at present, or only one, it would be discussed more objectively if the ECB and MCC were not living in each other's pockets in St John's Wood.

Where do Warwickshire get this money from? Birmingham City Council advanced a loan of £20m for the new pavilion, while Warwickshire in return renamed their T20 side the Birmingham Bears. An Ashes Test generates £7 million in ticket sales alone; a less attractive Test about one-third as much. Edgbaston has cornered T20 finals day, making use of its geographical centrality, and that is another £1.3m in ticket sales minus a 30% staging fee.

**

When you own the only cricket bat and ball, you tend to take first innings. If you happen to own the cricket ground as well, it is likely you are going to be the captain too.

The Edgbaston ground was leased to Warwickshire CCC by the Calthorpe family. A son of the eighth Baron Calthorpe, the Honourable Frederick Somerset Gough Calthorpe became Warwickshire's captain from 1920 to 1929. He was appointed captain of England too, on their inaugural Test tour of the West Indies in 1929/30: such a tour was a bit of a jolly in those days, languid and tropical, before lethal bowlers were unleashed. Only one man has served longer as Warwickshire's captain, Mike Smith or 'MJK' as he is usually known.

Freddie's players loved him, so we are told, and we have no reason to disbelieve it. He was so easy-going; it is said that in his four years up at Cambridge he never met his tutor.

On the field he would do whatever Warwickshire's senior professionals, or their committee, told him.

Calthorpe was therefore captain when the most amazing game of cricket – in the sense of the biggest turnaround – ever took place. Being a good swing bowler, Freddie personally took a hand in dismissing Hampshire for 15 in the 1922 Championship match at Edgbaston, by taking four wickets for four runs. Yet Warwickshire still lost the game so comfortably that you suspect match-fixing was involved; which, in a way, it was.

Edgbaston has often served up some of England's pacier pitches, as Warwickshire have been able to afford top groundsmen. On this occasion Hampshire's swashbuckling captain Hon. Lionel Tennyson sent Warwickshire in after winning the toss and dismissed them for 223, before Hampshire were dismissed for 11 runs plus four byes. The sight of their opening batsman having one of his stumps broken by Warwickshire's fast bowler Harry Howell did not encourage many of the Hampshire batsmen to hang around.

Calthorpe naturally invited Hampshire to follow on, and the game followed a predictable course as Hampshire in their second innings reached 98/3 by the end of day one, and 177/6 next morning, still 31 behind.

What happened next is a matter of dispute – not so much the content of the message sent out to Calthorpe but the identity of the sender. In *Summer's Crown* Stephen Chalke wrote that the sender was 'the Warwickshire secretary, wanting the game to last a little longer [and] asking his captain not to take the new ball'.

This Warwickshire secretary was Rowland Ryder, who had been in office since the club entered the County Championship in 1895. He did everything at Edgbaston for half a century – everything, that is, except delegate. When England played their first Test at Edgbaston in 1902,

Ryder organised it all without a telephone, a typewriter or an assistant, except for the head groundsman who helped Ryder count the gate takings long into the night.

Another version of this 1922 match has it that the Warwickshire committee had a meeting later on that second day and wanted to watch some cricket before then, and it was *their* collective message which was sent out to Calthorpe, to ease the pressure on Hampshire. So Freddie duly did. He gave 49 overs to Warwickshire's 50-year-old batsman Billy Quaife, who tossed up leg breaks. Hampshire's No.10 was Tennyson's valet, Walter Livsey: normally paid to serve his master, Livsey seized this opportunity to help himself to a maiden century. Hampshire followed their 15 by scoring 521. Warwickshire, set 314 to win, lost by 155 runs. Not only match-fixing of a kind was involved but gambling too: Tennyson had a large bet with Calthorpe on the first evening that Hampshire would go on to win. But was ever a losing captain more exonerated than Freddie?

If Ryder appears to have been a bit of a control freak, he did have an eye for a cricketer. During a walking holiday in the North Riding he saw a pace bowler, who had been born in Dewsbury and was playing for Hawes, and who possessed a fine action. England's Test bowling was horribly weak after the First World War partly because this bowler was killed in action after signing for Warwickshire and taking 199 first-class wickets at only 20.09 each: Percy Jeeves. He was only 28. Ryder's son, also Rowland, later wrote to PG Wodehouse and established that the cricketer Jeeves was the man after whom he had named Bertie Wooster's butler. It would have also been worth asking Wodehouse if he had based Wooster on Freddie.

However, Ryder, the Warwickshire secretary, did miss out on the two finest English bowlers ever, so it could be reasonably argued. His father had opened the bowling for the Wednesbury club with a chap called Syd Barnes, who played four games for Warwickshire before he went off firstly to Lancashire then to plough his own furrow, by playing for England but not for a first-class county. And in 1897 Ryder refused to offer a trial to a Yorkshire applicant called W. Rhodes: he went on to become the only bowler to take 4,000 first-class wickets.

***

As a Midlands centre of excellence, Warwickshire have always gone about their cricket in their own way, because they could afford to do so. When they were promoted to first-class status in 1895, they did not bring in a coach from Lord's but the best professional batsman in England, Arthur Shrewsbury of Nottinghamshire, to organise their pre-season practice.

Warwickshire have subsequently produced some of the most respected coaches: like 'Tiger' Smith, who kept wicket for England as well as the county, and coached Warwickshire till he was 77; Derief Taylor, who in the 1950s became the first non-white coach in county cricket (and, such has been the lack of diversity, still one of a small handful); Neal Abberley, who coached Ian Bell, the modern embodiment of orthodoxy; and Bob Woolmer, the coach who tore up the MCC coaching book and, with his own eyes, analysed.

Strange that two of this quartet died in Jamaica: Woolmer from what was probably a heart attack during the 2007 World Cup, rather than a conspiracy poisoning; and Taylor, who came from Jamaica and served in the Eighth Army in Africa. There he had met Tom Dollery, who was to become Warwickshire's first professional captain, and therefore the first professional to lead his county to the Championship title, in 1951. Warwickshire's coaching successes continued when Jeetan Patel, the former

Warwickshire captain and off-spinner, was appointed England's spin-bowling coach.

Dollery wrote, or 'wrote', a book the following winter about Warwickshire's first title since 1911, their second ever, and he assembled the data to explain how Warwickshire triumphed: a rare example of detailed county analysis in pre-laptop times. Warwickshire won, their captain explained, because they took a wicket every 9.58 overs: not quite the most penetrative of the 17 county attacks – that was Yorkshire, with their sporting out-grounds, who took a wicket every 8.31 overs – but fourth best; and only Yorkshire and Lancashire took their wickets at a cheaper average than Dollery's bowlers at 20.43 runs per wicket.

Warwickshire scored at 2.74 runs per over but Dollery, while admitting that quick runs were necessary in three-day cricket, considered that batting was less important than bowling. (Surrey, on the brink of winning the Championship annually, scored fastest at 2.96 per over, and Northamptonshire second-fastest under their zestful captain Freddie Brown at 2.87, with Warwickshire third; as limited-overs cricket has subsequently moved in, all counties now score at more than three an over in the Championship.) A nice human touch was that Warwickshire's own WG, William Quaife, came into their dressing room after their triumph and showed Dollery's men the gold watch with which he had been presented exactly 40 years before. Quaife died before the celebration dinner but at least it was a link.

***

Warwickshire have seldom attracted large crowds to Edgbaston, albeit England have. It will never be quite the perfect venue until it has a railway station, which would require an expensive diversion through the former meadows. It is at least half an hour's walk from Birmingham New

Street, whereas Nottingham station is an easy mile from Trent Bridge.

The stand beside the Rea, now the Hollies Stand, is like no other in English cricket. Headingley's Western Terrace can rival it for size, but too often spectators have expended their energy on their own amusements, such as making a snake out of plastic beer-glasses, rather than watching and reacting to the cricket.

A stabbing in the Hollies Stand marred the England v Pakistan one-day international in 1996 but in general the audience has been full of wit, bonhomie and passion – for England games. When Freddie Calthorpe was captain, the stand would confine itself to the odd shout like 'Put 'Arry 'Owell on!' Lugubrious Black Country humour, in which Eric Hollies himself specialised, has been the keynote for county games.

The 1981 Ashes Test was the first time I saw Edgbaston's passion not simply at work but probably affect the outcome. Australia were chipping away slowly at their target of 151 on a somnolent Sunday afternoon, and spectators were starting to accept that while the miracle at Headingley had been nice, Australia were going to go 2-1 up and take the Ashes. But, climbing so slowly, Australia were liable to stall.

When Ian Botham took the ball that afternoon as Michael Brearley's final fling of the dice, he began with one of his slower spells. What shattered Australia was the combined effect of Botham and the Hollies Stand once they had both warmed up. Botham ran in and roared for lbw, as did the ten thousand spectators sitting square on the leg side. The Australians were daunted, demoralised, scattered to the winds, five of their batsmen dismissed by Botham for a single.

The passion, or patriotism, of the Hollies Stand was needed no less in 2005 when, after a decade and a half of bending the knee, England rose up and punched Australia on the nose. On that final Sunday morning of the second Test at Edgbaston, Brett Lee, Shane Warne and Mike Kasprowicz did not go quietly. It was the most excruciating red-ball drama I ever saw because Australia's last-wicket pair worked gradually towards their target of 28, whereas Ben Stokes at Headingley in 2019, at the climax, charged over the line. I think England's fast bowlers would have flagged on that fourth and final morning if the crowd, and the Hollies Stand in particular, had not spurred them.

I tried to find out what made Edgbaston, and the Hollies Stand in particular, so vocal: because it was not only Tests against Australia that were so loud and dramatic but West Indies too. Edgbaston seethed in 1984 when the West Indian fast bowlers destroyed England by an innings and 180 runs. Warwickshire's debutant Andy Lloyd was hit on the head by Malcolm Marshall and never played Test cricket again.

The secret, if there was one, was that Edgbaston at that time used to stage the first England Test of the summer, in June. The city's students had done their exams but had not 'gone down'; indeed they were up for a party. Some students worked at the ground, bringing youthful zest to the merchandising and catering; others attended as paying spectators, usually in the cheaper seats of the Hollies Stand. The timing of the Edgbaston Test has altered; the zest in the Hollies Stand remains.

So overwhelmed had the Australians been at Edgbaston, not least by England in the World Cup semi-final of 2019, that by the Ashes Test later that summer it was re-branded 'Fortress Edgbaston'. This was the venue where Australia had failed to win any game since 2001. It was written in the stars that Jimmy Anderson would break down in his opening spell, and England would lose by 251 runs. Cricket hates hubris.

If I could re-live one cricket match all over again it would have to be that 2005 Test at Edgbaston when England turned the wheel after so long – since 1989 they had not simply lost to Australia by the end of every game, they had almost lost before the start.

That Test was so vivid, and remains so – a thrill a minute, if not from the moment when Glenn McGrath was injured in the warm-up, then when Marcus Trescothick took Brett Lee apart with his cover-driving and signalled England's new aggression. My choice is based partly on the fact that the press box at Edgbaston then was in the perfect position behind the arm at the City end, not too high up, not too low, and blessed with open windows. You were of the crowd but not in it, surrounded by spectators but with space to type.

Almost everywhere now the media are divorced from the crowd, kept behind glass, air-conditioned, unsocially distanced. As no mean recompense, Edgbaston offers by far the best lunches and teas on the circuit – breakfast too for the photographers who arrive very early – but the press box is too high up, on the top floor of the new pavilion. The numbers must have shrunk too. For the inaugural Test in 1902 Ryder single-handedly issued passes for 90 journalists.

* * *

Another feature of Edgbaston, whether you are playing or watching behind the arm, has been 'wobble'. I have never seen this phenomenon to quite the same extent as when Allan Donald was steaming in for Warwickshire from the pavilion end and Keith Piper was keeping wicket. Donald did not swing much either way before the ball bounced but after it had beaten the bat, and the stumps, the ball would often assume a life of its own. It would describe some crazy parabolas while heading down leg side, i.e., to Piper's left, and also dip: more a flying saucer than a ball, and controlled by men from Mars, if anyone.

This made a thrilling sight in the early 1990s: Donald tearing in, the batsman 'leaving' or more usually missing, Piper launching left or right and leaping. Bob Woolmer, of course, when coaching Warwickshire, brought crash mats out and had Piper practising his dives – possibly before any other keeper – and maximising his span. When he became South Africa's coach, Woolmer did the same with Mark Boucher. It was extreme gymnastics.

England's first regular wicketkeeper was a Warwickshire man, Arthur or more commonly Dick, Lilley. He worked as a lad at the Cadbury's chocolate factory which, being philanthropically run by a Quaker, had its own cricket team and coach, who was a former Warwickshire professional. He converted Lilley into a keeper and recommended him to Warwickshire, for whom he kept wicket from 1888 until 1911. Lilley was England's keeper too from 1896 until 1909, as reliable as they come, whether catching the ball or advising his captain or batting with the tail. Averaging 20 with the bat, as a keeper, was not bad in three-day Tests on uncovered pitches.

'Tiger' Smith succeeded Lilley as the Warwickshire keeper and, briefly, England's. He too had worked at Cadbury's – and lost the tips of two fingers in an accident. When he went for a trial at Edgbaston, he kept his hands behind his back.

No county outside the Big Six – Kent, Lancashire, Middlesex, Nottinghamshire, Surrey and Yorkshire – had won the Championship before Warwickshire did so in 1911, when Smith was their wicketkeeper. Their captain was only 22 years old, one of the game's mavericks, who drank heavily even by the standards of the age, and whose career was finished by a motorbike accident aged 25.

By then, however, Frank Foster had proved himself to be one of the game's most skilful all-rounders. I imagine a slightly taller and whippier version of Sam Curran. Foster would bowl left-arm round the wicket to a leg-side field: this was subsequently cited as the first version of Bodyline. He made the ball swing into the right-hander or cut it away from him to hit off stump. Tricky to face, and tricky to take: Tiger was brought into the England side for the second Test of the 1911/12 series in Australia, after England had lost the first, to replace Herbert Strudwick, who could not take Foster down the leg side.

England won the next four Tests. Syd Barnes took 34 wickets, Foster 32: England have never had such a successful pair of bowlers in Australia as these two, who might have both been bowling for Warwickshire as well. In 11 Tests together they took 118 wickets. Foster also hit 305 in a day in a county game. 'Mr Foster plays the game for the enjoyment of it,' Dick Lilley remembered, 'and always with that splendid nerve which in cricket is the halfway house to success.'

***

The bear has often slumbered. After 1911 it did not rouse itself to win the Championship again for 40 years. In the 1950s Warwickshire started football pools, and this money paid for the renovation of Edgbaston, to the point where it was restored to the list of Test grounds in 1957, having been demoted after 1929.

In 1972 they won the Championship for the third time, spending their extra money on overseas players again. In 1951 it had been three New Zealanders, in 1972 four West Indians, including Rohan Kanhai, Alvin Kallicharran and Lance Gibbs, all from Guyana.

In their 100th season as a first-class county, the Warwickshire bear rose to its full height, flexed its claws and enjoyed the most successful season any county has ever had, before or since. The stars were aligned. They had the best possible off-field set-up for a start: MJK Smith as the wise, old, seen-it-all president; Dennis Amiss, who had overtaken Quaife as Warwickshire's most prolific batsman and was now chief executive; and Bob Woolmer as coach. Has any other county had a CEO who has scored over a hundred first-class hundreds as Amiss did? Here was some thinktank to have on tap: this triumvirate scored almost 100,000 first-class runs.

They had the luck too, in two ways. The Indian all-rounder Manoj Prabhakar, who might have scored 500 runs and taken 30 or 40 wickets in the Championship, pulled out with injury, so Warwickshire replaced him with a chap who was running into form, having just scored 375 against England, Brian Lara. Secondly, by accident, an innovation came about 20 years ahead of its time. Warwickshire had two separate captains: when Dermot Reeve was injured, he concentrated on the limited-overs side, while Tim Munton took over the Championship team, won nine of his 11 games, and led by example as by far the leading wicket-taker.

But the collective stepping-stone to this success was the NatWest Trophy of the previous season, 1993, between Warwickshire and Sussex, the 53rd one-day final at Lord's and, according to *Wisden*, 'widely regarded as the greatest ever played'. At no stage were Warwickshire favourites. Sussex's total of 321 was, by all precedent, insuperable even if it had been scored off 60 overs. Off the last over Warwickshire still needed 15 to win, whereupon Dermot Reeve sealed his reputation as the limited-overs cricketer of his day.

After winning that final, anything was possible; and after signing Lara, everything was possible. Warwickshire in 1994 won their fourth County Championship, their second Sunday League and their first Benson and Hedges Cup.

They again reached the final of the NatWest Trophy but Worcestershire sent them in on a damp day and not even Lara could save them.

Lara scored six centuries in his first seven Championship innings, including his 501 not out against Durham, and 2,066 runs off 2,262 balls in all. Has anyone made batting look more gloriously simple than Lara in his prime? If he had a technical weakness it was the bouncer, as he was classically side-on, and he could barely score off Curtly Ambrose when he played against Northamptonshire; yet he still made 197.

'An extraordinary team of ordinary players' was Dollery's own summary of his side that won in 1951. Warwickshire's 1994 version was a team of ordinary players, plus Lara, at least by the England selectors' estimation: none of that uniquely successful side was chosen for a winter tour.

Warwickshire have subsequently won more than their share of trophies, including four more Championships to make eight in all. The good coaching has continued and a pathway for local talent has been created, which has made them slightly less dependent on signings – whether from other countries or counties – than their moneyed rivals like Nottinghamshire and Surrey.

And the scope for future growth exists literally: Warwickshire are so far using the land on only one bank of the Rea for their infrastructural developments, while the other bank is devoted to practice areas and nets. Once its cave is sorted out – when the cricket ground with the biggest footprint in the land is fully operational – the bear will be able to emit a mighty roar.

Worcestershire

ICON IS not a word I am tempted to employ outside its Orthodox context, but if an exception can be made for its usage in cricket, then it has to be reserved for that famous photograph of Worcester Cathedral – the one taken from the New Road cricket ground across the River Severn.

Now that the tree inside Canterbury's ground has gone, no image captures county cricket to the same extent. Photographs of Arundel, Abergavenny and Queen's Park in Chesterfield can also evoke the English and Welsh summer, but they are or were out-grounds staging county cricket once or twice a year.

Worcester Cathedral, like many churches, is built on a rise or hill so as to be seen more clearly from a distance, and to look more imposing (sports grounds usually go to the opposite extreme in valleys or at the bottom of hills). The nave is relatively recent, Victorian; nonetheless its stained-glass windows, which we see from the cricket ground, are magnificent in that they do magnify, whether the Lord or the light.

The original part of the existing cathedral dates back to the 11th century; the oldest book in the library (Bede's work on grammar and poetry) to the 7th century. King John – boo! – was entombed here in 1216; memorial services for Tom Graveney and Basil d'Oliveira – hooray! – held here. Neatest of all, in the crypt, is a leather boot, dug up in the churchyard and dated to the 15th century. Polish it up, and such was the craftsmanship that you could sell it in the shopping centre.

Back in the 1890s, the cathedral's dean and chapter leased the fields on the other side of the swan-strewn Severn to a fellow called Paul Foley, who converted them into Worcestershire's cricket ground. Foley employed a 23-year-old farmer from Berkshire (who had played cricket for Kent), called Fred Hunt, to turn these fields into a stage for first-class cricket. It was going to be quite a challenge, given that no other major cricket ground is subject to almost annual flooding.

On a wall below the cathedral, beside the river, lines have been cut into the stone to mark the heights which the Severn has scaled. Records show there were fewer floods in the old days, when meadows upstream would absorb rain-water, before they were turned into housing estates. Yet the water still peaked 16 feet above normal in 1672, 1770 and 1886.

'I came in September [1898],' Hunt recalled in a radio interview with John Arlott in 1964. 'It was just ordinary fields – three fields, hedge through the middle and a hay rick. There was no road, there was no path to the ground, there was no stand, there was nothing. And I thought to myself, well it looks like no first-class cricket ground to me!'

Appropriately, given the ecclesiastical proximity, it took a leap of faith to enter Worcestershire in the County Championship in 1899, to join 14 others (Northamptonshire, Glamorgan and Durham were subsequently added). At times since then it has looked as though the county would, like their ground in many a winter, go under. In 1919 Worcestershire became the only county ever to miss a season in peacetime, so many of their players having died in the Great War. Even today they are barely clinging on at times: the only county without floodlights, and without an indoor school (they have to go to Malvern College), and often without a chief executive (cheaper to make do without one).

Worcestershire CCC is nevertheless part of our heritage and consciousness. The image of the New Road cricket ground, with the cathedral behind, is up there with the music of Elgar or the words of Housman as an intrinsic part of the west of England; and, like an icon, some people may cling to it in time of despair.

***

It is only appropriate that when a photographer today takes a picture of New Road, he or she does so from the balcony outside Foley's cafe, which stands at wide third man or deep midwicket, next to the new pavilion. No first-class county has been the creation of one man so much as Worcestershire was the work of Paul Foley. But for him it might well be just another minor county (or 'National County' as they have been renamed) like Staffordshire or Shropshire.

Foley was an Old Etonian ready to plough everything he had into making Worcestershire a first-class county: it was no mere vanity project of which he tired. The natural course would have been to let Gentlemen of Worcestershire continue as the premier club in the county, based at Boughton Hall outside Worcester, but Foley's ambitions were loftier. Worcestershire's winning of five County Championship titles, and seven other trophies, would suggest those ambitions have been fulfilled.

Foley bankrolled Worcestershire for 30 years until it was strong enough to stand on its own two feet, or at least until Viscount Cobham's family – the Lyttletons – were ready to chip in. And has anyone turned his hand to so many roles at a county club? For a start Foley employed the professionals, and paid them out of his own pocket, in order to win the Minor Counties Championship four years in a row in the 1890s; and he inaugurated this competition precisely because it gave Worcestershire the springboard to first-class status.

In addition Foley painted the sightscreen, rolled the pitch between innings, acted as scorer and as secretary, paid for the first pavilion at New Road, and conceived the logo of three pears, as well as engaging Fred Hunt as the first groundsman. (Fred not only made the ground, he produced absolute belters, as if Don Bradman needed any encouragement to make a century on all four of his visits to Worcester from 1930 to 1948.)

Most audacious of all, Foley almost signed the greatest batsman of his day, Victor Trumper. The correspondence between Foley and Trumper, who toured England with Australia in 1899, has been unearthed by the Australian writer Gideon Haigh and it is fascinating how close Worcestershire came to signing Trumper. The nearest equivalent would have been Devon signing Don Bradman when they applied to join the Championship in 1948. Only when he was told that he would not be able to represent Australia again did Trumper pull out.

Foley had one local advantage: the family of Fosters, who attended Malvern College and kept the Worcestershire team liberally supplied with amateurs. Frank Foster, a contemporary Warwickshire bowler of distinction, was no relation but that still left loads of Fosters who were qualified for Worcestershire: most notably Reginald or 'Tip', the only man to captain England at cricket and football. His name was mentioned again when Zak Crawley scored 267 against Pakistan in 2020. The only higher maiden century for England was Foster's 287 in Sydney in 1903/04, which remains the highest individual innings for England in Australia.

Not until Foley married, and had children, and a cricket ground of his own at his Stoke Edith estate, did his enthusiasm for Worcestershire begin to wane. By then he had propelled his county up to second place in the County Championship in 1907: some effort, given the size of Worcestershire's population, although the county has always tried to enrol Dudley, Kidderminster and a bit of Black Country money.

***

As New Road is unique among first-class cricket grounds, its head groundsman cannot be imported like a player. He has to grow up there, to read all the warning signs, even now that radar can tell him, to within a minute, when it is going to rain. He has to be more experienced than Noah in dealing with floods.

Tim Packwood joined the groundstaff as a lad in 1989 and stayed there until the middle of 2022. In normal years he had a staff of five, including himself, so when the floods arrived a couple of the catering staff chipped in – and some players at least offered to lend a hand. 'I always said if we can get through to Christmas without a flood, the new grass will be established and strong enough to withstand any flooding afterwards.'

In the winter of 2019/20 the ground was flooded six times, a record, and spent 75 days under water. Crucially, the first of those six floods was in October, so the seed that had just been sown was washed away. When the waters finally receded, the square was bare. Cricketers could have come out of the ark in pairs, one to bat and the other to bowl, but there was no grass on which to play.

Clearing up once is bad enough: the silt dumped by the overflowing Severn goes everywhere. In Fred Hunt's time, a flood would only cover the square by a few inches and what it left behind was natural, and beneficial. According to the Worcestershire and England bowler Fred Root, who was the son of a groundsman himself, Hunt would 'produce wickets which are a veritable batsman's paradise' and was 'the prince of groundsmen' (no wonder Bradman never rested himself for a game at New Road). But this was before pesticides entered the water supply on an industrial scale.

'You sometimes see these oil slicks,' said Packwood, 'and you're not sure if it's cooking oil or engine oil – and you're not allowed to wade in and find out.' Worcestershire's annual budget for clearing up floods is £20,000, some of which is spent on hiring high-pressure hoses to wash down everything at ground level – and however many feet above that the water has risen. Some winters the highest mark is only a couple of inches below the floor of the Ladies' pavilion where afternoon tea is served.

Six times! To go through all that hosing, and brushing, and shovelling the sludge down the drains with a spade (nothing hi-tech) six times! Old Fred claimed to have once caught a 45-pound salmon swimming on the outfield, in the days when cricket nets were employed as another kind of net; these are more toxic times. I have watched Worcestershire's groundstaff clearing up in winter and resolved to appreciate their manual work more.

***

'We never start later than 7.30 on matchdays,' Packwood said. 'I was up at half-five to see the kids for a few seconds before I leave for the ground. The match covers have to be off the pitch by eight o'clock according to ECB regulations.'

It is true. One matchday during the Bob Willis Trophy, I opened my curtains shortly after 7.30am on the top floor of the Premier Inn at New Road (when the club sold the land for the hotel, they got the new building adjoining it in return for their offices). No view of the cathedral, but there were the Malvern Hills, undulating in the distance, which I had never seen from ground level. And there were the groundsmen hard at work.

In order to maintain biosecurity, Tim Packwood and his team could not use the normal nets beside the Severn but set them up on the outfield. The players staying in the hotel could therefore go straight from the rooms on their floor, through the fire exits, and on to the ground without meeting anybody outside their bubble.

Some of us might be used to setting up nets in April then taking them down in September, but the New Road groundsmen have to do it almost every day, certainly match-days. All those ropes, and metal pegs to be pushed into the turf (no ready-made holes), after the roller and mower have prepared two strips on the other side of the square. Then creases have to be marked out in the nets at both ends. Then a couple of wide strips of netting have to be set up on the outfield for fielding practice.

'We don't actually stop for a break till 10am when the players are practising. We have 15 or 20 minutes for a quick cup of coffee and a bacon roll, then we take the nets down ready for an 11 o'clock start and watch the first 20 minutes or so of play, to get a feel for how the pitch is playing and how the game is going. Then we clean the machines and re-mark the nets [the ones beside the Severn that are used in normal times].' And someone has to keep an eye on the umpires all the time to see if they have requirements, like wanting foot-holes repaired.

The lunch interval is time for everyone to have lunch, except for the groundsmen. They have to sweep the creases, re-mark the lines and roll a pitch for the next game – with a mechanised roller. Old Fred always used a horse-drawn roller, and mysteriously kept refusing the committee's offer of a mechanised one (which other counties were using by the 1930s) right through until his retirement after the Second World War.

An hour after play finishes – and how many counties complete their overs in time? – and once the square is covered, the groundstaff can go home. Old Fred said he was sometimes up at 3am to roll in the dew – and Sir Everton Weekes, who as a lad in Bridgetown would help out the groundstaff at Kensington Oval, said the secret behind those mirror-like West Indian pitches of yore was rolling in the dew. But current regulations state the pitch has to be covered at night and today's groundstaff can sleep through, right up until 5.30am, before starting again their 12-hour day.

The Pakistan tourists came to Worcester at less than a fortnight's notice in the summer of 2020, and not one touring team but two: their Test squad and their white-ball squad, 30 players in one bio-bubble. So Packwood and his team in July had to provide 'double-sessions' of nets for them, in the morning and the afternoon, and two pitches for their intra-squad games which were up to international standard. 'They were very appreciative and a pleasure to work with.'

Any extra money for helping the touring team's preparations? No. 'It was very hard work but a really good opportunity for the club. They [the Pakistanis] were on the ground 24/7, with the club providing all their food – breakfast, lunch and dinner – and a gym for them in a marquee,' said Packwood. 'You were just happy to play your part.'

Worcestershire seems to inspire devotion even more than most first-class counties. Moeen Ali grew up at Edgbaston but transferred to Worcester, and always spoken fondly of the club before going back to Birmingham. Moeen was the captain when Worcestershire won their first T20 final in

2018, telling his players before the semi-final: 'Prepare to play two matches today.'

Members were so loyal that the club chairman Fanos Hira said that only 6% of the 3,300 asked for a refund when they were not allowed to attend any games in 2020. One of the most devoted is Andrew Thomas, who is the club's de facto historian, indefatigable in his researches.

Why did Fred Hunt persist in using a horse to pull the roller at New Road? Because the club had contracted to pay him £40 a year for equine expenses, so Thomas reveals in his book *Pears 155*. This was in addition to Hunt's salary of £310, which was 'more than the WCCC secretary and any of the professional players'. Plus, all the salmon Fred could catch.

I would be tempted to leave all the flood damage until the spring then clear it up in one go, but this is not possible: conferences or wedding receptions are booked, and the ground has to look – and smell – decent. It has helped that New Road itself, running beside the ground, was raised 18 inches by Worcester council, but nothing has yet been invented to halt the tide of nature. As Packwood said: 'It's a cricket ground built on a flood plain and you've got to live with it.'

***

Under-arm bowling came to be outlawed after Trevor Chappell rolled the last ball of Australia's ODI against New Zealand at Melbourne in 1981 along the ground.

Worcestershire produced the last under-arm bowler, or 'lobster', to play Test cricket (and Foley himself had bowled lobs in the 1890s). Back in 1909/10 England selected George Simpson-Hayward for their tour of South Africa and he took 23 wickets in the five Tests at only 18 each. At school in Malvern Simpson-Hayward had learned how to bowl flat off breaks, rather than lobbing up leg breaks as most lobsters had done; and he even bowled a kind of carrom ball underarm, with his thumb underneath the ball and flicking it out, which turned from the off. South African pitches then were all matting, so Simpson-Hayward must have made his offies grip and turn: 14 of his 23 Test wickets were right-handed batsmen who were bowled.

The recent law that makes any ball that bounces twice or more into a no-ball would have been sufficient to stop rolling along the ground: no need to ban under-arm (now both captains have to agree in advance of a game for under-arm to be allowed). I think some bilateral white-ball series would be enlivened if Simpson-Hayward were imitated, and someone – I can see Joe Root volunteering with a mischievous smile – came on for the final over to bowl lobs.

**

Being the first-class county with the smallest population after Northamptonshire, as the boundaries were traditionally defined, Worcestershire have been more entitled to imports than most. Victor Trumper may have fallen through, but the arrivals of Tom Graveney, Basil d'Oliveira and Graeme Hick – from the outposts of Bristol, South Africa and Zimbabwe – made for delicious icing on the cakes in the Ladies' stand. Worcestershire were propelled to all five of their Championships by one or other of these three batsmen.

Graveney, having under-performed for England while at Gloucestershire, acquired steel in his soul when he moved to New Road. He was far and away the leading batsman when Worcestershire won their first title in 1964; and as soon as he was restored to the England side after a long hiatus, he made not only handsome strokes but major hundreds.

Graveney told me he might have fulfilled his talent earlier if, during the Lord's Test of 1953, he had not obeyed Len

Hutton's advice to block towards the end of a day when they had Australia on the ropes. The advice suited Len himself, not Graveney. Next morning England's captain went on to his hundred, but Graveney fell early for 79, and it was not until 1966 that he cracked Test level.

D'Oliveira, in his first county season of 1965, matched Graveney run for run and together they took Worcestershire to their second Championship. Don Kenyon, as forthright when batting for his county as he was nervous for England, captained the county to both triumphs. They also had a fine battery of seamers led by Jack Flavell, who had succeeded Reg Perks as attack-leader. Perks lost his prime to the Second World War yet still took 100 wickets in a first-class season 16 times, the most by any bowler of his pace.

D'Oliveira was the county coach when Graeme Hick arrived and helped to assemble the team that won the Championship in 1988 and 1989. His special quality as a coach was to understand when a young player was ready for the next step up. As much as batting, coaching is about timing.

Hick wanted somewhere tranquil, away from publicity, akin to Zimbabwe, and found it at New Road. Who else could the new pavilion be named after when Hick hit 50 first-class centuries on the ground in 301 innings?

Hick did not do the same for England. In retrospect, I would say the biggest single factor was that, for England, he batted at No.3 only 35 times in his 114 Test innings. Three was his position: he could just go out and bat irrespective of the game situation.

After an uncertain start – well, it would be, if you faced the West Indian pace attack of 1991 – Hick almost cracked it in the Ashes Test at the Oval in 1993. At three he motored to 80 off 107 balls, smashing the Aussie bowlers, before being out caught at backward point in the most sickening manner (because the batsman can see his downfall from the moment it leaves the top edge of his bat). For the next Test Hick was demoted, a well-meaning move to protect him from the new ball, but it did not suit him. He averaged 34 at No.3 for England, against a modest 31 overall, even though he was never secure in his familiar position.

At the other extreme comes Worcestershire's worst player: the Reverend Reginald Heber Moss. Or maybe this is unfair. He was 57 years old when he played his one and only Championship game in 1925, setting a world record of sorts for the longest gap between first-class appearances. His previous game, as a pace bowler, had been for Liverpool and District against the 1893 Australians.

I wonder what sort of life Moss had led in between those games. A fine red-brick rectory near Malvern or Ledbury? Nothing too arduous apart from a weekly sermon; a spot of cricket at the weekends for his local club; visit his parishioners once a year to talk about their children but, like the vicar in *Lark Rise to Candleford*, never mention religion? The Almighty must have been watching with a kindly eye when Moss made his comeback, 38 years after his first-class debut, and had a trundle against Gloucestershire, because he took a wicket in his three-over spell. Might have stiffened up overnight, and needed a vicar to stand in his pulpit next Sunday.

＊＊＊

Worcester has been a home for yeomen, for fine cricketers never picked for England, but had they played for one of the home counties and been selected, they would surely have done a job. Like Daryl Mitchell and Alan Richardson.

Had he been given a run as an England Test opener, Mitchell might have been the most successful after the two Sirs, Andrew Strauss and Alastair Cook, his technique a lot less quirky than that of some of those tried. Excellent slip fielder, a bit of all sorts medium-pace, always chipping in, a thorough cricketer.

Richardson had to go round the houses before ending up as Worcestershire's opening bowler. That whirly-arm action did not impress coaches. He went from Derbyshire back to his native Staffordshire, on to Warwickshire, then Middlesex, and finally New Road, where he ended up being a *Wisden* Cricketer of the Year: to gain such an accolade, without having represented your country, you have to be a real yeoman.

The press box at New Road can lay claim to being the wittiest on the county circuit; but if you can tear yourself away from the banter you can sit beside the boundary and talk to Richardson about bowling and coaching as he does his rounds. For instance, this fashion of 'wobble-seam' which has made batting against the Dukes ball in England so awkward: he first saw and heard about it from the Australian pace bowler Stuart Clark when they were both at Middlesex a decade ago.

Richardson now has a wonderful stable of pace bowlers to coach, all local lads, none of them poached. Some of them are studying at the University of Worcester, which is building a state-of-the-art indoor cricket centre with some contribution from Worcestershire CCC so they will not have to use Malvern College in future. Lads like Josh Tongue and Dillon Pennington, Pat Brown and Adam Finch, and a rare left-armer Ben Gibbon, and more besides.

Not all hail from Worcestershire but they come from thereabouts. 'Paul Pridgeon is now a club vice-president,' Richardson says of another yeoman, who was a successor to Perks and Flavell, and a new-ball predecessor of himself. 'Pridge still pops into Shrewsbury school and keeps an eye on Shropshire for us.'

WORCESTERSHIRE

Everything ephemeral changes. Yet Worcester Cathedral still looks down benignly on New Road, the Severn still flows alongside, and the swans still glide serenely over its surface, not flapping like the rest of us.

Yorkshire

THERE HAS, it would appear, never been so much trouble at t'mill.

Firstly, the allegations of racism, made initially by Azeem Rafeeq, a former captain of Yorkshire's T20 side. The number of days when he was not racially abused amounted to 60 by his own count – and his career spanned a decade. 'The remainder of my time at the club has been filled with many dark moments where I have been left isolated, lonely, bullied and targeted because of my race,' Rafeeq claimed in his written statement.

Much of what Rafeeq alleged has been challenged, and many allegations levelled at him for incidents that occurred during an upbringing, which, at least, everyone can agree was troubled. But whatever Rafeeq has said or done is, surely, secondary. What matters is whether there was racism in English cricket as a whole and Yorkshire cricket in particular, and whether everything possible is being done to eradicate it.

Another manifestation of this same phenomenon might be that the number of Yorkshire's non-white players, who are not overseas registrations, has dwindled to almost zero. When not required by England, Adil Rashid does not hasten back to represent Yorkshire, as Moeen Ali hastened to Worcestershire. Rashid has won two World Cups and is the best wrist-spinner in Britain by many a street, but he has not played a first-class or Championship game for Yorkshire since September 2017, or a List A game for Yorkshire since April 2019. In 20-over cricket, his speciality of late, Rashid has played 16 games for Yorkshire from August 2017 to date (yearly 2023), or three per year.

A decade or so ago, not only Rashid and Rafeeq but another England bowler, if only briefly, in Ajmal Shahzad were playing regularly for Yorkshire; and another pace bowler, Moin Ashraf, more occasionally. The county was making the most of its human resources: Yorkshire won their last two Championships in 2014 and 2015 under Jason Gillespie, the Australian coach whose USP was to make a cricket club, so far as the inevitable frictions allow, into an extended family.

In another respect, there is trouble at the mill. The West Riding is drying up. Yorkshire's cricketers tend to hail from the North and East Ridings in a far higher proportion than ever before.

The West Riding was the original hotbed of professional cricket in England. At one point in the 1880s, 30-odd members of the village near Huddersfield called Lascelles Hall were employed either as Yorkshire players, groundsmen or coaches at clubs and schools. I would be surprised if, at that time, there were as many as 300 people making a profession out of cricket in the world, never mind England.

Yorkshire, or the West Riding in effect, soon overtook Nottinghamshire and Surrey as the main force in the land. Starting in 1893 Yorkshire have won the County Championship 32 times, and shared the title once. Between 1893 and 1968 inclusive they won the Championship 29 times and shared it once. Thus, in the space of 68 seasons and once the war years are deducted, Yorkshire won the Championship almost every other season.

It was said that 'when Yorkshire is strong, England is strong' but this was not quite right. When England were strong – in the early 1950s and early 1970s they were unofficially number one – they were strong because they had numerous Yorkshire players in their team; but Yorkshire, denuded, were not winning the Championship as usual. A strong Yorkshire leads to a strong England, but not simultaneously.

Like everywhere else in England, the standard of league cricket in Yorkshire is not what it was, for multifactorial reasons. Some counties have a Premier League all their own, like Derbyshire and Northamptonshire, Surrey and Sussex, but Yorkshire is too big: players cannot be expected to drive two hours on a Saturday morning for a 50-over game and back home again. There are so many leagues – especially in the West Riding, whether racially segregated or unsegregated – it has become complicated for cream to reach the top.

Yorkshire's past is glorious, unrivalled in its splendour so numerous have been the masterful cricketers; and, above all perhaps, relatively simple. Herbert Sutcliffe averaged 60 for England, Sir Leonard Hutton 56, and Joe Root too has touched 50. Wilfred Rhodes and George Hirst were the ultimate all-rounders. Fred Trueman held the world record for the most Test wickets. Darren Gough was the English bowler who pioneered reverse swing. Never has an England batsman been so blistering as Jonny Bairstow in 2022. Three of the most famous Ashes victories were led by Yorkshiremen – Sir Stanley Jackson in 1905, Len Hutton in 1953 and Michael Vaughan in 2005 – although none was ever appointed captain of Yorkshire, such were the politics.

Yorkshire cricket was tribal in a healthy way. The community took great pride in it, the role models kept on coming, youngsters were inspired to follow in their footsteps and play in the county's streets, alleys and snickets. County cricket, I would guess, used to be more deeply ingrained in Yorkshire than anywhere else in England or Wales.

When Yorkshire ended Surrey's seven-year reign in 1959, by chasing down a target in Hove, their players had to drive that evening to Scarborough for a game next day. They arrived in their cars about 2.30am. According to their batsman Bryan Stott, quoted in *Through the Remembered Gate* by Stephen Chalke, 'Everybody was waiting up for us, all along the streets and outside the hotel. It will stay with me forever.' The Yorkshire public were starved, not having won a Championship for 13 years.

The first traffic jam I recall being stuck in was outside Harrogate on 31 August 1966. Yorkshire had to win their final game against Kent to win the Championship, and they needed all the support they could get because Kent had Derek Underwood to bowl for them on a damp pitch. It seemed that every member of the tribe wanted to get into the ground; cars snaked back for miles, on a weekday morning. The White Rose meant summat alright.

***

I was brought up as a member of this tribe, initiated by being born in Yorkshire. In those days Sheffield was not a cricket backwater. Bramall Lane had been a Test ground, if only in 1902; it used to stage four of Yorkshire's 14 Championship home matches per season, usually more than Bradford or Headingley. And it was little more than a mile's walk away, so that you could hear the cheers and roars, and feel the urge to hurry there.

On Saturday mornings, instead of lying in bed, I would run downstairs to pick up the *Sheffield Telegraph*, thrust through the letterbox and lying on the doormat (it subsequently tried to become more posh and regional as the

Morning Telegraph). I spread it out on the coconut matting on which visitors wiped the mud off their feet: no time to be lost in finding somewhere hygienic before discovering how Yorkshire had fared. To help my parents and sister enjoy their weekend slumber upstairs, I would shout out the Championship table. As I was looking downwards at the newspaper on the mat, downstairs, they were probably unable to distinguish a word.

'Yorkshire, Gloucestershire, Hampshire, Middlesex, Kent!' Pause for breath after reading out the top five in the table. Alliteration then kicked in. 'Essex, Sussex, Surrey, Somerset! Worcestershire, Warwickshire, Lancashire, Leicestershire! Glamorgan, Derbyshire, Nottinghamshire, Northamptonshire …'

To this day, when I have to run through the list of first-class counties in my head, I recite them in this order, not alphabetically. Sometimes I remember to add Durham.

No Championship season, I have discovered, ever ended with the counties in exactly this order. But around 1960 and 1961 there must have been one or two times per season when the table was such or thereabouts. Anyway, the main thing was that Yorkshire were on top of the table, ahead of Surrey, who had recently won seven consecutive titles. The natural order of the universe was restored.

I painted three white lines on the wall in our backyard and batted and bowled when friends came round or my family could be persuaded. Never once, so far as I can remember, did it occur to me that I could exercise my birthright and play for Yorkshire. Such ambition was so remote it was vanity. The cricketers who bestrode the turf at Bramall Lane were demi-gods.

The former Yorkshire and England captain Norman Yardley lived round the corner, little more than a hundred yards away. He owned a wine shop or two in the city centre and, when sent on an errand, I would sometimes see him stroll back home with the gait of a cricketer: broad-beamed, as Fred Trueman was wont to say. Primarily a batsman, Yardley could bowl some canny inswing and topped the England bowling averages on their understandably disastrous tour of Australia in 1946/47, dismissing Don Bradman thrice in a row. He was captaining England in 1948 when he led the three cheers for Bradman in his last Test at the Oval. At a distance Yardley looked genial, and sounded as much as a summariser on *Test Match Special*. But me, a ten- or 12-year-old, speaking to Him?

***

We all know how keen on cricket Yorkshiremen are, but I never realised how keen, and for how long they have been keen, until a few years ago when I read an interview with Schofield Haigh. Along with his Edwardian contemporaries George Hirst and Wilfred Rhodes, Haigh is one of three Yorkshire bowlers to have taken 2,000 first-class wickets.

'I often think that around Huddersfield is the most splendid zone for the game that I have ever known; everybody is so keen on the sport,' Haigh told George Wade. 'Why, I've heard them tell how Thewlis, Ulyett, and Greenwood used to play at the bottom of an old quarry at six o'clock in the morning; and I myself have known my father play a match at Christmas. A queer season for cricket, the month of December, eh? But then, you see, when it "runs in the blood" you've got to play everywhere and always.' George Ulyett playing cricket in a quarry at 6am? He used to be England's finest professional all-rounder, if you count WG Grace as an amateur.

'To play everywhere and always': the implementation of this motto made Yorkshire supreme in England. Now perhaps the county needs to update this motto: 'To enable everyone to play everywhere and always.'

Hirst, left-arm, was England's first swing bowler. He grew up in Kirkheaton, where the cricket ground is exposed on top of a hill, and the prevailing wind comes from mid-off, which enabled him to swing the ball from round the wicket into right-handed batsmen 'like a fast throw from cover'. (Only in the last decade or so have left-armers in T20 clicked that this is the way to go at the death.) Hirst's record will always remain: that of being the only man to score 2,000 runs and take 200 wickets in a first-class season, the double 'double', in 1906.

In the absence of academies and indoor schools, Rhodes perfected his game by bowling in a barn all winter, and by becoming a pro in Scotland, like Haigh. Rhodes will always hold the record for the most first-class wickets, 4,187, or 4,204 if you accept the recent amendment by statisticians; and for the most 'doubles', 16 to Hirst's 14. I doubt whether any England spinner will again have such economical figures in a Test series as Rhodes in 1929/30: he bowled 251 overs for 453 runs. It was West Indies' first home series, but Rhodes was 52 at the time, the only Test cricketer above the age of 50. If Rhodes had a secret, it was that he was naturally lithe and extremely athletic – on England tours he used to win every game on board ship – and thriftily accurate, as only a Yorkshire bowler could be.

***

In the 1960s, when I was a lad, Yorkshire not only won the Championship six times, they beat the Australians by an innings, and the Indians by an innings, and the New Zealanders by an innings, and the West Indians comfortably. The Australians called their game against Yorkshire 'the sixth Test', and it was often more challenging than some of the other five which were fated to be bore draws.

It was an education to sit in the football stand at Bramall Lane for the morning session. In the second over of one Roses match Geoffrey Boycott stroked the ball three times through the covers for four: big outswingers by Ken Shuttleworth, which Boycott's left elbow and front foot had to reach for. Years later I asked him about it – three fours at the start of a Roses match! – and he said: 'They were there to be hit.' I wonder if he would have been so assertive if it had been a five-day, or four-day, not three-day game.

In the afternoons I would sit on the terraces opposite the Grinders' stand, while the Victorian pavilion – built for the Test of 1902 – dozed, and factories outside the ground hummed. Yorkshire's cricket was almost pitch-perfect not least because the pitches at Bramall Lane were perfect: green for the seamers on the first morning, flattening out for batsmen, spinning for Ray Illingworth and Don Wilson on the last afternoon.

This setting in itself was dramatic: a green field amid the grime, *rus in urbe*, a ground that had accommodated 68,000 spectators for a football match. The Yorkshire team of that era, on this ground, could beat anybody at home, and they did. Their bowling was relentless, especially Fred Trueman and Ray Illingworth. Their fielding was world-class in the hands of Phil Sharpe and Brian Close in the slips, John Hampshire and Trueman at short leg, Ken Taylor in the covers. In retrospect I understand that they did not make unforced errors, they played virtually flawless cricket.

* * *

But there comes a time when pride in the tribe can get out of hand and become excessive, when it spills over into a dislike of others and a mistrust of alien ways; as when patriotism turns to nationalism. Yorkshire cricket has inspired plenty of books. One of its recent histories was entitled *The Sweetest Rose*; but recently it has become more bitter.

One on-field example of the way that Yorkshire cricket has failed to adapt is the paucity of limited-overs trophies. They have never won the T20 competition. For the one and only time, they won the Sunday League in 1983 and the Benson and Hedges Cup in 1987. Of their three wins in the longest one-day format, under various sponsors' names, only one has been achieved since the 1960s. A total of three limited-overs trophies since 1970, and one since 1990, for a county of so many resources, is plain poor. The White Rose has never adapted to the white ball.

Trouble, meanwhile, has been frequently breaking out in Yorkshire's mill. It is the nature of tribal politics. Sometimes the energies and passions lead to creative tension, provided everyone pulls together on the field, sometimes to self-destruction. Either way, the refusal to give professionals anything longer than a one-year contract until Illingworth upped and left after the 1968 season, and the reluctance to select anyone born outside Yorkshire (a few amateurs were exempted before 1990): both acts of stubbornness which were self-defeating in the end.

No other county has suddenly lost its best bowler through being banned for life. Bobby Peel was also England's best spinner, the first bowler to take 100 Test wickets against Australia. The story about his team-mates having to stick him under a shower to sober him up in Sydney in 1894/95 is too strong to discredit. It had rained so much in the night that Peel had gone on a bender, yet again, but the sun came out, Peel somehow sobered up, and he bowled England to victory by ten runs. Not until Headingley in 1981 did another team win a Test after following on.

Another of Yorkshire's outstanding left-arm spinners, Johnny Wardle, was omitted by England for the 1958-59 Ashes tour and ever after, for criticising the Yorkshire club in print, from captain to committee. He was the best left-arm wrist-spinner England have had and could have achieved wonders on that winter's tour of Australia, which no finger-spinner has done for a century. Wardle, trying wrist spin for the first time in a Test, had tied Australia in knots in the last Test of England's previous tour in 1954-55, taking eight wickets for 130.

To this day, Peel and Wardle survive in the top six of England bowlers who have taken 100 Test wickets with the lowest average.

Still-feudal attitudes decided the pivotal moment when Yorkshire lost Illingworth to Leicestershire and a world-class county fell apart, never to be reassembled. The club's officials and committeemen were the masters; players were servants who had to be content with one-year contracts, because that was the way it had always been. Illingworth dared to ask for longer and was refused. He departed to guide England to No.1 in the unofficial Test rankings, and Leicestershire to their first trophies.

But of all the feuds and controversies, none was so vicious – until the Rafeeq affair at any rate – as the one that began with the sacking of Brian Close as captain in 1970. An authoritative book about it, by Stuart Rayner, was called: *The War of the White Roses – Yorkshire Cricket's Civil War 1968–1986*. The book ended with the date when Geoffrey Boycott retired, but the fall-out – the legacy of disunity – could be said to have lasted even longer.

Close was called into the Yorkshire offices at Headingley and, in true feudal fashion, told that he had ten minutes to make up his mind: did he prefer to resign as captain immediately or be sacked?

Yorkshire had just lost Illingworth, and Jimmy Binks their immaculate wicketkeeper, and Fred Trueman, who had retired at the end of 1968. Close, in these circumstances, had done well to win the Gillette Cup in 1969 and finish fourth in the Championship in 1970. The core of a great side had gone, but Close was still there to rebuild.

Geoffrey Boycott was appointed captain in 1971 after Close had departed to invigorate Somerset. Boycott's batting was not affected; Yorkshire's results were. 'It is with regret that your Committee has to report that the season of 1971 was, without doubt, the worst in the history of the Club, both from a playing and financial point of view.'

In *The Sweetest Rose* the author David Warner, who covered Yorkshire as the cricket correspondent for the *Bradford Telegraph and Argus*, came to this judicial verdict: 'Boycott gave clear evidence for the first time [i.e., in 1971] – and certainly not the last – that the weight of captaincy upon his shoulders would not in any way affect his ability to score runs. Indeed, the greater the pressures upon him personally the more he was able to push them to one side when he arrived at the crease.

'This ability to consistently stack up the runs while the team as a unit failed to make any sort of impact was one of the biggest single reasons why the club was to split into pro and anti-Boycott factions ... Some felt that he put self before team and was pre-occupied with his own batting to the exclusion of everything else but others saw him as being gloriously successful at a time when those around him could not match his own standards.'

Boycott himself used to say: 'You are either for me or against me.' In my opinion the issue always seemed to be a shade of grey.

He played in a media match in Jamaica on England's 1985/86 tour of the West Indies. The opposition was the Red

Stripe Brewery in Kingston, who had some decent players. Somehow, perhaps through being temptingly slow through the air, I've never got so many wickets as in the West Indies – mostly stumped, swiping – and I got a few more this time, but not when a thick edge looped towards extra-cover where Boycott was fielding and preferred not to dive. The Brewery team recovered and scored sufficiently.

When the media XI batted, Sir Geoffrey scored 30-odd with characteristic dedication. We were always behind the required rate, however, and lost. At the end of the game he could not find his batting gloves. Normally so full of life, he was utterly forlorn. I helped him search in the dressing rooms. When he eventually found them, he was a child reunited with a favourite toy, or even a parent with a child.

***

Every proper tribe has its sacred texts. I came across Yorkshire's in my mid-teens, after going to a dentist in York, when I saw in a second-hand bookshop a complete run of the *Yorkshire CCC Yearbook* from 1898 to 1940.

What more could a Yorkshire lad want? I mean, what was the attraction of girls, pop music and alcohol compared with the scorecards of every Yorkshire game? And what about 'Exceptional Bits of Bowling' in the records section? How could you possibly want to go out on a Saturday night when you could be reading that Ted Peate took eight wickets for five runs against Surrey in 1883 at Holbeck?

Rather less exciting in the *Yorkshire CCC Yearbook*, though nonetheless revealing in its own quiet way, was the list of members which took up the second half of the book. It told you where Sir Donald Bradman lived: 2 Holden Street, Kensington Park, South Australia. And where Wilfred Rhodes had retired to: 4 Beaumont Road, Canford Cliff, Bournemouth. And Sir Leonard Hutton was another of the eight Honorary Life Members, at Ebor House, Warren Road, Kingston-on-Thames. He went to live in exile away from the tribe, for golf and a quieter life.

So many members were listed – 60 per page for more than 200 pages, i.e., more than 12,000 in all – that they were divided into sections: Barnsley, Bradford etc., Halifax, Harrogate, Huddersfield and Hull. Yorkshire, as they did not own Headingley, played a home Championship game in many of these 'sections'. So it made sense to be a member; you could see the high priests in action every summer at no additional cost. There was a 'Ladies Section' too, with over 1,200 members, four by the surname of Miss Hirst alone.

Success went hand in hand. By playing all round the county – from Middlesbrough and Harrogate and Hull to Bradford and Leeds, to Scarborough and Sheffield – Yorkshire kept the flame burning in front of the whole tribe. Cannier still, the pitches at these grounds, used mainly for club cricket, were 'result pitches': unlike Trent Bridge or the Oval, they were not too hard and true for three-day matches. The Roses match might be the one home game that Yorkshire would draw; for the rest of the home season their finger-spinners made hay.

Hence the extraordinary bowling averages of Hedley Verity, who took his first-class wickets at 13 runs each for Yorkshire; and Peel, Haigh, Bill Bowes and Bob Appleyard who averaged 15; Rhodes who averaged 16; and Hirst, Wardle and George Macaulay who averaged 17. Most were left-arm spinners or off-spinners who bowled at a decent lick, driving their off breaks into damp and subtly under-prepared turf.

***

It might never have come to this present pass. Around 1980 Yorkshire put up a team to play an XI picked from the Quaid-e-Azam league, based around Bradford and Dewsbury. Lord Patel of Bradford, who played for this combined league team and eventually became an ECB director before being parachuted in as Yorkshire's chair, recalls that the Quaid-e-Azam team won. Another player says this fixture was held a couple of times, before the league team began to lose badly: favourites were picked, not the most promising Asian players.

In any event, this was one huge opportunity to connect Yorkshire mainstream cricket with Asian cricket in Yorkshire. Even if nobody is keen to mix socially, at least play an annual fixture, and get to know each other gradually, and build a bridge so the best youngsters have a chance of being seen and reaching the top. Play for mainstream clubs on Saturday, to achieve the highest standard, then with your mates on Sunday for fun.

Yorkshire were asked if they would care to participate, at no cost, in a project organised by Sport Diplomacy to promote cricket among the county's diverse communities. 'Sport transcends national borders with its ability to bring together people of different backgrounds, cultures, genders, races, and places, but it can also help to foster community,' says its founder Dr Simon Rofe, Reader in Diplomatic and International Studies at SOAS in London.

Sport Diplomacy had already made an impact in Luton. The project started by bringing to town the 2019 World Cup which England had won, so that all possible stakeholders could see it and meet. The second project was aimed at Huddersfield, which has so many social challenges, and one obvious partial solution: cricket is popular among all communities or would be if they were enabled to play the sport. It would be some progress if, 150 years on from the time when Huddersfield's cricketers had to practise in a quarry, facilities were available for everyone in the West Riding to play. Yorkshire might then revive former glories.

Otherwise the petals of the White Rose will fall off. Yorkshire were demoted to Division Two of the Championship at the end of 2022, having somehow managed to lose their captain Steve Patterson in mid-season. A pitiful sight they made in the field, at an almost deserted Headingley, when they were defeated in their final game by bottom-of-the-table Gloucestershire. Anything but a rose.